MARBLE PALACE

JOHN P. FRANK

MARBLE PALACE

The Supreme Court in American Life

Alfred A. Knopf: *New York*

1968

L. C. Catalog card number: 58–12628

© John P. Frank, 1958

THIS IS A BORZOI BOOK,
PUBLISHED BY ALFRED A. KNOPF, INC.

PUBLISHED SEPTEMBER 15, 1958
REPRINTED TWICE
FOURTH PRINTING, MARCH 1968

TO MY MOTHER,
BEATRICE ULLMAN FRANK

PREFACE

Perhaps the oddest aspect of the recent uproar over the Supreme Court is the sense of surprise that goes with it. The Court has been a tame tabby for so many years that apparently some observers are astonished to discover that it still has power, teeth, and muscle. It is, after all, the head of the third branch of the federal government, and it has duties to perform and the means to do the job.

It is true that the Court and the Constitution were dormant in the post-war years. I published an article on the 1946–51 Court called "The Passive Period," and I cannot improve on the title. Because it was a passive period, there were those who took both the Court and the Constitution for granted. In the recent period of contraction of individual liberty, from which we may now be emerging, it was supposed that each act of the executive and legislative branches would be gravely examined by the Supreme Court, but also supposed by their sponsors that each would be upheld; that the task of judicial review was a ceremony which would lend sanctity to the deed being done, but never impede its accomplishment.

Such a supposition required a forgetting that there are three, not two, branches of the American government, and that the black-robed third branch was still capable of action. It required a forgetting that the Constitution of the United States is a very tough document, framed by men who had but recently won a revolution against tyranny, and who were determined to restrict the acts that the government they were creating might inflict upon their own posterity.

When the founding fathers created a government which could declare war and regulate commerce, they gave that government a great deal of power. But when they declared that that government might not restrict freedom of speech or of press or of religion, or subject its people to unfair trials, they laid down some very substantial restrictions. When they set up, to police that system, a body of judges appointed for life, they gave great power to those judges.

These are facts never to be forgotten even when the non-use of that power may lull the unsuspecting into forgetting that it is there. It is a power that is not rendered insignificant by a lack of daily use. John Marshall was Chief Justice when the Court first invalidated an act of Congress, and it was more than fifty years before the Court used that power again. Almost twenty years passed before the power was once more seriously invoked. There are many other ways in which Justices may exercise great power besides invalidation of statutes, and these other powers may be called upon at any time. In concluding my 1951 piece on "The Passive Period," I pointed out that my report was "not meant as a requiem. There is power latent in passivity." That power is now being used. The legion of the astonished should not have been surprised to discover that some vitality is left in the old Bill of Rights. Indeed, millions of Americans feel that it has been a distressingly long time in showing itself.

In this book I will tell how the Court's power is exercised. I intend neither a discussion of current cases nor a description of current personalities. I do intend to tell how the Court is organized, how it does its work, and what its relations have been and may be expected to be to the main streams of American life. For these purposes I shall draw freely for illustrations on the entire history of the Court. The many-sided questions that I hope will always be present in the mind of the reader are "What contribution has the United States Supreme Court attempted to make, or actually made, to American life? What can be expected of it? What is the relation of nine men in a distant marble palace to the daily lives of each of us?"

It will be most convenient to refer to the Justices themselves sometimes by full title, sometimes by full name, and sometimes only by last name; it would be unnecessarily clumsy if every reference had to be to "Mr. Justice ———." Footnotes will be few except where it would be ungenerous to fail to give credit to another writer; and I shall occasionally and unblushingly steal from random essays of my own. Some of what I say will be based on gossip or hearsay—but I would not put it down if I did not believe it—and some on personal observation. Basically, my purpose is not to reveal newly discovered facts, but to integrate some old ones—though some of the material is new.

My wife, Lorraine W. Frank, my partner, Paul M. Roca, and my friend David Brinegar have gone over the manuscript and made many suggestions, and my secretaries, Jane Manley and Helen Johnson, have worked over several drafts with uncomplaining devotion. Ex-Senator William Benton of Connecticut helped to spark the project.

JOHN P. FRANK

CONTENTS

MARBLE PALACE

Chapter I

TO THE HIGHEST COURT

IN THE LAND

New atomic-energy plant construction announced. Battle continues to rage over testing atomic bombs.

Defense Department expands satellite program.

War prospects with Russia diminished (or increased, depending upon which day of the week it is). Does dropping of Bulganin affect international situation?

Trade with Red China to increase. Trade with Red China to diminish.

Revised plans for next census announced.

Congress and President in budget tussle. 72 billion dollars too much, says Senator.

Inflation is greatest menace, says Treasury official. Inflation increase needed, Congressman asserts.

Grand Canyon hotels to be renovated.

Draft age to be lowered. Draft age to be raised. The draft to be suspended. The draft to be expanded.

Congressman denounces seniority system in congressional committees.

New commemorative stamp announced.

The foregoing hodgepodge consists of miscellaneous recent news items which have two facets in common. First, each of them involves some activity of the United States government of substantial interest, or even of vital concern, to large numbers of American citizens. Second, the Supreme Court of the United States has nothing to do with any of them. For, large as is the swath the Supreme Court cuts in American life, it is by no means as broad as that of the President or Congress.

The list repays closer examination. Atomic energy and space exploration, the developments of the 1940's and '50's for which this little moment in world history is most likely to be remembered, have been completely outside the scope of the Supreme Court function. Able and conscientious men firmly believe—or disbelieve, as the case may be—that atomic-bomb tests may render impossible or at least severely impair the future existence of humanity. Here are problems for the Atomic Energy Commission, for the President, for the Defense Department, for the Congress, for the American people—but not for the Supreme Court. This is also true of the satellite program.

So, too, with the great questions of war or peace. Hundreds of thousands of Americans died or were injured in our wars of these two decades. Our troops saved the population of the world from one set of dictators only to find the country confronted with another. In the course of those wars the entire face of America was radically changed by vast new industries and by the largest migration of human beings in the history of the world. None of this made business for the Supreme Court. In another chapter the phases of international relations in which the Court does play some part will be discussed, but the larger questions of war or peace are the concern of the State Department, the President, the Congress, the Defense Department—but not the courts. The same is true of very large lesser questions such as the pattern of trade with this country or that.

4

The housekeeping functions of the government, from the taking of the census to matters of budgetary and financial policy, are not judicial. Similarly, the important service activities of the government, such as the administration of the National Park Service, only occasionally give rise to lawsuits, and hence rarely give the Supreme Court anything to decide.

Like the basic questions of international relations, questions of military policy are outside judicial review. Whether we should have created a second front in France or attacked through the soft underbelly was a matter for the President or General Marshall to decide and might be a fit subject for later inquiry by a congressional committee; courts had nothing to do with it. The same applies to what might be called internal military matters, such as the draft. The Court had a basic decision to make on the constitutionality of the draft, but, once that decision was made, the details of the age groups and classes to be covered, the length of service, and what should be done with the soldiers after they were called up all lay outside the function of the Supreme Court. It is left only comparatively minor questions of interpretation, such as whether this or that individual person is covered by the draft law.

The internal operations of the Congress itself—to filibuster or not to filibuster, seniority or no seniority, organization of committees, and so on—are in the hands of Congress, not of the Court. So are the operations of that government function which so intimately reaches all of us, the postal service. The hard-fought question of whether the mail is to be delivered on Saturday may provoke a battle between the Postmaster General and the congressional appropriations committees, but the Court cannot settle the matter.

On the other hand, consider the sizable areas of American life in which the Supreme Court has a great deal to say. I have chosen illustrations from one year in the mid-1950's to show how wide is the range even in a short period of time.

For example, a good many Americans are chiefly interested each summer in the pennant races of the major baseball leagues. Of concentrated concern East and West was the question of whether the Dodgers and the Giants would move to California. The power of the owners of the teams to keep their iron control over the sport and its players, in the light of the anti-trust laws, was reviewed by the Supreme Court only a few years ago, and at the 1956–7 term the Court considered the rights of the owners in professional football as against professional baseball, reaching the intellectually odd but highly practical conclusion that baseball is not subject to the anti-trust laws and football is. The reasons are lost in the history of the two sports and their relation to the law, but the results will be felt in the amusements of most Americans.

Another common but less highly regarded amusement is the viewing of dirty books and dirty pictures. A New Yorker was enjoined from peddling a paper-covered booklet called *Nights of Horror* and thereby triggered a Supreme Court decision that he was subject to injunction for that act. In related cases the Court went into detail on the problems of the publication of what the judges referred to as "sexually impure" publications. Unquestionably the decisions will be felt at newsstands, and in the course of time the reading habits of Americans will probably be altered, at least a little, as a result.

Most Americans drive cars; the price and the source of the paint on those cars may be affected by the Supreme Court's decision in the du Pont-General Motors anti-trust case. Many Americans are members of unions, and the whole field of labor relations involves federal laws that the Supreme Court interprets. The decisions on the right to picket and on the right of the states to regulate labor relations in the larger industries engaged in interstate commerce will have very substantial effect on union practices. Many Americans either work for or invest in the construction industry, and so much construction is done today by the federal government that a decision limiting the rights of the states to regulate which companies can engage in federal projects within their borders will affect many dollars and many jobs. Many Americans invest in securities, and securities sales practices are directly under Supreme Court review; and while basic matters of taxation, such as the rates, are left entirely to Congress, lesser but still important interpretative questions are left to the Supreme Court, which affects many pocketbooks by its decisions in that field.

Millions of Americans work directly for the government; in the 1956–7 term the Court put some restriction on the manner in which those employees might be discharged for security reasons. More than half of all adult Americans vote, and the Court reviewed the important question of campaign contributions and also gave to state legislatures and the Congress a firm reminder that Americans have a traditional right to cast their votes in private, without any subsequent investigation or inquiry into how they voted. A great many Americans have either directly felt the bite of, or been deeply interested in, the program for inquiry into "un-American" activities and in the trial of persons charged with subversive activities. The means of making such inquiries and the ground rules for such trials were very thoroughly reviewed, with results that rapidly began to affect the proceedings. In a colorful case the Court held illegal a search and seizure in which the F.B.I. had marched off with, quite literally, everything in a house. The Court took eleven pages of tightly spaced small print simply to list the items that had been acquired in this zealous bit of detection; included were such as articles as "one mirror, two sides, for shaving"; one "plastic soap dish"; a package of matches "advertising Schneider's Donuts"; and "one bra—pink."

Family relations received attention. Many Americans are divorced, and many of them obtain divorces in states in which they do not really live—for instance, Nevada. The home state may be burdened with problems of support of the children while one of the spouses enjoys the fruits of a Reno divorce. The Supreme Court had something to say about that. American troops are stationed all over the world, and some families of the soldiers wish to be abroad with them. Two wives who chose to be with their husbands in England and Japan then murdered them. The Court searchingly reviewed the problem of how the law is to be applied to civilians with our armed forces abroad.

One more illustration: ten per cent of the population of the United States is colored, and the problems of members of that colored minority are grave both for themselves and for the communities in which they live. These problems have much occupied the Supreme Court. In the year in question they did again.

So it is clear that while the Supreme Court does not have a *universal* impact on American life, many questions being wholly outside the scope of its powers, its impact on American life is nonetheless very large.

The comparison of the areas in which the Supreme Court does function with those in which it does not shows that the individual Supreme Court Justice probably has more actual power than any other individual in American public life except the President. It is true, for example, that the Postmaster General and the head of the House of Representatives appropriations subcommittee relating to the postal department each has infinitely more power than the Court in matters concerning the postal service; but when they have used up this authority they are about done. They have a bit of concentrated power, but little general power.

It follows, therefore, that in terms of the degree of concentration of power in one individual, probably the only officials who can compare with members of the Supreme Court are the Secretary of State, the head of the military establishment, and the head of the Atomic Energy Commission, and this because those individuals have power concentrated into particular areas, power that directly affects the actual lives of the citizens. The powers of the Supreme Court Justices (except for specialized criminal situations) are not powers of life or death.

But one cannot really compare the power of a Secretary of State, whose success or failure in a crisis may affect every home in America, with that of a Supreme Court Justice, whose decisions on a race-relations problem may have some impact on millions. All that it is really useful to conclude is that in our system a Supreme Court Justice has a very large measure of authority. Because the Justice is appointed for life, and because important cabinet members or key committee chairmen tend to serve for much shorter periods, the appointment of a Supreme Court Justice conveys to him immense power.

It was not always so. When the first Court met in 1790, it had nothing to do. The first President immediately on taking office settled down to the pressing business of being President. The first Congress enacted the first laws. The first Supreme Court adjourned.

From 1790 through 1800, the Court decided a total of only fifty-six cases. This was natural. The Supreme Court is largely a court of appeals, and there could be no appeals until there were decisions in the lower courts, created at the same time, to appeal from. State courts already existed from which appeals might be taken to the Supreme Court, but the habit of doing so had first to be established. At this early stage the work seemed so unimportant that John Jay resigned as the first Chief Justice to become the Governor of New York.

This does not mean that those years were one long vacation for the Justices. Then and, indeed, for most of the nineteenth century the Justices of the Supreme Court were also trial judges, and traveled about the country on circuits to preside at trials. These circuit duties were extremely onerous, particularly in view of the travel conditions of the time. Justice Iredell of the first Court, who described himself as a "travelling postboy," rode the southern circuit, which required a round trip of two thousand miles twice a year. One of the first Justices quit rather than endure such travel.

But though the early cases were limited, not so the quality of the issues. The first serious matter before the Court was a suit by the State of Georgia over questions arising from the settlement of debts with Great Britain, a matter affecting a good many pocketbooks. The second case established a great constitutional principle concerning the *types* of cases which from that day to this the federal courts will hear. In the third case the Court made its first great error by holding that a state could be sued, without its consent, by a private citizen. Perhaps the states should be sued in such circumstances, but the states have not traditionally taken this view. The Eleventh Amendment to the Constitution quickly reversed this decision, reminding the Court at the very begin-ning that the people themselves retain the final veto on important rules of law.

This business consumed the time of the Court to 1793. The official Court reporter tells us that in the latter part of that year "the malignant fever, which during this year raged in the city of Philadelphia, dispersed the great body of its inhabitants, and proved fatal to thousands, interrupted, likewise the business of the courts; and I cannot trace, that any important cause was agitated in the present term."

After the germs permitted the Court to reassemble, its principal business had to do with the shipping industry, particularly in regard to ships or cargoes seized during the Revolution or the Napoleonic Wars. In deciding these cases, the Court was performing one of its most clearly anticipated functions, the determination of those special questions of international relations which can arise in lawsuits and which need to be settled for the country as a whole. The founding fathers, in establishing the Court, said that Georgia could not have one policy toward foreign ships and Pennsylvania another. In these early cases the Court's responsibility was to walk a line between the French and the English which would not unduly involve the country with either.

After this trickle of a few important matters there finally moved in from the lower federal courts a wave of ordinary routine cases. As volume increased, national importance went down. The Court's great cases began to be rare nuggets in a mass of conventional litigation. The Court was on its way to becoming a typical court of law. Between 1790 and 1800 some twenty cases involved problems of business, insurance, and property. Between 1800 and 1815 that number rose to well over a hundred. There were no insurance cases between 1790 and 1800, when the insurance industry barely existed in the United States; in the next fifteen years there were forty such cases.

The most important change in the volume of business came when Congress created the District of Columbia in 1800. The Supreme Court of the United States then became also the Supreme Court of the District of Columbia, and in that connection the Supreme Court of the United States heard all of the little problems of the people of the District in the same fashion that the Supreme Court of, say, Illinois, might hear the problems of the city of Springfield. The District furnished over thirty per cent of all of the cases in the Supreme Court from 1800 to 1815.

An observer describing the United States Supreme Court at the end of its first twenty-five years of existence might very well have summed it up this way: The Court was composed of judges who both heard appeals in Washington and tried cases around the country. Its business was small, but included occasional very important national matters. With perhaps twenty exceptions in the first twenty-five years, all of its cases could about as well have been decided by other courts. Most of the business problems could have been left to the state courts. A special local appeals court could have been created for the District of Columbia. Yet the handful of important cases of nationwide concern included enough really serious business to justify the creation of the Court.

Fifty years later, in 1875, vital changes had occurred. The country had expanded to its present national borders and had increased its population and its business enormously. The business of the Supreme Court expanded with the growing country. In 1875 the Court heard approximately two hundred cases, or almost four times as many in one year as in its whole first decade. The Court membership, which had previously varied, had become, apparently permanently, set at nine. We now know from long experience that two hundred is approximately the maximum number of opinions that nine Justices can be expected to turn out in a term.[1]

Just under half of the cases of 1875 involved conventional business matters such as bank drafts, contracts, insurance, or property. There were also important public matters, such as a case on the freedom of interstate commerce, another on the power of the United States to take private land for public purposes, a case on the right to trial by jury, and two basic decisions on the rights of Negroes after the Civil War.

There was one major trouble with this flood of business: it was too much. The Court could not keep up with its work, and by 1875, when Congress added a new load of cases in the lower courts, the Supreme Court was more than three years in arrears. The Justices struggled hopelessly to keep from falling even further behind. Just after Christmas of 1877, Chief Justice Waite wrote a friend: "We have had a holiday, vacation as it is called, but my vacation has consisted in writing nine opinions." As he added to another note, without undue exaggeration or excess of self-pity: "A Chief Justice is simply a slave." [2]

This was the situation of the Court toward the end of the nineteenth century:

1. The Court had important work to do, which could be done only by a national tribunal.

2. It was still a court that dealt with little questions as well as big ones, and the sheer volume of the little questions

---

[1] The 1875 figures and some figures for the 1890's shortly following are taken from Felix Frankfurter and James Landis: *The Business of the Supreme Court* (New York: The Macmillan Company; 1927).

[2] Bruce Trimble: *Chief Justice Waite* (Princeton: Princeton University Press; 1938), pp. 271, 272.

was so overwhelming that it was likely to prevent the Court from performing its national functions.

3. Experience had established the approximate capacity of the Court. Hard work could not remedy the situation; the Court itself, without some congressional relief, could have cut through its burden only by some ruthless device that would have wholly changed its own nature, such as splitting into two or three courts or divisions and having the whole bench adopt the opinions of the divisions; or abandoning written opinions altogether; or creating large staffs to write its opinions.

The condition was destined to grow worse before it got better. Between that date and the present time, however, two basic reforms have enabled the Court to do its work.

In 1891, Congress, after years of deliberation, finally established a new set of federal appeals courts. It divided the country into circuits and established a little regional supreme court for each one. Then appeals from the federal trial courts could go to a court of appeals instead of directly to the Supreme Court. The system, with some changes, continues to this day; for example, the states of New York, Vermont, and Connecticut have been grouped together into a circuit, and if a litigant is dissatisfied with a decision of a federal district judge for Manhattan, he can take his case to the circuit judges for the three states. A case can still go on to the Supreme Court, but Congress, by giving a different outlet for appeals, tremendously relieved the situation. In 1890, before the Act, 623 new cases came before the Supreme Court. In 1892 the number dropped to 275.

The 1891 Act kept the work of the Court up to date until well into the twentieth century. Lesser reforms helped from time to time. For example, an Act finally met the District of

Columbia problem by creating a special appeals court for the District. Up to that time the Supreme Court was still getting approximately ten per cent of its cases from the District; now it has almost none.

By 1925 the Court, despite the best efforts of the Justices, was in the same old trouble. It took almost two years to bring on a case to be heard. This lag was already acute when William Howard Taft became Chief Justice in 1921. As a former President, Taft was accustomed to making proposals to Congress, and he was not reluctant to do so again. He appointed a committee of his own Court to prepare a bill, known publicly as the Judges' Bill, which became law in 1925.

This is the law under which we live today. The Judges' Bill cut to the heart of the problem by giving to the Supreme Court almost unlimited discretion to decide for itself what cases it would hear.[3] This means that the Court for more than thirty years has been taking cases subject to two limitations: first, it takes no more cases than it thinks it can handle reasonably quickly; and, second, it attempts to restrict itself to matters of some general importance. Like a great dam, the Act of 1925 cut the flood to a trickle.

Here is a quantitative picture of just what the Supreme Court today means in relation to all of the quarrels of American citizens who wished to go to Court in 1956:

[3] Basically the jurisdiction is divided into two types, for which the technical names must be used: most of the cases come up by writ of certiorari, which is to say that the appealing party in effect asks the permission of the Court to bring up the case before the Court agrees to decide it. Second are the appeals, or the cases which the Supreme Court is supposed to have to take, whether it wants to or not. The Court has found ways of cutting down on these appeals either by dismissing them or by affirming the decision of the lower court summarily, without any oral argument and without full briefs. Thus, as a practical matter, today its control over what cases it will decide is nearly absolute.

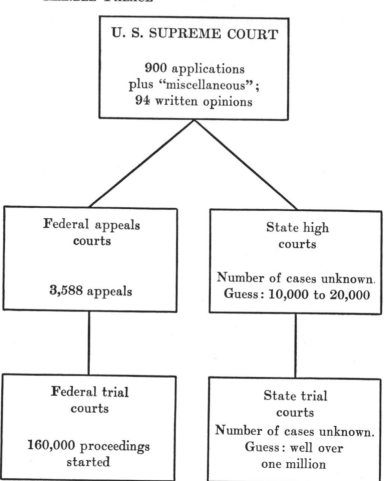

As the diagram shows, the Supreme Court gets its business from two basic sources. (In the interest of simplicity we will not mention the special courts or the cases that bypass one link or another of the system.) The great bulk of the cases originate in our state trial courts. This includes divorces, wills, criminal cases involving everything from murder to speeding, quarrels over property, and quarrels over accidents. It includes juvenile and sanity cases. It includes more cases than anyone has ever counted up because most states lack any statistical system for keeping track of how many there are; the number is astronomical.

Only a small proportion of these cases goes to the supreme courts of the respective states. Again, no one knows how many because of lack of adequate statistical systems. Probably the number is between ten and twenty thousand.

Which of all those cases can ever go to the United States Supreme Court? Only one type: those which turn on the interpretation of the federal Constitution or an act of Congress or some related federal source of law. These constitute a very small fraction of one per cent of the whole number. For example, the ordinary divorce does not involve the federal law at all, but in a few rare instances it may. Suppose that a couple gets a Nevada divorce and goes home to North Carolina and each person marries the spouse of his second choice; and then suppose that each is put in jail in North Carolina for bigamy because North Carolina does not recognize the Nevada divorce. Such a case, arising from a divorce, will pose a question of the duties of the states toward each other, and become federal. Again, almost no state criminal cases involve serious federal questions; but if a state defendant in a robbery case contends that he was beaten into a confession, there is a federal question as to whether his right to due process of law may have been denied. If a state sues a businessman to collect taxes, that is a state question; but if a businessman contends that the state tax interferes with the free flow of commerce among the states, then there is a federal question that may go on to the Supreme Court.

Illustrations could be multiplied, but the general principle is clear: the only cases originating in state courts which can ever be considered by the United States Supreme Court are the cases in which federal questions are involved. Of the more than one million cases that originate in the state courts in the course of a year, and of the ten or twenty thousand that go to a state supreme court, about two hundred go to the United States Supreme Court.

On the federal side, a first-class statistical system permits us to know just what our courts are doing. Beginning in the lower federal courts are the civil cases, the criminal cases, and the bankruptcy cases. Altogether, 160,000 cases started in the lower federal courts in 1956. Federal civil cases are of two basic types. First are those which involve citizens of different states, as when a citizen of Indiana collides with a citizen of New York in an auto accident. All that is "federal" about these cases is that the parties live on different sides of a state line. Second are the cases that involve the interpretation of federal statutes or the federal Constitution, as, for example, cases under the tax laws, the labor laws, the securities laws, the food-and-drug laws, or anything else in the wide-ranging code of federal statutes or regulations.

The first big cut in the load comes when the cases move from the federal district or trial courts to the courts of appeal. The total number of these appeals in 1956 was 3,588. In other words, out of 160,000 cases started in the lower federal courts, over 156,000 stayed there. Approximately 675 cases went from the federal courts of appeal to the Supreme Court.[4]

4 To keep the figures from becoming too complicated, some practical adjustments have been made. First, for purposes of showing the cases going to the Supreme Court on the federal side, all of the federal cases have been lumped together even though a few of them do not come from the courts of appeal. Second, the so-called miscellaneous cases have been ignored altogether. These are the informal petitions of prisoners for relief from their imprisonment. They are processed specially. In those instances in which they came before the whole Court for decision, they are included in the figures given above. Yet they cannot be ignored altogether, because they

18

To the Highest Court in the Land

The most obvious fact about the United States Supreme Court, statistically considered, is that with the growth of the country the Court has become a very small mahout on a very large elephant. Of the stupendous number of cases begun in the United States in a year—160,000 on the federal side alone—about 900 got to the United States Supreme Court. Yet the sifting and winnowing process only begins when the cases knock on the Court's door. Exercising its discretion to determine which cases it is willing to hear, the Court chose to hear arguments in only 123 of the 900 cases that sought to be heard, and in the end it rendered only 94 final written opinions. Speed is no longer a problem; the Court has cut its load to a size it can handle, and most appellate cases are disposed of in well under a year after filing.

When a citizen says in a burst of rage: "I'll carry my case to the highest court in the land," it is almost certain that he won't. In the nineteenth century most of the cases were of primary interest only to the persons directly involved, and were of secondary interest to the country as a whole. Today there are many more cases of far-reaching significance to the country at large, although there is still also a large number of secondary importance. The work load has been cut to a manageable size or even less; unlike its predecessors, the Court of today is wholly free to be quick and decisive.

---

do add to the burdens of the Court. There were some 550 such petitions in the 1955–56 term. Third, cases in the district courts in 1956 will not reach the Supreme Court until a year or two later. However, the relative figures remain approximately the same.

Chapter II

THE PRACTICALITIES

OF POWER

In this vast, unruly, undisciplined country of ours, the fact that as few as five men in distant Washington may say that something is to be done does not always automatically mean that it will be done. It is one thing to order, and another to be obeyed. When is the Supreme Court most and when least effective?

The Supreme Court's most obvious effect is on the actual case being decided. When in the case of the West Coast Communists in 1957 the Supreme Court said that certain of the cases should be dismissed, that was the end of the matter, and the cases were dismissed. If in a controversy over money the Court directs payment, generally speaking, the amount will be paid. When at the time of the post-World War II coal strike the Court held that John L. Lewis had to pay a fine of ten thousand dollars, he paid.

The Court is not invariably effective even in the particular or concrete case. Sometimes the situation has changed so drastically that the decision has no effect, as when the Court decided a case about a criminal who had been drowned in an escape attempt while the decision was pending. No one had bothered to inform the Court of this. If a lower court is determined to frustrate the Supreme Court and takes the bit in its teeth, on occasion it may successfully do so; and occasionally when the order of the Court is not effectively carried out, the matter may be abandoned because of either lack of funds or declining interest. A few years ago the Supreme Court of Nebraska decided against a prisoner on a particular ground. The Supreme Court of the United States reversed that decision. Thereupon the Supreme Court of Nebraska took the matter up again and redecided the case against the petitioner on some other ground that, for technical reasons, was beyond the Supreme Court's reach. This is not a unique example. Nonetheless, day in and day out, it may be expected that most of the time the Court will have its way in the particular case.

The Court may also have very far-reaching effects in the lower court on matters of general principle quite apart from the particular case. This is so, however, much less often than non-lawyers might suppose.

To illustrate the general effectiveness of the Court: when it declares an act of Congress unconstitutional, that ends it. The lower courts thereafter will not enforce the statute in other cases. Again, if the Supreme Court uses its rule-making power to make general rules for the conduct of cases, there will be an effort on the part of all the lower courts to obey such rules. Inevitably there will be conflicts of interpretation and mistakes, but these will not arise from resistance to the Court. Also, when well-publicized general principles of law are announced by the Supreme Court, the lower courts commonly attempt to apply them. A good current example is the ruling of the Supreme Court on the duty of the government to produce reports made to the government by its own eyewitnesses. The widespread publicity given to the decision resulted in the general application of the rule all over the country.

But this acceptance and enforcement of Supreme Court general principles by the other courts of the country is far from universal. There is an imperfect bridge between the 100 to 200 opinions filed by the Supreme Court and the 160,000 new cases filed in the lower federal courts in a year.

The illustrations just given in which the Supreme Court has been undoubtedly effective are cases in which it has enunciated well-publicized broad general principles. If the principles are less broadly stated or less well publicized, there is the solid practical possibility that the lower-court judges may never know that they exist. The trial and appellate judges of the country by no means carry the teachings of the 350 or more volumes of the United States Supreme Court Reports in their heads, nor do they commonly stand anxiously at the mailbox to receive the new wisdom ground out weekly. If a principle is not called to its attention by counsel, the lower court may not know that it exists.

Particularly when the Supreme Court sets off on some new course or opens up some new subject, it may take reversal after reversal to get the word about the country. A few years ago the Court enunciated certain principles on the respective powers of the state versus the national government in the field of labor relations. How those principles should be applied to concrete cases was not wholly clear. In 1957 the high courts of Idaho, Ohio, Utah, and California were each reversed for not following the earlier decisions. Now they know. But sometimes the matter never gets back to the Supreme Court. Remember that something under two per cent of all the cases started in the federal system ever gets to the federal appellate courts, and only a small fraction of those goes the rest of the way to the Supreme Court. As a result of the mammoth size of the country, Supreme Court decisions on lesser points may be ignored.

Quantity creates the problem. The largest single example is a colossal experiment undertaken by the Court a hundred years ago, now largely regarded as unsuccessful. In 1842 Mr. Justice Story, a publicist in his spare time, had completed a book on checks and other commercial paper. At that time each state was free to make its own law on these subjects. Story felt that there should be national law on commercial paper—along the lines of his book—so that the businessman giving a check in New York or getting a note in Mobile would be subject to identical principles of law. Therefore in the famous case of *Swift* v. *Tyson*[1] Story announced that the federal courts, including the Supreme Court, would establish a uniform system of federal commercial law. He hoped that the courts of the several states would follow this lead, so that the law on these important financial matters would be the same all over the country.

The Story experiment was tried for almost a hundred years and was junked because, among other things, it did not work. Justice Brandeis, who wrote the opinion overruling Story's initial decision, said: "Persistence of state courts in their own opinions on questions of common law prevented uniformity."[2] The situation reduces to this: when immense masses of cases are involved in the lower courts and one single general principle can decide them all, and when that general principle is extremely clear-cut and precise, the Supreme Court is effective. The best example is when a law is declared unconstitutional. On the other hand, when the Supreme Court declares general principles that are not at all precise, and when the proper application of those general principles to particular cases is difficult to determine, the Court may be ineffective. In those situations the lever with

[1] 16 Pet. 1 (1842).
[2] *Erie Ry. Co.* v. *Tompkins,* 304 U.S. 64 (1938).

which the Supreme Court attempts to move the world is simply not big enough to do the job.

Perhaps the greatest single failure of the Supreme Court is in relation to the patent system. In the running war between the Patent Office and the Supreme Court, there are zealots for each side. In turning to it now it is necessary to put aside altogether the question of whether one *likes* the Supreme Court approach or the Patent Office approach. The sole question here is whether the Supreme Court is able to make the Patent Office respond to its mandates.

As usual, the underlying difficulty derives from the quantity of cases to be decided. The Patent Office is a branch of the United States Department of Commerce. The Constitution of the United States provides that Congress "to promote the Progress of Science and useful Arts" may give inventors "the exclusive Right to their" discoveries. To carry out this duty, Congress has provided for the issuance of patents to inventors. The Patent Office frequently issues over fifty thousand patents a year.

The problem arises in determining what is patentable and what is not. Real, honest-to-God inventions should have patents; this is what the system is meant to encourage. On the other hand, mere imitative gimmicks or copies of other men's work should not have patents, because each patent operates as a tax on the public that pays the royalties, and this the public should pay only when it gets a fair return. If someone believes that the Patent Office has made a mistake and that it has given a patent for something which is not really an invention at all, then the courts and eventually the Supreme Court must decide whether the patent is good.

There is your war. The Court's standard of invention, or of what it considers patentable, is infinitely higher than the standard of the Patent Office. For example, the Court invalidated a patent on a three-sided wooden frame used by cashiers in supermarkets to pull groceries forward in order to ring them up. That the gadget is useful, no one doubts. That it is an invention in the sense that the telegraph and the combustion engine and the radio are inventions, no one believes. The Court also held invalid the patent on a most deceptive toy pig. Perched on the edge of a child's breakfast bowl, its tail buried in cereal, the pig could be fed alternate spoonfuls of cereal ("See, junior, piggy takes a spoonful too"), which it then deposited through its tail back into the bowl.

For the last forty years the Supreme Court has regularly invalidated far more patents than it has upheld, and from 1936 to 1940 it held thirteen patents invalid and none valid. In the supermarket-counter case, Mr. Justice Douglas observed:

> The patent involved in the present case belongs to the list of incredible patents which the Patent Office has spawned. The fact that a patent as flimsy and as spurious as this one has to be brought all the way to this Court to be declared invalid dramatically illustrates how far our patent system frequently departs from the constitutional standards which are supposed to govern.[3]

Among what Douglas thought were the more worthless patents of Supreme Court history, stretching back to before the Civil War, were a clay doorknob shaped slightly differently from other doorknobs; a collar made of parchment paper where linen paper and linen had been previously used; fine threads placed across the squares in a hairnet to keep the hair in place; a stamp for impressing initials on the side of a plug of tobacco; a revolving cue rack; rubber hand-grips

[3] *Great Atlantic & Pac. Tea Co.* v. *Supermarket Equipment Corp.,* 340 U.S. 147 (1950).

on bicycle handlebars; and a toilet-paper roll made oval instead of round to facilitate the tearing off of strips.

One of the best of the lower-court patent judges once estimated that about fifty per cent of the patents issued by the Patent Office were invalid. One of the country's leading patent lawyers has said that it is "deplorable" that the office grants so many invalid patents.[4] Yet what is to be done? It is beyond the resources of the English language to word a general standard that can be applied with exactness to devices as different from one another as a store tray, a toy pig, and a toilet-paper roll. If the Supreme Court did nothing at all but handle patent cases, abandoning entirely all the rest of its work, it could not deal with even one per cent of the patents that the Patent Office issues in a year. As Justice Jackson once gloomily observed,

> I doubt that the remedy for such Patent Office passion for granting patents is an equally strong passion in this Court for striking them down so that the only patent that is valid is one which this Court has not been able to get its hands on.[5]

At the other end of the production line, the Patent Office, which controls this endless sausage-grinder, rolls out the product and refuses to budge. An intensive reading of ten years of the *Journal of the Patent Office Society* reveals that the Office has taken every attitude about its invariable reversals in the Supreme Court, except one: nowhere has there been an expression of a desire to comply with the decisions from on high. Instead the Court is regarded as The Enemy, to be thwarted by every ingenuity of which the Office is capable.

[4] Davis: "Proposed Modifications in the Patent System," 12 *Law & Contemporary Problems* 796 (1947).
[5] *Jungersen* v. *Ostby & Barton Co.,* 335 U.S. 560 (1949).

The Practicalities of Power

Editorials and articles in the *Journal* are a measure of the militant hostility of the Patent Office to any checks by superior officers in the federal system. With reference to Supreme Court decisions, the *Journal* enthusiastically admonishes its readers to "check the torrent of baleful judicial action." With reference to one Supreme Court decision that appeared to put a restriction upon unlimited patents, a 1943 editorial proudly announced that the patent lawyers "took a dislike to this new character, and either refused to accept him into their scheme of things, dismembered him by analysis, attempted to show him up as an impostor . . . or merely noted his existence and ignored him."

Another issue of the *Journal* noted that the decision of the Supreme Court was being treated as a "fiction on Mt. Olympus." A few years later, referring to a Supreme Court opinion, an article in the *Journal* said: "What effect this admonition will have on the Patent Office remains to be seen." [6]

To sum it up, in the war between the Patent Office and the Supreme Court, the Supreme Court has lost. Almost incessantly for a hundred years the Court has attempted to raise the standard of invention. Yet it is more than probable that in the year 1958 ten thousand new patents will be issued which, to paraphrase Justice Jackson, would be invalid if the Supreme Court could get its hands on them.

The Court has been more successful in maintaining a free flow of interstate commerce. The United States of America is one of the largest free-trade areas in the world. There are practical impediments on this free flow of commerce; for example, the freight rates may be rigged to favor one section as against another. However, at least some possible

[6] The four quotes are from the *Journal of the Patent Office Society,* Vol. 26 (1944), p. 151; Vol. 25 (1943), p. 773; Vol. 26 (1944), p. 275; Vol. 33 (1951), p. 102.

extra charges are knocked off because this is one big country instead of forty-eight little ones.

The Supreme Court has assumed the job of policing this system,[7] and we have now something over a hundred years of experience with its efforts. Prior to 1851 there was considerable difference among the Justices as to whether the maintenance of the free flow of commerce was a task primarily for the Court or for the Congress, it being agreed that the Congress was free to operate in that field if it wished. Since 1851 it has been largely accepted that this job should be done by the Court.

Chief Justice Stone sized it up this way: the Constitution "affords some protection from state legislation inimical to the national commerce. . . . Where Congress has not acted, this Court, and not the state legislature, is under the commerce clause, the final arbiter between the competing demands of state and national interest." The Chief Justice noted that Congress could operate in this field if it wished, but said: "In general Congress has left it to the courts to formulate the rules thus interpreting the commerce clause in its application, doubtless because it has appreciated the destructive consequence to the commerce of the nation if their protection were withdrawn."

Stone declared that the states do not have "authority to impede substantially the free flow of commerce from state to state, or to regulate those phases of the national commerce which, because of the need of national uniformity, demand that their regulation, if any, be prescribed by a single authority." [8]

Since 1851 the Court has made many rules as to the cir-

---

[7] For fuller discussion, see Chapter XII on the relation of the Supreme Court to the business life of the country.

[8] *Southern Pac. Co.* v. *Arizona,* 325 U.S. 761 (1945).

cumstances and manner in which the states may regulate commerce. Taking the general position that the states may not unreasonably burden commerce, the Court has held that the State of Arizona cannot restrict trains going through it to a maximum of fourteen passenger cars or seventy freight cars. On the other hand, South Carolina was allowed to restrict the width of trucks operating on its roads. Madison, Wisconsin, cannot bar milk from Illinois, and in the reverse situation, New York cannot forbid the shipment of milk to Massachusetts. The Court held in 1876 that the State of Missouri could not put a license tax upon peddlers in Missouri of goods produced outside the state, thus giving rise to the whole series of peddler cases.

In the field of taxation on interstate sales—as, for example, whether New York can charge a sales tax on goods delivered there but purchased from out of state—the Court has followed a winding course, with the result that in a large number of situations businessmen and states do not really know whether a given tax can be collected. The same is true as to the almost infinite number of taxes on the motor-transport industry.

Most people will probably agree that the Court has done a fair job with this self-imposed assignment, but not a great one. On the one hand, our internal commerce is not chopped up like that of Europe or South America. On the other hand, not only are there many impediments to free trade, but on some occasions the Court has leaned over too far, depriving the states of needed regulatory or taxing power. As George Braden, a close student of the subject, has said of taxes on commerce, the Court is the only body in our system which so far has attempted to control the situation and "its endeavors have by and large been unsuccessful." Even more seriously, Mr. Braden concludes: "In the nature of things, the Supreme Court can never exercise successfully the control required." [9]

Why the partial but not complete success? It is the old quantity problem. There are an endless number of slightly different ways of affecting interstate commerce; the Supreme Court, which decides only one case at a time, simply cannot cover all of them. Every time one restriction is stricken, a dozen new devices spring up in its place. The mass of the job gets ahead of the men available to perform it.

The Supreme Court has, however, been far more successful in regulating commerce than in regulating patents, where it has had no substantial success at all. Why? There are two basic reasons. First, the quantity of regulations in the commerce field, large as it is, is not nearly so large as the number of patents. Burdens on commerce may spring up by the dozens or by the hundreds, but not by the tens of thousands. Quantitatively speaking, the Court is fighting an enemy a little nearer its size. Second, for all of its critics, the policy that the Court is advancing in the commerce field is more sympathetically received and hence more co-operatively treated by the lower courts and other bodies that operate in the same area. There is not that determined and entrenched resistance which meets the Court in the Patent Office. Generally speaking, these controversies are reviewed first by the state supreme courts. Most state judges accept in greater or lesser degree the philosophy of the Supreme Court: that commerce ought to be as free as possible and that courts ought to act to secure this result. In this field the United States Supreme Court finds in the various state supreme courts a host of loyal allies instead of foot-dragging

[9] George Braden: "Interstate Taxation," 18 *Ohio State Law Journal* 57 (1957).

resistance. Indeed, the United States Supreme Court occasionally finds in the commerce field that the lower courts go further in the direction of the Supreme Court's own policy goals than the Supreme Court itself wants to go, while in the patent field the opposite is true.

Jury trials are a third example of the quantity problem, this time in a field directly under the Court's control. The Seventh Amendment to the Constitution of the United States provides in effect that anyone who wants a jury trial in a suit for damages may have one, at least in the federal courts. When that constitutional provision was adopted, it meant substantially what it says—namely, that juries and not judges were to decide the factual questions in lawsuits. In practical terms this would mean today that if there is an automobile collision and each driver says that the other was negligent, it is for the jury and not the judge to decide who is right.

The Supreme Court left this matter as it was for about the first sixty years of the country's history. Then, bit by bit, it began to move in on the jury's function, allowing more and more responsibility to be transferred to judges. Thus, judges were allowed to comment on the evidence and influence the juries to come to one decision or another. More important, judges developed the right of taking a case away from the jury entirely if they felt that the facts pointed all one way; either the judge directed the jury to decide a particular way or he reversed it after it had decided. By approximately 1930 the jury function had withered away to a point in which trial by jury was very rapidly becoming trial by judge.

This practice is objected to by Justice Black, who was a jury lawyer before he went to the Senate in 1926. When

Black came to the Court in 1937, he brought with him a determination to reverse this trend and to give juries the full play of their constitutional power.

As a result, the Supreme Court has for the past twenty years been turning the law back to its original channel and increasing the effective authority of juries. A group of like-minded associates, in the persons of Justices Murphy, Douglas, Rutledge, Clark, Warren, and Brennan, took up the cause, in large part because of a widespread general feeling that judges' control over juries had gone too far. For the last fifteen years the Supreme Court has worked diligently to compel federal trial judges to leave juries alone.

But in 1956 there were about 2,000 jury trials in the lower federal courts, and in about 150 of them, judges took the cases away from the juries. If the Supreme Court reviewed all of those 150 cases, it could do nothing else. Yet if the Court gives only one or two decisions on this point, the lower courts will scarcely know what they are being told. Remember that in these cases the Court is going against what has become an established way of doing things, and it meets the passive resistance that always confronts change.

Moreover, the Court has been handicapped because it has not been unanimous within itself, several of the Justices believing that it should not attempt to interfere with judge-controlled juries. Foremost among these has been Justice Frankfurter, who regularly says that the jury questions are not worth the Supreme Court's time, and that it should have nothing to do with them.

Because of these internal divisions, the Court has never been able to draw a sharp, clear line, such as stating that trial judges should never be allowed to reverse juries. So clear a ruling, whether right or wrong, would be obeyed. Instead the Court has not been able to go further than saying that *in most cases* the trial judge should leave the jury alone, with the result that there has been room for argument as to whether each individual case is within or without the rule.

The Court majority has attempted to solve this problem by the device of mass reversals. It has set out to bring every federal district judge in the country into conformity by a steady stream of reversals where the district judges do not comply with the policy. Between 1941 and 1949 the Court reversed twenty-three lower courts that intruded on the jury function in cases of injured railroad workers. After a slackening of activity in that field following the deaths of Justices Murphy and Rutledge in 1949, the Court re-entered the zone with vigor in 1955, reversing three cases in 1955–6 and several more in 1956–7, four of them in one day.

It would be a dull-witted federal district judge indeed who, in these circumstances, did not perceive that the Supreme Court wants him to leave juries alone, and further that he has almost no chance of being reversed by the Supreme Court if he leaves a case to a jury and a very good chance of being reversed if he takes it away.

The results are unimpressive. In this situation the Supreme Court is using full power. It has given an extraordinary amount of attention to this question. Yet the federal trial judges are consistently directing verdicts in about the same percentage of cases every year. Taking the available statistics for the dozen years prior to this writing, the number of directed verdicts was approximately ten per cent of the number of jury verdicts in every year but three. In one year it was markedly more and in two markedly less than this. Full statistics are unavailable, but I believe that, compared to the 1920's and 1930's, the Supreme Court has undoubtedly had *some* effect in increasing the effectiveness of juries. Moreover, if the Court consistently keeps at this reversal policy for some years, it will probably make itself felt. Nonetheless, to date the result is not proportionate to the effort.

The Court in its power position is like the pass-thrower on a football team. When there is someone to catch the ball and run with it, wonders can be accomplished; otherwise, the passer throws out his arm for nothing. In one decision at the beginning of World War II, the Court, by almost forcing Congress to pass a vital act on war profits, helped cut not millions but billions from the war costs. A few decisions unleashed and backed the Securities and Exchange Commission and the National Labor Relations Board, respectively, enabling them to revolutionize financial and industrial practices. A mere sentence uttered from the bench established that corporations as well as individuals were entitled to the protection of the due-process clause. These are all cases of broad exercise of power for co-operative institutions.

Passive resistance by other agencies of government occurs where the Court is unable to hit hard, where it lays down some rule dependent on little factual variations and does not cut to the heart of the matter, or where the other agency of government, instead of resisting passively, attempts actively to change the rule the Court has made.

There are two ways of changing a Court-made rule: by changing the law, or by changing the judges who interpret it. Sometimes the change in the law is effected by a change in the Constitution itself—as, after the Court had held that the income tax was unconstitutional, the income-tax amendment was adopted. The greatest single example is the rule laid down in the *Dred Scott* case in 1857, where it was held that slaves could not be kept out of the territories. It took a war and a constitutional amendment to end that doctrine.

The Practicalities of Power

Abraham Lincoln, then a prairie lawyer and politician, expressed an attitude toward the Court itself which has not been uncommon since:

> We believe as much as Judge Douglas (perhaps more) in obedience to, and respect for, the judicial department of government. We think its decisions on constitutional questions, when fully settled, should control not only the particular cases decided, but the general policy of the country, subject to being disturbed only by amendment of the Constitution as provided in that instrument itself. More than this would be revolution. But we think the Dred Scott decision is erroneous. We know the Court that made it has often overruled its own decisions, and we shall do what we can to have it overrule this.[1]

Where statutes rather than constitutional provisions are involved, Congress can change the law if it doesn't like it. A good example was the controversy in the 1950's over the Federal Power Commission's control of certain phases of the natural-gas industry. The Court held these matters subject to that Commission's jurisdiction. Doughty friends of the gas industry in 1956 persuaded the Congress to pass a law changing that, which the President vetoed; and the effort continues as this volume is written. Such an effort was successful in respect to the control of the tidelands oil, which was held by the Court to belong to the nation as a whole but which was then given by the Congress to the states adjacent.

The other method of altering the decision of the Court is by changing its personnel and inducing the new appointees to come to a different result. The most spectacular instance of this was in 1870, when the Court held the Civil War

[1] A. Lincoln, Springfield, Ill., June 26, 1857, in Roy Basler, ed.: *The Collected Works of Abraham Lincoln* (New Brunswick: Rutgers University Press; 1953), Vol. II, p. 401.

financing system, known as legal tender, unconstitutional. A short time and two new Justices later, it reached the opposite decision by a margin of one vote.

The same result was achieved much less spectacularly in the shift of Court personnel from the 1870's to the 1890's, the earlier Court of Chief Justice Waite holding that the Civil War amendments to the Constitution were intended primarily to protect the ex-slaves and not to protect private corporations from state regulation of business. The Court of the '90's, with radically different personnel, abandoned much of the effort to use the amendments to protect the Negroes and increased the interpretation of those same amendments as a protection of the corporate enterprise of the country.

In the 1930's, when the so-called Old Court had invalidated most of the important legislation of the New Deal, President Roosevelt, immediately after an overwhelming re-election, proposed to solve his problem by adding as many as six Justices to the Court. This so-called Court-packing plan of 1937 ran into immense resistance and was finally abandoned; but not until the Court itself had reversed some of its most critical decisions, thus occasioning the famous aphorism: "A switch in time saves nine."

An even more thorough way of changing judicial personnel is the proposal of Senator Jenner of Indiana, before the Senate Judiciary Committee in 1957 and '58, to take away the decision-making responsibility of the Supreme Court altogether in important areas by abolishing or limiting the right of appeal to it. This device, which was used by the Reconstruction Congress to keep the Court from getting its hands on some reconstruction legislation, now has very limited appeal but is earnestly sustained by a small number of Senators. It was almost totally eliminated from the Jenner bill before that bill passed its first committee hurdle in April 1958, and it was expected that even this element would be eliminated if the Jenner bill were to make any further headway. Under this device there would be no Supreme Court on many questions, and final decision would rest with the various lower courts around the country.

The practical problems of enforcing their decisions ofttimes induce the Justices to mix discretion with the business of judging. They are in varying degrees aware that if they bite off more than they can chew, the mouthful will never be digested. They are aware that they are powerful but not all-powerful, and that even in the Supreme Court of the United States it is dangerous to confuse oneself with God.

One way to solve this problem is to damn the torpedoes and go ahead, with all possible dignity and unanimity. When another course seems necessary, the Court has developed three key solutions:

The Court avoids a good many controversies. It has developed whole groups of rules as to what it will and what it will not decide. Particularly in the constitutional field it has learned that caution may be more profitable than haste, and has found ways of dealing with problems that might get it into trouble.

Sometimes the Court yields altogether to what it conceives to be the temper of the times. Thus, the Court abandoned its efforts in the late nineteenth century to uphold Negro rights. One who reads the history of that time and the role the Court played in it ends with the conviction that the Court concluded that the tide of opinion was running so heavily against the rights of the Negroes that the Court could not effectively fight it; and, indeed, many of the Justices themselves had no wish to fight.

One of the most unfortunate phases of this latter approach to the business of judging—that is, judging in terms of what the public will bear—is that the Justices are not really qualified to know what the tolerance point of the community is. It is an approach to the job which at its greatest level may be statesmanship, but which at its lesser levels may be nothing but timidity. It can result in a total failure to do the job assigned by the Constitution. The danger that individual whims may underestimate the extent of public support of the Constitution is best balanced by the size of the bench: a timid response of one Justice may be neutralized by the courage of others.

Finally, the Court can avoid trouble by controlling the actual order it enters in a particular situation. The first great example in our constitutional history was Chief Justice Marshall's device in his famous case of *Marbury* v. *Madison*.[2] In that case Marshall was called on to pass upon acts of the Jefferson administration, which had but recently been swept into office after an exceptionally bitter campaign. One of its first acts was to repeal a statute of Marshall's own Federalist Party which had created numerous judgeships for Federalists; another was an attempt to impeach one of the Justices of the Supreme Court itself. The Jeffersonians also abolished one year's term of the Supreme Court for the very purpose of keeping Marshall from getting his hands on their program. In these difficult circumstances, in 1803 Marshall had to pass upon the rights of a Federalist to a minor judicial position.

The possibility was extremely strong that if Marshall decided the case against the Jeffersonians, they would pay no attention to him. All the Court can do is call upon the President of the United States to enforce the laws; if he will not enforce them, the Court is helpless. Sixty years later, during

[2] 1 Cranch 137 (1803).

the Civil War, President Lincoln refused to pay any attention to certain orders from Chief Justice Taney.

Marshall faced his problem by doing what he could. He held that the Jeffersonians had done wrong in all respects, but then he removed his own neck from the block by holding, on an ingenious technical ground, that his Court did not have power in this particular case to do anything about it. In short, by renouncing for the moment the exercise of power, Marshall lived to fight another day.

This problem of nonenforcement by the President has largely disappeared as the Supreme Court has gained stature in our system of government. It is true that Lincoln ignored a directive from Taney; and in a great controversy over the Indians of Georgia, President Jackson is supposed to have exclaimed: "John Marshall has made his decision, now let him enforce it." But for the last hundred years the problem of utter defiance has not been a real one.

In disposing of the recent segregation cases the Supreme Court gave great thought to the practical limitation on its power. It proceeded to hold segregation in the schools unconstitutional. It moved very gradually, chipping away at segregation for approximately twenty years before the final blow.

A court that cannot control a single isolated unit of the federal government such as the Patent Office, or the interstate-business situation involved in burdens on commerce, or even the lower federal district judges on a matter of jury trial, was obviously facing a supercolossal problem in pressing its interpretation of the Constitution upon a whole region determined, in varying degrees, to resist. The Court realized that its operating effectiveness might well be limited to the exercise of a determined moral leadership. If it had not scored a smashing success a few years before in upholding Negro voting rights, the Court might not have attempted to outlaw segregation. But the decision of Justice Reed, after a great battle within the Court concerning voting, had been a success; under it the number of Negro voters in Southern states had increased fivefold.

In these circumstances, the Court waited an entire year after it had decided that segregation was unconstitutional before it decided what should be done—whether its rule should take effect immediately or in a delayed fashion, and whether the order would be declared by it or applied and worked out by the lower courts. It then entered a "soft" order that in effect remanded the problem to the lower courts for disposition.

The practical consequence is that in terms of the actual lawsuits decided by the Supreme Court in the segregation cases the results of the Court's opinion in the deep South has been very nearly nothing. The particular cases decided involved school children in South Carolina, Virginia, Kansas, Delaware, and the District of Columbia. In Kansas, Delaware, and the District of Columbia the communities were close to abandoning segregation; the impetus of the cases helped to push them over, and segregation was abandoned. However, in May 1958, on the fourth anniversary of the segregation decision, in Virginia and South Carolina the Negro children who "won" the segregation cases were as far from unsegregated education as ever.

The segregation cases are a measure of the effectiveness of a Court in a highly turbulent situation. The decision followed from twenty to thirty years of national examination of the country's greatest internal problem. Large sections of the country were morally vibrant to the issue, and an overwhelming majority of Americans felt a sense of wrong about segregation. The Supreme Court's decision put the Court at the head of a moral force, and by the same token added its weight to the increase of that force, so that in the so-called fringe areas, such as the District of Columbia, Kentucky, and parts of Kansas and Missouri, segregation stopped.[3] A little farther to the south, in Tennessee and Arkansas, segregation began to crumble. This by itself is a great deal. The hard core remains, to date, thoroughly stirred up but not as yet practically affected by the ruling from Washington.

To sum up: The Court normally can decide the case before it, and that conclusively. Exceptional situations exist, but they are rare. When the Court lays down broad general principles, clear and decisive, as when it declares a law unconstitutional, its mandate is widely effective. When the decision, though more minute, governs a co-operative agency of government, it is also likely to be effective.

But when the Court moves into an area of highly qualified decisions in which cases depend on fine details, then the effectiveness of the Court is largely dependent upon the responsiveness and co-operation of the lower courts, agencies, or legislative bodies that must apply the Court's general principles. The Court has power, and great power, but it is no puppet-master pulling the strings of American life.

---

[3] A St. Louis *Post-Dispatch* editorial, May 10, 1958, said: "Even if desegregation were inevitable here, what realistic Missourian would argue that it did not come much sooner than expected because of the Court's ruling?" The editorial quotes statistics showing that of 3,113 school districts in seventeen southern and border states, 540 had moved toward integration by the first anniversary of the school decision in 1956, 685 by 1957, and 764 by 1958.

Chapter III

THE JUSTICES

The first and most obvious fact about the Supreme Court Justices is that there are not many of them. At any one time there are 96 United States Senators and 435 members of the House of Representatives. From 1790 to 1957, including the present bench of nine, there have been 92 Justices. Since 1900, 35 have been appointed.

Necessarily this means long average service. The term of a member of the House of Representatives is two years, of a Senator six years, of a Supreme Court Justice life. A good many Justices serve from twenty to thirty-five years, and about half have served over fifteen years. Senator A. H. Garland of Arkansas, who had practiced before the Supreme Court for a long time, told President Cleveland that he regarded himself as disqualified for appointment because a man should serve at least twenty years and he doubted if he would live that long.

The Court of 1958 is made up of relatively young men, though even with four Eisenhower appointees the average service is over six years, or more than a Senate term. Only Justice Black has served for a full two decades. When Black was appointed to the Court, he took the place of a man who had served over twenty-five years and joined a bench that included two fifteen-year veterans and two of more than twenty.

Incredible as it might seem to President Eisenhower, who has declared a preference for appointees of previous judicial experience, history proves that the best Supreme Court Justices are likely to be those who have *not* been judges before. Choosing "great Justices" is a little like choosing pretty girls: there is considerable room for personal taste in the selection. Nonetheless, there are certain commonly accepted estimates. The outstanding pre-Civil War Justices on almost anyone's list include Chief Justices John Marshall and Roger Taney, and Associate Justices Joseph Story, William Johnson, John McLean, Benjamin Curtis, and John Campbell. None of them had previous judicial experience. The very best among them, Marshall, Taney, Curtis, and Campbell, might well be included in the list of ten or twelve outstanding Justices of all time. At the time of their appointment two were practicing lawyers and the other two were cabinet members.

The post-Civil War list includes Chief Justices Morrison R. Waite, Charles Evans Hughes (at the time of his first appointment), and Harlan Stone, and Associate Justices Miller, Harlan, Bradley, Moody, Brandeis, Sutherland, and Pierce Butler. None of these had any significant previous judicial experience.

This does not mean that previous judicial experience is an absolute bar to great success on the Supreme Court. Of the 1958 Court, Justices Brennan and Whittaker have substantial and Justice Harlan has a little lower-court experience. None of the three needs to turn in his robes with a hopeless expectancy that he can make nothing of the job, for a few outstanding Justices have come up from lower courts. The greatest example is Holmes, who had abundant experience in the Supreme Court of Massachusetts, and into this little circle come Justices Field, Brewer, Cardozo, and Chief Justice Taft. That, however, comes very close to completing the list. David Davis, Lincoln's campaign manager and a Justice with some real claims to distinction, had been the local trial-court judge before whom Lincoln practiced, but had had no previous appellate experience.

There have at the same time been many Justices with previous judicial experience, and the list includes some notable ciphers. Take for example Ward Hunt, who went to the bench from the New York Court of Appeals in the nineteenth century, or Willis Van Devanter, a twentieth-century Justice appointed from the federal bench whose most peculiar achievement is that for perhaps his last ten years on the Supreme Court he averaged some three opinions a year; or Joseph R. Lamar, who had served briefly on the Supreme Court of Georgia and who is remembered, if at all, only by his grandchildren; or Justice Sanford, appointed from the lower federal bench, who was known at the time of his appointment as "a little slow" in getting out his work, and who disabused no one thereafter.

This is not an argument that all experienced judges are poor and all inexperienced ones are good. Some poor Justices have been appointed who did not have judicial experience—Chief Justice Fuller, for example, a Chicago lawyer appointed in the nineteenth century, who adorned the bench with personal charm but with negligible accomplishment, or McReynolds, a Tennessee lawyer who did not bring even charm to his task. The clearest lesson which history teaches is that there is no way of making sure in advance that a man will become a valuable member of the Supreme Court. Demonstrably, however, previous judicial experience is not the answer. For a final example, Charles Evans Hughes once listed eight outstanding Justices prior to the bench of the 1920's. Only two had had previous judicial experience.[1]

Indeed, its unpredictability is almost the clearest feature of the appointment process. Some Presidents have chosen Justices who thereafter performed just as the appointing Presidents expected they would. Chief Justice Marshall, chosen by the outgoing John Adams, impressed the Federalist spirit of Adams into the law for thirty-five years. On the Anti-Federalist side, Peter V. Daniel was chosen by the defeated Martin Van Buren only a few days before the latter went out of office. As Van Buren wrote his predecessor, Jackson, with some glee, he had left the Court with someone who had been a Democrat *"ab ovo,"* or from the egg; and this is exactly what Daniel was. Harding's Butler, F.D.R.'s Black, and Jackson's Taney were just what those Presidents wanted.

Nonetheless, the number of surprises is great, and no President can be sure of what he is getting. Wilson chose McReynolds, who proved to be the total antithesis of everything Wilson stood for and became the most fanatic and hard-bitten conservative extremist ever to grace the Court. Coolidge chose his own Attorney General, Harlan Stone, and Stone is commonly regarded as one of the great liberal Justices. Anti-Federalist Presidents sent Justice after Justice to the Court only to see them captivated by Marshall; among the more amusing stretches of American legal history are the papers flowing between Justice William Johnson, a Jeffersonian appointee, and Jefferson as Johnson attempted to account for his deviations from good Jeffersonian faith. Chief Justice Chase, Secretary of the Treasury during the Civil

---

[1] Charles Evans Hughes: *The Supreme Court of the United States* (New York: Columbia University Press; 1928), p. 58.

War, handed down an opinion invalidating the very financial system that as Secretary he had administered; and Holmes, who had been the choice of Theodore Roosevelt, bitterly disappointed T.R. by going against him on the heart of his anti-trust program, the *Northern Securities* case.[2]

The lifetime appointment is intended to, and does, emancipate a man from many of the pressures to which he had been subjected. That great corrupter of the conscience, the local constituency, is gone, and a man once appointed to the High Court need consult only the law, his conscience, and his aspirations for his country. This freedom may not merely broaden, it may also alter the vision. One of the most penetrating comments I ever heard a Supreme Court Justice make was a remark to a colleague whose life was being consumed in a series of minor pressures from persons who had helped to elevate him to his ultimate station. When the victim of these pressures pointed out the obligations, the Justice to whom he was speaking said: "Yes, but you are here now."

There is solid reason why the record of judicial success is so largely unrelated to previous judicial experience. Indeed, the situation is not radically different from that in other branches of the government. One of the Presidents most experienced in the executive department was Buchanan, and he is commonly regarded as the most ineffective occupant of the office; and one of the most effective was Lincoln, who had no such background. The most dynamic of the twentieth-century Presidents, Wilson and the two Roosevelts, had only brief previous experience in the executive department. In the ultimate positions of power, the most valuable qualities are wisdom, judgment, and great energy. Experience can aid but it can also diminish any of these

[2] *Northern Securities Co.* v. *United States,* 193 U.S. 197 (1904).

qualities. The man who works his way up from the bottom has to be a man who is willing to start at the bottom. The Supreme Court sheds so much prestige upon its members that, while appointment to it from time to time has been refused, ordinarily any lawyer will proudly accept the post. This is not true of some of the lower benches. On those courts the work may be intellectually gratifying, the association delightful, and the opportunities for self-expression very satisfying. Nonetheless, the positions have traditionally paid very little, and able men who did not have independent means have frequently been unable to accept them. There are repeated instances of Justices having a hard time with their salaries; Wilson in the 1790's was in real debt trouble, and Waite had to borrow repeatedly. Yet the number of men who have either left this highest bench or refused appointment to it for reasons of money is small.

From another standpoint, one can know so much about one's job that he does it badly. The man at the top makes policy. Great policy-making often requires a bold transcendence over practice, precedent, and experience. A man conditioned to the daily workings of a bureaucracy is dangerously unlikely to conceive of the building of one hundred thousand airplanes in the nation's hour of need, or the buying of the vast Territory of Louisiana from France, or the creation of an international league of states, or the freeing of a slave population by executive order. The same thing is true—in a more limited way, of course—in the judiciary. When the question "What shall we do tomorrow?" is asked, the judge answering it must be able to answer without being limited altogether by the answer to "What did we do yesterday?"

Since the appointment, once made, requires confirmation by the Senate, the appointing President must give some consideration to the attitude of that body. Normally, confirmations go through without much question, but the Senate rejects an appointee just often enough to remind the country that it knows how. The most recent example was the rejection by one vote of Judge John Parker, appointed by Hoover. When Parker was rejected, Owen Roberts was appointed in his place. By the cosmic irony of such events, it was the Senate liberals who defeated Parker, and on the basis of the comparative subsequent careers of the two men, they would have been much better off if they had supported him.

Usually the confirmation process either functions without controversy or simply raises a quarrel without affecting the ultimate result. However, there are some colorful by-products. Justice Brennan of the present Court was opposed waspishly and ineffectively by the late Senator McCarthy. An earlier Catholic appointee, Pierce Butler, encountered some opposition on religious grounds; a person wrote the Senate that "it may create happiness in Tammany and other Pope domains in the U.S. to have an Irish Catholic appointed to the Supreme Court." [3] The confirmation of Justice Frankfurter brought before the Senate Judiciary Committee an amazing collection of eccentrics. The anti-Semites sent their Senators mail by the bagful. Some of these were acknowledged Fascists, such as Ernst Goerner, a Nazi of Milwaukee, Wisconsin. Goerner contended that Frankfurter was a spiritual colleague of Justice Brandeis, an evil man who allegedly during World War I "had at his disposal a secret cable that connected him with various battle fronts." The Senate Committee heard numerous witnesses, also, on Frankfurter's alleged radicalism, including Mrs. Elizabeth

[3] Quoted by me in "Appointment of Supreme Court Justices," 1941 *Wisconsin Law Review* at 480.

Dilling, author of *The Red Network*, who indicted the nominee, most of the Senators present, and five Supreme Court Justices as Communists. The following dialog took place.

> SENATOR NEELY: Is it not a fact that in your book *The Red Network*, you criticized Chief Justice Hughes, Justice Brandeis, Justice Cardozo, Justice Roberts, and Justice Stone as vigorously as you have criticized Dr. Frankfurter?
>
> MRS. DILLING: I didn't know Hughes was in it. I know the rest of them were. I don't keep all these radicals in my mind.

As a consequence, when one of the witnesses told the Committee that he had facts which were "really surprising," Senator Neely replied: "The Committee does not want you to restrain yourself because of any fear of its being startled. The Committee became shock proof long before you appeared." [4]

In comparatively recent years one practice has arisen which could be most dangerous. The first nominee to be called to testify himself was Justice Stone in 1925. Up to that time the Committee, if it desired to make inquiry, carried out its own investigation, and on occasion a nominee fed material to the Committee. For example, the first Justice Harlan submitted an extended autobiographical letter to the Committee, when it was considering his appointment in 1877, in answer to allegations that he was not a good enough Republican to be worthy of the post.

Pierce Butler and his friends also fed the Committee much material for his hard-fought struggle for confirmation. Butler as President of the Board of Regents of the University of Minnesota during World War I had ruthlessly dominated that university, prying into private affairs of faculty mem-

[4] Many of the appointment episodes are detailed in my "Appointment of Supreme Court Justices," 1941 *Wisconsin Law Review*.

bers. He was also responsible for the discharge of a Professor Schaper during the war, to whom the university many years later made apology and gave reinstatement. These and many other items came up during the Butler hearings, and Butler directly furnished answers to the charges without appearing personally.

Bringing a nominee up for direct examination is quite another thing. Stone as Attorney General was in the midst of prosecuting Burton K. Wheeler, then recently elected Senator from Montana, for alleged participation in an oil-land fraud. (When the trial was eventually held, Senator Wheeler was found not guilty by a jury that was out of the box for ten minutes.) Senator Walsh of Montana used the hearings on the Stone appointment to examine the Department's handling of the Wheeler case. During the hearing Walsh and Stone in effect abandoned their functions as Senator and appointee, respectively, and simply became opposing counsel, so that the record contains the actual dickering between the two as to just when and where the Wheeler case should be tried.

In Frankfurter's case the questioning was of a very different sort. Senator McCarran made a direct examination into the ideas and attitudes of Frankfurter about particular matters, such as Communism. Frankfurter was keenly aware that a most important and perhaps most injurious precedent might be established, as the confirmation process neither has been nor should be used to determine how a Justice is going to decide particular matters which may come before him. He therefore advised the Committee that he did not care to "express his personal views on controversial issues affecting the Court" and asked it to make its judgment on the basis of his record over the years rather than its impressions of the moment.

McCarran's questions revealed that Frankfurter had not read some of the works which McCarran thought desirable, such as the report of the Dies Committee and the report of the American Legion on Communism in the American Civil Liberties Union, of which Frankfurter was a member. McCarran then dug hopefully into the possibility that Frankfurter's father had not been properly naturalized and that Frankfurter was thus not a citizen, but the facts were against him. When the questioning finally became what Frankfurter regarded as badgering, Frankfurter said: "Senator, I do not believe that you have ever taken an oath to support the Constitution of the United States with fewer reservations than I have or would now, nor do I believe that you are more attached to the theories and practice of Americanism than I am. I rest my answer on that statement."

When the Committee expressed a desire to interrogate Justice Minton, Minton avoided appearance, suggesting doubts as to the propriety of the whole business. Justice Brennan did appear to answer questions that came to nothing.

As a result of the appearances which have been made, it is now established that an appointee can be called and can be questioned. The potential evils in the practice are so obvious that it can at least be hoped that the Senate Judiciary Committee will be chary of using the privilege.

The real significance of the confirmation process is twofold. First, it gives the country a chance from time to time to think about the Supreme Court and to get information about it. The battle over the appointment of Charles Evans Hughes to the Chief Justiceship in 1930 on the grounds of his alleged excessive conservatism is a case in point. The first instance of a direct economic controversy over an appointee was in 1881, when Hayes appointed Stanley Matthews, a railroad lawyer, to the Court. The anti-monopoly leagues and granges of the country opposed the appointment bitterly, and Matthews was confirmed by a one-vote margin. From then to the time of Hughes, the charge that an appointee favored "the interests" has been frequent. Such charges, whether or not they were well taken, have done at least a little to educate the public at large on the work of the Court.

The public discussion may be extremely blunt; a Georgia newspaper commented on the appointment of Justice Wayne in 1835: "We live in an age of wonders. The man who was at best but a second rate lawyer at the bar of Georgia; who was a third rate judge in his native state, is by some strange freak of fortune, or of folly, transmitted to a seat with the Rabbi [Marshall] of his profession!" [5] It may also be merely scandalous or sordid, as shown by the hostility to Grant's Attorney General Williams because Mrs. Williams had offended Senate wives, and by the hullabaloo over L. Q. C. Lamar and his relations with a certain female government clerk suspected, among other things, of arson.

Second, and more significant, the process may affect the choice of a President who wishes to avoid a possible fight. While Supreme Court appointments are very rarely defeated, they are very frequently fought over. A President who is in no mood for a struggle may on occasion bypass a strong or colorful possibility in order to choose someone less controversial or to conciliate a faction.

In making these appointments, Presidents retain a very large degree of personal discretion. The choice of federal district judges may be left to the Senators, to the party organization, or the bar association, in some combination, of

---

[5] Quoted in Alexander A. Lawrence: *James Moore Wayne* (Chapel Hill: University of North Carolina Press; 1943), p. 80.

a particular state. The choice of the court-of-appeals judges may or may not come from the same sources. For example, Franklin Roosevelt kept more personal control of these appointments than did Truman. The Supreme Court appointments, however, are for the President to make, although Eisenhower did ask for the views of the American Bar Association before appointing Justice Brennan. They require consideration of several factors.

One is geography. Earlier in the Court's history this was of controlling importance. It is no longer. For the first hundred years of our history the Justices were in varying degrees responsible personally for a circuit or area of the country, in which they also sat as trial judges. It was usually thought that a Justice must come from the circuit in which he was to serve. When, for example, a new circuit was created for California during the Civil War, the number of Justices was raised to ten to make room for a Californian on the bench. Justice Miller maneuvered his own appointment by having the Iowa congressional delegation get through a new circuit arrangement in 1862 to make a space for him.

An extreme example of the operation of this system was the appointment of Justice Peter V. Daniel by Van Buren, referred to earlier. Daniel was to fill the vacancy of the deceased Justice Barbour, whose circuit consisted of Virginia and North Carolina. The Whig Party in the lame-duck session of 1841 did not have enough votes to defeat the Daniel appointment, though it would have enough immediately after March 4, when a new President and a new Congress would take office. Hence, if they could keep the appointment from being made until after March 4, it would fall to their own party.

The device they chose was based upon then accepted notions of geographical necessity. The Whigs offered the Democrats of the Southwest the creation of a new Southwestern circuit, breaking up the Virginia-North Carolina circuit and putting those two states into adjacent circuits that already had Justices. This would leave no circuit for Daniel to serve and would require a new appointment from the Southwest. The scheme very nearly worked, as the Southwesterners agreed to hold up the confirmation. When, however, it became apparent that there was not time for the redistricting bill to pass, they yielded and Daniel was confirmed on March 2, 1841, only a few hours before the expiration of the Congress. The Whigs very shortly got their revenge—they created a Southwestern circuit anyway, abolished Daniel's circuit, and left him nothing to serve except the region of Mississippi and Arkansas. The travel and hotel conditions of the time made this an almost mortal punishment.

Today some attention is paid to geographical considerations, but only in an approximate way. Thus, for a time in the 1930's New York had three justices, Hughes, Stone, and Cardozo. The Roosevelt administration gave representation on the Court to the Far West only by the device of having Justice Douglas abandon the Connecticut residence that he had long claimed. Douglas reverted to his original residence in the state of Washington, and has made a real thing of this affiliation by again becoming a Westerner. In the year 1958, geographical representation for the various sections of the country is at least fair: Chief Justice Warren and Douglas can be regarded as from the West Coast, Clark the Southwest, Whittaker the West Central states, Burton the East Central states, Brennan the mid-Atlantic states, Frankfurter New England, Harlan New York, and Black the Southeast. The most nearly unswerving geographical line on the Court has been the tradition of a New England seat, Frankfurter holding a seat that—except for his immediate predecessor, Cardozo—has been held by a New Englander from the very foundation of the Republic.

Other general considerations are those of religious and political affiliation. There has more often than not been a Catholic Justice, and except for two brief interruptions this has been invariably the case since 1894. There is no similar tradition of a Jewish seat, though there have been three Jewish Justices, one or more of whom has been on the bench from 1916 to the present time. Truman filled a "Catholic" vacancy with a Protestant, indignantly and emphatically rejecting the notion that there should be any religious tradition involved. The Democrats have made practically no effort to appoint across party lines. From Jefferson's day in 1801 to the close of the Truman administration in 1953, the only non-Democrat appointed by any Democratic President was Truman's choice of Justice Burton, and this selection is probably attributable to Truman's deep loyalty to his old friend and companion of the Senate War Investigating Committee. The Republicans have not been so parochial— in part, it may be suspected, because it has been easier for them to find conservative Democrats than for the Democrats to find liberal Republicans. As a result there have been several Republican appointments across party lines, the most recent of which is Eisenhower's choice of Brennan, a liberal Democrat.

The appointments are frequently political in a much more profound sense than that of mere party affiliation. A President is free, if he wishes, to serve some grand political purpose of his own. George Washington carefully filled the first Court with good solid Federalists for the purpose of setting the government off on the course he wished it to follow. As has been mentioned, John Adams's choice of John Marshall, his Secretary of State, came at a time when the Adams party had been defeated and when Adams was consciously trying to protect his policies. F.D.R. chose Black, perhaps in part to spite the Senate conservatives opposed to his Court-reform program, who could not refuse to confirm a fellow Senator; but he also made the choice for the purpose of giving the Court a strong push in the New Deal direction.

An appointment may also be made for more mundane political reasons. Prominent Republican Senator Allison in 1890 unsuccessfully asked Harrison to appoint Senator Spooner of Wisconsin, just defeated for re-election, to take care of a good lame duck. Senator Plumb of Kansas in 1889 expressed a willingness to let a Kansas appointment go to Missouri if added patronage would help carry that state, though he thought it would make no difference.

An example of shrewd political judgment was the selection of Chief Justice Chase by Lincoln. Chase was a radical Republican who had been Lincoln's Secretary of the Treasury. Vain, pompous, and assured, he must have been one of the most difficult men personally ever to hold a high public office. In 1864 he left the administration and for a time appeared a likely rival to Lincoln for the nomination for the next term. Although Lincoln controlled the nominating convention and was easily chosen, it was by no means clear that he would be re-elected. He needed the help of Chase as a campaigner, and was in no position to ask for it. At this fortunate moment Chief Justice Taney died. Lincoln passed the word that he would not make the appointment to the Chief Justiceship until after the election, but that he had made up his mind that the right man for the job was Chase. This was sufficient: Chase campaigned hard for Lincoln's election. The course of military events had so changed by the time of the actual election that Lincoln no longer needed the help of Chase—but Chase was appointed nonetheless.

There are numerous other instances of appointments to serve some purpose of either political convenience or political warfare. Cleveland engaged in a political vendetta with Senator Hill of New York, refusing to appoint a New Yorker satisfactory to Hill. Hill retaliated by causing Cleveland's first two choices from that state to be rejected. Cleveland then cut the ground from under Hill by choosing a Senator as appointee, as senatorial courtesy would not permit a Senator to be defeated; and thus Edward D. White of Louisiana went to the Court. It is sometimes suspected that Wilson chose his Attorney General, McReynolds, for the Court principally in order to end the closer association, but there is no concrete evidence. In 1937 it was universally believed that F.D.R.'s first appointment would go to his Senate majority leader, Joseph T. Robinson of Arkansas, as a reward for services rendered, but Robinson died before the question could be put to the test.

For the past forty years no appointment has been so obviously political or so obviously personal as some of those which preceded. There is no current equivalent of the best-told story of any of the political appointments, Lincoln's selection of David Davis, his 1860 convention campaign manager. Lincoln was under acute pressure to appoint another. His good friend Leonard Swett went to Washington to see him. As Swett described the episode twenty-five years later:

> In the morning about seven o'clock, for I knew Mr. Lincoln's habits well, [I] was at the door of his room at the White House and spent most of the forenoon with him. I tried to impress upon him that he had been brought into prominence by the circuit court lawyers of the old Eighth

Circuit, headed by Judge Davis. "If Judge Davis with his tact and his force had not lived, and all other things had been as they were, I believe you would not be sitting now where you are sitting." He replied: "I guess that is so." "Now," I said, "it is the common law of mankind that one raised into prominence is expected to recognize the force that lifts him, or, if from a pinch, the force that lets him out. . . . Here is Judge Davis, whom you know to be in every respect qualified for this position, and you ought in justice to yourself and public expectation to give him this place." We had an earnest pleasant forenoon, and I thought I had the best of the argument and I think he thought so too.

I left him and went to Willard's Hotel to think over the interview, and there a new thought struck me. I therefore wrote a letter to Mr. Lincoln and returned to the White House. Getting in, I read it to him and left it with him. It was in substance that he might think, if he gave Davis this place, he, when *he* got to Washington, would not give him any peace until he gave me a place equally good. That I recognized the fact that he could not give this place to Davis, which would be charged to the Bloomington faction in our State politics, and then give me anything—I would have [to] be just to the party there; that this appointment, if made, should "kill two birds with one stone"; that I would accept it as one-half for me, and one-half for the judge; and after that, if I or any of my friends ever troubled him, he could draw that letter as a plea in bar, on that subject. As I read it, Lincoln said: "If you mean that among friends, as it reads, I will take it and make the appointment." [6]

As may be expected, the Justices themselves sometimes take an interest in who is to sit with them. They may wait to be asked or they may attempt to persuade the President, depending upon their temperament and upon their relation-

[6] Swett to William Herndon, August 28, 1887, in Emanuel Hertz: *The Hidden Lincoln* (New York: The Viking Press; 1938), pp. 339–40.

ship with the White House. At the time of the appointment of Justice Rutledge by F.D.R. in 1943, Attorney General Biddle did consult several of the Justices as to their preferences, and at least some of them suggested that they would like to have Rutledge with them. The role of Chief Justice Taft in appointments is described in the chapter on Chief Justices. In the nineteenth century Justice Miller made constant efforts to get a like-minded colleague, and it may be presumed, although it is not known, that Truman consulted Chief Justice Vinson in connection with the appointments of his administration.

The influence of the Justices themselves upon the choice of their co-workers is less than might be supposed. By the very nature of the lifetime appointment and the long tenure of office, the Justices very rapidly grow apart from the party in power, even if it is their own. To take an extreme example: assuming that Justices Black and Frankfurter, the senior Roosevelt appointees on the Court, are on the bench at the time of the election of the next Democratic President, it is quite possible that there will be no acquaintance at all between these Justices and the new President. Of the Eisenhower appointees, none ever had any particular intimacy with any key members of the administration, and they are likely to have very little, if any, influence to wield even in the administration that chose them. Justices of the past have frequently been isolated from the administration in power, and, it may be added, this is just as it should be. Coupled with this is a general reluctance to ask favors or to risk rebuff; so that the number of Justices who, like Miller, attempt to influence the choice of their associates is small. This does not mean that the Justices may not have marked preferences; for example, Justice Rutledge strongly desired the appointment of Lloyd K. Garrison, of the New York bar, to the Chief Justiceship, which went to Fred Vinson. There was, however, nothing practical he could do about it.

The object of appointment is, basically, to get "competent" judges. There is every possible shading of competence among those appointed. This means plain technical competence, without any relation at all to the results generally reached by a particular judge. The ranking of the qualities of competence is impossible, and, indeed, one man's list of its elements may be different from another's, but there are some generally accepted factors.

For example, there is the capacity to reason cogently and clearly from the problem to its solution. In our system almost no factor is more important than this, because the opinions themselves (as distinguished from the results) are laid out for the acceptance of mankind, or at least so much of mankind, now or hereafter, as is willing to read them. An opinion which, given its major premises, is faulty in its logic is unconvincing, and to that extent is a technical failure.

In this respect, some Justices are infinitely better than others. One of the strong, forceful Justices of the Court was the first Harlan, whose dissent in the leading segregation case of the nineteenth century, including the famous passage "The Constitution is color blind," became the law in the twentieth century. The devastating comment of Justice Holmes on this brother was: "I never troubled myself much when he shied." His mind was like "a powerful vise, the jaws of which couldn't be got nearer than two inches to each other." [7]

Many of the most sympathetic readers of Harlan's opinions will agree that Holmes was right. Anyone who attempts

[7] Mark De Wolfe Howe, ed.: *The Holmes-Pollock Letters* (Cambridge: Harvard University Press; 1944), Vol. II, pp. 7, 8.

to follow, link by link, the reasoning of some of Harlan's outstanding opinions will end up with gaps in the chain.

Harlan was an immensely valuable judge who was occasionally shaky in his reasoning. He was infinitely superior, even in this regard, to the rock-bottom type that tends to abandon logic altogether and become simply oracular. An extreme example was McReynolds, who got over the hard spots by drawing a line across the center of the page (literally) and going on to another topic. Other Justices have used the purely agglutinative or paste-pot approach to the method of judging, their opinions consisting largely of quotations linked by very little reason.

At the other end of the stick was Justice Bradley, who, whether right or wrong, was always clear. A fine example of a first-class mind at work was Cardozo, about whom Judge Learned Hand wrote:

> There were indeed times when I dared to question the paths by which he reached his goal, but it seems to me that almost never did I venture to say that he came out at the wrong place. His results had an unerring accuracy, which, in my case at any rate, usually left me altogether reconciled, and which curiously contrasted with his tentative, at times almost apologetic, approaches to them. He never disguised the difficulties, as lazy judges do who win the game by sweeping all the chessmen off the table: like John Stuart Mill, he would often begin by stating the other side better than its advocate had stated it himself.[8]

What Hand describes as the lazy judge who sweeps the chessmen off the table is a common enough type. He is the judge who assumes the point actually in issue; who reasons his way through all of the points that do not matter, but slides over the one that does.

[8] Learned Hand: *"Mr. Justice Cardozo,"* 48 *Yale Law Journal* 379, 1939.

Of the Justices of the past whose work particularly commends itself for its clarity of reason, Justices Curtis and Campbell of the pre-Civil War period and Justice Sutherland of the 1920's and 1930's may particularly be mentioned. By the standards of our own day, Sutherland was almost always wrong in his conclusions; but he faced his problems very fairly.

More important than reason is the quality of creativeness. Creativeness is the capacity to come up with basic new answers to new problems, the capacity to see the farthest horizon as well as the matter immediately at hand. It is the opposite of the tendency to stop thinking when some past bit of experience has been found.

Court commentators have almost invariably, whether consciously or not, based their appraisal of Justices on this quality. Marshall had the greatest opportunity to be creative because he came at the beginning; he hit the Constitution much as the Lord hit the chaos, at a time when everything needed creating. Nonetheless, only a first-class creative genius could have risen so magnificently to the opportunity of the hour. Marshall made new law all the time, and yet seldom recklessly. For example, in his basic early opinions about the commerce clause Marshall went very far indeed to uphold the power of the federal government to regulate commerce and to restrict the states from burdening it; and in so doing he on occasion went much further than the necessities of his cases. That is to say, he could have decided his cases on narrower grounds than he did; he deliberately headed for the big questions. At the same time, his answers to those questions were flexible, giving subsequent generations free rein to make their own discoveries and decisions.

It is from this creative quality that Taney derives much

of his eminence, as do the late-nineteenth-century Justices Field and Miller. Stephen J. Field was one of the most powerfully creative Justices ever to sit on the Court. He came to the bench from California in Lincoln's administration. The post-Civil War amendments gave him an opportunity to bend the Constitution in a way that would make it protect business from government regulation. He must have greatly surprised those who had voted for the amendments on the assumption that they were simply freeing the slaves and giving them civil rights. By force of logic, creative imagination, energy, and intellect, Field more than anyone else created the due-process clause as it became known in the twentieth century, when it was used regularly to nullify state and federal regulations. More is said of this in the chapter on the Court and business.

Among the great creative minds in the twentieth century have been Holmes, Brandeis, Hughes, and Black. It was the task of Holmes and Brandeis to lay the foundations for our rejection of much that was Field. Brandeis's imaginativeness shows nowhere to better advantage than in the field of public-utility regulation, where, against the tide of his times, he merged law and economics into modern public-utility regulation. The creative powers of Hughes were particularly evident in the civil-liberties field; especially in respect to freedom of speech, he led the way to a restoration of the belief that Americans can be left to speak their minds.

On the contemporary Court, Black belongs in this company because he is never intimidated by the new ideas of anyone else simply because they are new, and because he is highly capable of creating new ideas himself. Black mingles a deep respect for history with an absence of fear of it. He draws liberally on seventeenth-century English experience, and his Livy is marked from one end to the other with his own notes, but his view is still forward. To the public-utility field, state regulations of business, the patent system, the right to counsel, the obligation of the states generally to honor all of the civil rights established in the Constitution, freedom of speech, and, most recently, to the right to practice the professions, Black has brought more new ideas than anyone else who was ever a member of the Court.

In addition to reason and creativeness, a judge must be possessed of endless industry. Moreover, this industry must be harnessed to objectives: the job of judges is to decide, and the job of opinion-writers is to get out opinions. A judge who is indecisive or who cannot get his work done is not of much use, no matter what his wisdom may be in occasional flashes. In the 1940's the lion's share of the "opinions of the Court" was written by Roberts, Black, Douglas, and Chief Justice Stone. Today the docket has become so light that this unevenness is balanced out; where those Justices were capable of doing from twenty to thirty opinions for the Court each year, today the quota is down to ten or twelve. In the past, Hughes, Brandeis, Miller, Waite, and particularly Marshall were immense workers. This is a quality that, standing by itself, can easily be overglorified; for example, Justice Story was a great worker, but it might be contended with a touch of fairness that he was merely an industrious hack. Yet great industry is a foundation to any accomplishment on the Court.

And a judge must be clear and persuasive. In this regard, most lawyers regard Holmes as pre-eminent. There is a thoughtful minority which feels that Holmes was too elliptical, that his lovely prose glided over hard spots and created obscurities by its brevity; but in any general vote he wins hands down.

Finally, a judge must possess scholarship. Creativeness

and policy-making may be important factors in High Court judging, but so is the capacity to find out what the law has been, the capacity to analyze the precedents and to find all of the materials that bear on a given point and then make intelligent use of them. The good judge may reject the lesson of history, but first he should find out what it is. This is immensely difficult; it requires, among other things, knowing where to look. It is a quality best nourished by the training of a lifetime; it is largely alien to the skill of either a Marshall or a Miller. The great scholars of the bench include Story, Gray, Brandeis, Stone par excellence, and, on the present Court, Frankfurter. Stone deserves extraordinary rating because of his great patience and because of the creativeness that went into his researches. His efforts outran merely the casebooks; he thought of new places to look.

It will be apparent that these are all Easterners. This is probably not accident. Because the East is the oldest region, it is the region in which there is the longest tradition of scholarship. For a time in one of the great rooms in the Supreme Court building there stood at opposite ends of the room a bust of Miller, the frontier Justice from Iowa, and a bas-relief of Gray, the scholar (and perhaps pedant) from Massachusetts. The appearance of the two confronting each other in the image of death as they did on the Court on which they served together dramatizes the medley that is the Court; the bookman is balanced by the first-class, energetic mind.

A basic difference among Justices is the degree of "judicial temperament" with which they approach the job. This term is usually applied to the objectivity of the judge, to his capacity to consider all sides of a question before he makes up his mind. The most obvious lack of judicial temperament, or objectivity, occurs when a judge has been bribed. Such a person is of course not a judge at all; he is simply a hired lawyer in a strategic position who has departed altogether from his obligations. It is a glory of the Supreme Court that there has not been a single known case of money bribery from the beginning. Some Justices have been very hard up. James Wilson, one of the members of the Constitutional Convention and a member of the first Court, was, for example, an out-and-out fugitive from his creditors. Nonetheless, if any Justice has ever been paid, the incident has been unrecorded, though William Allen White gives very circumstantial evidence that Justice Brewer, as a trial judge, was subject to influence through a relative.[9]

A second form of bribery, and one considerably more subtle, is social lobbying or pressure. To this the Court may at some times in the past have been a little vulnerable. There was the great Gaines case of the mid-nineteenth century, a controversy over a large estate, in which a charming lady claimant actively maintained a social lobby in Washington for the purpose of kindling the ardor of Supreme Court Justices in her behalf; and she lit some fires.[1] Carl B. Swisher has very well described the fashion in which Justice Field was absorbed by the social lobby of the Western railroads when he was in California.

In modern times, however, these pressures have been largely insignificant. The Justices make for themselves the kind of social life they like. A Vinson or a Burton who takes pleasure in trotting Diplomatic Row on Massachusetts Avenue, a Stone who savors the feasts of Lucullus, or a Black who would rather stay at home, can each indulge his preference. Today the predisposition of the judge makes his social

9 William Allen White: *Autobiography* (New York: The MacMillan Company; 1946), pp. 439, 440.

1 Noland Harmon, Jr.: *The Famous Case of Myra Clark Gaines* (Baton Rouge: Louisiana State University Press; 1946).

pattern; the pattern does not move in on him for some purpose of its own.

The ultimate in delicate corruption is that corruption which comes from hope of preferment. If the Justice has his eye on another place, if he wishes to become either Chief Justice or President, there is always the possibility that his votes or views may be affected by that ambition. This problem is discussed in some detail in Chapter XIV, and will be put aside here with the note that if this lure does influence the otherwise free mind, it does so in a manner which cannot be measured or assessed.

If judicial temperament means that in almost all cases the mind of a Justice can be compared to a perfectly balanced scale which is not moved until each authority and each argument has been carefully weighed, then in the tradition of the Supreme Court there has been very little judicial temperament. One of the most extreme examples of the opposite was Pierce Butler, of whom Attorney General Jackson said in his memorial proceedings: "He was relentless in bringing the lawyer face to face with the issues as he saw them. I think I never knew a man who could more quickly orient a statement of facts with his own philosophy. When the facts were stated the argument was about over with him—he could relate the case to his conceptions of legal principles without aid of counsel." The Attorney General continued: "His judicial attitude was not one of frosty neutrality, but one of intensity and certitude of conviction; I have known no one of more affirmative and immovable and masterful character than Mr. Justice Butler." [2] Which is to say, less politely, that presenting an argument to Mr. Justice Butler was like shooting darts at a brick wall.

On occasion the Justices have been out-and-out zealots.

[2] Supt. Ct. Proceedings, May 20, 1940.

As has been noted, the first bench appointed by President Washington was composed of Federalists who were chosen for that reason, and who in their capacity as trial judges moved about the country giving splendid stump speeches on behalf of Federalism under the guise of grand jury addresses. Chief Justice Marshall was admired for many qualities, but open-mindedness was scarcely one of them. Justice Daniel was so passionate a states'-rights Democrat that on one occasion when he had to shake the hand of Webster he felt positively physically polluted, and in 1851 on New Year's Day he declined to pay the normal respects at the White House because he preferred damnation to showing any respect for Whig President Fillmore. In the late nineteenth century those powerful figures Miller and Harlan were approximately as aggressive as grizzly bears; and while a few of the friends of Justice Brandeis attribute to him a considerable objectivity, this is not one of the softer virtues for which he is acclaimed by most scholars.

It will be noticed that judicial temperament was not characteristic of a good many of our greatest Justices. Great exceptions are Cardozo and Holmes. On the present Court a foremost example of judicial temperament is Justice Burton, a fair man who apparently does not make up his mind until he has considered every aspect of a problem, and who as a result, though basically conservative in his instincts, is highly unpredictable.

It is essentially a virtue on a bench of nine that it should have divergent talents, a set of qualities all mixed up. A bench of men all of whom made up their minds only after extended research and much contemplation might never get the job done; and it must always be remembered that the first job of judges is to decide. There are times when to ask a question is to answer it, when protracted thought would be a waste of time. There is an anecdote, almost certainly apocryphal, that at one Saturday conference Justice Murphy was unable to make up his mind on a four-to-four case and asked that the matter go over for the week end. On Monday he met Chief Justice Hughes, who asked whether he was now ready to cast his vote. Murphy confessed that he was still in doubt, that he had prayed for divine guidance on Sunday but had not felt it. Hughes's beard is supposed to have bristled as he replied: "Never mind prayer, have you read any cases?"

On the other hand, a group of Justices all brilliant, all willful, all ruthlessly decisive, could either precipitate drastic conflict within the Court or carry the country much too precipitately in one direction or another. The best bench consists of a mixture of talents—a hard and practical Miller with a highly scholarly Gray, a ruthless Field with an objective Waite and a profoundly thoughtful Bradley, in the company of a militant Harlan to intensify vigor of decision and color of exposition. These men, along with Samuel Blatchford, William Woods, and Stanley Matthews, all generally serviceable men, made up the Supreme Court of the 1880's. One may fairly believe that this was the ablest all-around Court that ever sat.

Chapter IV

THE CHIEF JUSTICES

The salary of an Associate Justice of the United States Supreme Court is $35,000 and that of the Chief Justice is $35,500. These salaries are the result of recent raises, and when the raises were made, it was first proposed to make that of the Chief $5,000 more than those of his Associates.

That proposal, more than any other, held up the judicial-pay-raise bill. While the many congressional friends and admirers of ex-Congressman Vinson, then the Chief Justice, would happily have given their old companion this special remuneration, others thought it a long step in the wrong direction. It seemed undesirable to magnify the margin between the Chief and his Associates by more than the $500 long before established. As a result, the proposal for the marked difference was quietly scuttled.

The Chief Justice of the United States is not the number-one man among a group of subordinates. He is *primus inter pares*, first among equals. He casts only one vote, and that vote carries no more authority, no more weight, than that of the most junior Justice, except as his own personality and abilities influence other members of the Court.

This puts it a little too simply. His office carries some pre-rogatives. His formal title is a trifle different: he is Chief Justice of the United States, and his fellows are Justices of the Supreme Court. He administers the oath of office to the

President. He presides when the Court is in public session, and at its secret conferences. He also presides over the judicial conference of the judges of the lower courts, and he has the not inconsiderable duty of assigning the writing of most of the opinions to his brothers. He is the chief administrative officer of the Court.

All of these together are not very important. By themselves, they do not account for the fact that periods of the Court's history are likely to be known by the names of the Chief Justices who presided. They do not explain why the country at large regards the Chief as more significant than his brothers.

The great and yet intangible difference between the Chief and his Associates is the prestige that, rightly or wrongly, tradition attaches to the Chief Justiceship. Popular mythology makes the Chief Justiceship much of what it is, in part because there have been some very great Chief Justices whose personal glory has rubbed off on the office, and partly because of popular esteem for the very idea of "Chief." There have been Chiefs who gained their prestige, such as it was, entirely from the office; Fuller, who presided at the turn of the twentieth century, is an example. But for the very reason that the Chief Justice sits where John Marshall sat, any holder of the office enjoys an almost hereditary status.

Popular esteem for the title is such that many believe that if Charles Evans Hughes, who resigned as an Associate Justice to run for the Presidency in 1916 and lost in a close election, had been Chief Justice instead, he, rather than Woodrow Wilson, would have been President during World War I. In some states with an elective judiciary there is an amiable practice of rotating the state chief justiceship so that the justice next up for election serves as chief justice and can be introduced and referred to as chief justice during his campaign. This is because the public attaches special value to the label.

For much the same combination of reasons, the Chief Justices are chosen with special care and usually come to the bench with particularly distinguished backgrounds of public service. As two Senators accurately summed it up in 1873, "The country seems to require that the Chief Justice should possess high character, sound principles, great capacity and wide celebrity." [1] An occasional Associate is extremely obscure. For example, when Attorney General Wickersham began to make inquiries leading to the appointment of Joseph R. Lamar, Wickersham had only a vague impression of where to find him; and Justice Miller was widely confused with another person of similar name.

The Chiefs are usually prominent. John Marshall, Roger Taney, and Salmon P. Chase were cabinet members either at the time of or shortly before their appointments. Edwin D. White was a Senator when he was appointed an Associate Justice, from which position he moved to the center seat. William Howard Taft had been President, Charles Evans Hughes had been an Associate Justice, a cabinet member, and a presidential candidate, Stone and Vinson had been cabinet members, and Warren had been a Governor and a presidential candidate. Of all of the Chief Justices from 1801 to the present time, only Waite and Fuller came essentially from the bar, and the appointment of each was due to exceptional circumstances. Waite, appointed in 1877, was President Grant's third nomination, the Senate having raised objections to his first two choices, each of whom was eminent. Cleveland appointed Fuller because an unusual po-

---

[1] Quoted in Bruce R. Trimble: *Chief Justice Waite* (Princeton: Princeton University Press; 1938), p. 131.

litical exigency made him extremely eager to choose a man from Illinois and the most obvious choice from that state was financially unable to accept the position.

Nonetheless, fame is not enough; the Chief Justices cannot solve tomorrow's problems with yesterday's press clippings. A Chief Justice comes into a situation in which some of his Associates may be unsympathetic to him, and in any case may have reputations that in legal circles are at least as great as his. Take, for example, the appointment of Fuller as Chief Justice in 1888. Shelby M. Cullom, senior Senator from his home state of Illinois, appraised Fuller as one of the "five best lawyers of Illinois belonging to his party." At the time this was not exactly overwhelming praise. Fuller's Court already contained the considerably more famous Field, Miller, Bradley, and Harlan. As Fuller, with fair modesty, wryly observed, "No rising sun for me with these old luminaries blazing away with all their ancient fires." [2]

As difficult a situation as any was that of Chief Justice Waite. The appointment came as a considerable surprise to Waite, an obscure Ohio lawyer, leading one legal wag to observe: "Waite is that luckiest of all individuals known to the law, an innocent third party without notice." Waite proved to be a splendid Chief Justice. When he came to Washington, his supposed unfamiliarity with the practice and methods of the Court led Justice Clifford to suggest that Waite stand aside for a few days and let Clifford preside in the meantime. Waite turned for counsel to a good friend, who said: "I would go up there tomorrow, get on the box, gather up the reins and drive, and give them to understand that I was the Chief Justice."

[2] Willard L. King: *Melville Weston Fuller* (New York: The Macmillan Company; 1950), p. 127.

The next afternoon Waite appeared again in the office of his friend and, when asked how the day had gone, said: "Splendidly, splendidly. I acted on your suggestion literally. I got on the box as soon as I arrived there this morning, gathered up the lines and drove, and I am going to drive and those gentlemen know it." [3]

When a Chief picks up the reins to drive, his most conspicuous task is presiding in the courtroom itself. He handles the little ceremonies. When a lawyer is admitted to the bar of the Supreme Court, his sponsor, already a member of the bar, stands before the entire Court and asks the Chief Justice to order the admission. As there are a good many hundreds of these each year, Chief Justice Warren has astonished the onlookers by managing to give each individual lawyer a sense of personal welcome as he gestures the newcomer over to the clerk's desk to take his oath. Of somewhat greater importance, the Chief has a limited control over the length of time for argument and over other niceties of the courtroom procedure.

Administratively, the Chief is the head of the institution in the sense that if the clerk or the marshal has problems to take up with the Court as a whole, he takes them up through the Chief; and by practice the Chief decides minor matters for the Court. To someone like Warren, who has been Governor of a great state, these little problems are trifling.

More important, the Chief presides over the conference of the senior circuit judges. This gathering of the top federal judges from lower courts all over the country reviews and considers how to improve the entire court system of the United States. A worth-while and serious project, this judicial conference was originated in 1922 by Chief Justice Taft, who, as a former lower-court judge, knew the need for

[3] Trimble: *Chief Justice Waite,* p. 135.

some co-ordination among the federal judges. Warren regards it as a significant part of his work, and so did his predecessor, Vinson. It is not, however, a large part of the work of the whole Court, for very little that happens in this conference bears on the Court's main job, which is to decide cases.

The two really meaningful functions of the Chief in relation to his brethren are his chairmanship of the Court's own conference (as distinguished from the general conference just described) and his assignment of the writing of opinions. When the judges gather in their conference room to decide the cases, the Chief, as chairman, opens the discussion by giving his own views on the questions at issue. The task of thus stating the case and indicating the questions to be decided is a genuine power, because in any discussion the first analysis of a problem will more often than not affect the analysis of everyone else. The man who selects the issues to be talked about very frequently dominates the end result.

With some Chiefs, this skill reached the point of genius. The outsider who knows most about how Chief Justice Hughes handled his statements to the conference tells us that Hughes viewed this ability to state the cases "as very important, for it gave him the opportunity to fix the relative importance of the case against the perspective of the Court's deliberations, and to suggest (if not to determine) the amount of conference time which should be spent on each." The same author reminds us that in the Hughes administration an average petition for certiorari could not be given more than three and one-half minutes of conference time. On that basis, the first statement was very likely to be the last.[4]

[4] Edwin L. McIlwain: "The Business of the Supreme Court as Conducted by Chief Justice Hughes," 63 *Harvard Law Review* 12 (1949).

By every account, Hughes performed this function better by far than any other Chief Justice. As a result of superb preparation he was usually able to state the cases from memory, or with very few notes. Perhaps the greatest tour de force ever accomplished by a lawyer was Hughes's statement of cases at the end of the summer recess when some three hundred petitions for certiorari were up for decision; his complete mastery of the materials enabled him to state every case accurately without reading any matter to the conference. With Chief Justice Stone, much depended on the skill and brevity with which a clerk had prepared the notes from which he worked, and the legend is that when Stone had two clerks, the other Justices could tell which one had prepared the notes from the length of time Stone took to state the cases. Under Vinson, the effectiveness of the statement system largely disappeared and was replaced by a good deal of plain mumbling.

Because the Chief is chairman, he has the greatest opportunity to control the occasional acrimony which is bound to come up in discussion among men of strong character and convictions. In this respect Fuller was one of the best Chief Justices, able to turn the discussion tactfully after flare-ups; and his skill was greatly appreciated by his strong-minded colleagues. Hughes achieved much the same result by the discipline that emanated from his stern personality and by the quick pace at which he ran the meetings, while Chief Justices White and Taft relied heavily on jolly good nature of the sort traditionally attributed to the fat men they were. For Taft, this effort at times exhausted his supply of good nature, and he sometimes betrayed his own irritations by very sharp remarks in letters.

The most important duty of the Chief Justice in relation to his Associates is his assignment of the writing of opinions.

He must distribute the work load and so ride herd on its completion that by the end of the year the Court will have done the job which was before it. In this respect Hughes was the greatest success the Court has known since its docket began to grow heavy about 1850. The writing of opinions is not rotated in order nor selected by chance, as in some state courts; the Chief, if he is on the majority side in a given case, designates or assigns the Justice who is to write the opinion, and it thereupon becomes the duty of that Justice to perform.

In making assignments the Chief may have any one of a variety of purposes in view and can often affect the resulting opinions. Sometimes his purpose is public relations, as when Chief Justice Hughes assigned "liberal" opinions to "conservative" Justices in order to disabuse the public of the notion that the Court was divided along simple liberal and conservative lines. Thus, for example, right-winger Sutherland was assigned the task of writing the opinion upholding the Scottsboro Negroes' right to counsel. The assignment may also be used as a reward, the new members of the Court receiving the gentle hazing of the duller cases, such as those dealing with taxes or fair labor standards, while the plums are often saved for seniors. Stone, for example, rarely received a good assignment from his own first Chief, Taft.

Most importantly, the assignments control the whole nature of the Court's opinions, and may very radically affect the status of a judge. Because Chief Justice Stone had very little confidence in Justice Murphy, he practically never assigned him anything of importance. Murphy's opportunities came only when all Justices senior to Black were in dissent; Black then became the senior, or assigning, Justice and could and did give Murphy big cases. Black has pronouncedly unfavorable views on the patent system, and

Stone, though he assigned Black many good cases, never assigned him one that had to do with patents. Again, the power of a Chief to choose the writer of an opinion gives him the power to select for the purpose that Justice whose views are closest to his own, just as it permits him to assign to himself the cases on which he is most anxious to speak for the Court. The assignment power can lead to much exasperation when a Justice feels he has been passed by. Justice Harlan wrote Chief Justice Fuller in 1898: "Two Saturdays in succession you have not assigned to me any case but have assigned cases and important ones to Justice Gray. I was in the majority in each case assigned to him." [5]

The power of self-assignment means that a Chief can make or break himself as well as make a good deal of law if he is of a mind to. John Marshall almost invariably spoke for the Court in the great cases that came before him. Chief Justice Fuller, on the other hand, assigned himself so little of consequence that he wrote almost nothing of contemporary significance. By now it has come to be accepted as traditional that in the majority of the most important matters the Chief should speak for the Court. Thus, it was particularly appropriate that Chief Justice Warren should give the opinion in the segregation cases; and in 1957 Warren very properly assigned to himself the writing of the opinion in which the Court finally put a sharp check on the House Committee on Un-American Activities. [6]

All these special powers of the office of Chief do not amount to a great deal; a Chief must get his real eminence not from the office but from the qualities he brings to it. He must possess the mysterious quality of leadership. In this

[5] Quoted in King: *Melville Weston Fuller*, p. 245.
[6] A most revealing discussion of the headaches of the assignment system for a Chief, including some complaints from the Justices, is contained in Trimble: *Chief Justice Waite*, pp. 259 *et seq.*

respect the outstanding Chief was Marshall, who for thirty-five years presided over a Court largely populated by Justices of an opposing political party. Moreover, his Court, because of the very newness of the Constitution it was expounding, dealt with some of the greatest questions of history. Nonetheless, Marshall dominated his Court as has no other Chief Justice. He wrote most of its important opinions, and his dissents are remarkable for their rarity.

Marshall's leadership has intrigued every Court historian. His record of valor in the Revolution, his distinguished public service, and the superb quality of his personal simplicity undoubtedly contributed to his standing. Chief Justice White, a century later, was as simple and unostentatious a man and had a good, if more modest, military record; yet, while everyone liked White, no one ever supposed him to be an outstanding Chief Justice.

More important, Marshall brought a first-class mind and a thoroughly engaging personality into second-class company. The Court when he came to it was lazy and quite willing to let him do the work. Johnson, one of its members, told Jefferson that "Cushing was incompetent. Chase could not be got to think or write—Patterson was a slow man and willingly declined the trouble, and the other two judges [Marshall and Bushrod Washington] are commonly estimated as one judge." [7]

Later appointees to Marshall's Court, with one or two distinguished exceptions, were weak. From what we know of the lives and see of the work of most of them, Marshall's superior powers must have filled the conference like the rush of air into a vacuum. This condition, which has not existed to the same degree at any other time, was intensified because

[7] Johnson to Jefferson, December 10, 1822, quoted in Donald G. Morgan: *Justice William Johnson* (Columbia: University of South Carolina Press; 1954), p. 182.

in those early days most of the Justices lived together in a common boardinghouse in Washington.[8] They were thus constantly in the company of the ablest among them. From the standpoint of sheer technical competence, Marshall had a dominance which was denied, for example, to a Vinson, whose unfamiliarity with many of the matters that came before the Court made his effective leadership impossible.

A further factor making for a strong and significant Chief is the capacity to get along happily with his colleagues. The late Chief Justice Stone is a notable example of a judge completely competent in his own individual duties of judging who was yet unable to function well as a Chief. As Associate Justice from 1925 to 1941, he had been one of the most distinguished members of the Court. When Stone was originally appointed in 1925, Senator George W. Norris opposed his confirmation. When he was nominated as Chief Justice in 1941, Norris, still in the Senate, arose to confess his error and to applaud the elevation. The promotion of Stone from Associate to Chief was accompanied by as nearly unanimous an accolade as ever occurs in our turbulent public life.

Yet Stone was not a satisfactory Chief Justice. During his tenure the high efficiency of the Court began to deteriorate, the Court was much more frequently divided than usual, and the opinions of at least some of its members indulged in a stridency of tone which diminished the prestige of the tribunal. Personal relations within the Court were most unhappy.

Why? Stone's occasional testiness and vanity made him very difficult to work with. A partisan battler himself, he could not rise above the fray to bring calm leadership into the controversies of others. As his biographer Alpheus T. Mason observes, he was a "loquacious Justice"; and he was

8 This system is described in Chapter XIV.

given to tactless comment about his colleagues. Stone condemned almost every colleague he had, whether Republican or Democrat, both in the Old Court and in the New Deal days. For example, he regarded the Nuremberg war trials, in which his brother Justice Jackson was prosecutor, as a high-grade lynching party. Perhaps they were, but it was not tactful of Jackson's Chief to say so.

Stone's relations with his own first Chief, Taft, were strained, and he felt great hostility toward his next Chief, Hughes. It may have been an old man's malice, but Chief Justice Taft was quite right when he wrote in 1929, when Stone was being considered as his own successor, that "Stone is not a leader and would have a good deal of difficulty in massing the Court."

Under Hughes the conference of the Court was usually a four-hour affair; under Stone it sometimes ran for four days. Discussion became wrangling. As the Justices emerged from these interminable meetings they were irritated and exhausted, with pride of opinion inflamed from excessive argument. Hughes was perhaps too dominant a Chief, and it is usually said that this explains why Stone swung so far in the opposite direction; however, he did not find a happy mean.

Chief Justice Taney, who served in the post for thirty years—from the days of Jackson, who appointed him, almost to the end of the term of Lincoln—represents a certain intermediate degree of success. His strengths and his weaknesses highlight what the office requires. Like Marshall, he achieved an easy eminence because he brought to the bench a mind many degrees better than those of most of his colleagues. Justices Story, Curtis, and Campbell, who served with Taney, were first-class judges. Otherwise, Taney's superiority to the other members of his Court in terms of ability gave him much of the automatic leadership that was Marshall's. (I put aside the very strong men appointed by Lincoln at the very end of Taney's service.)

At the same time Taney was thoroughly companionable, at least with his like-minded Justices, and was able to evoke immense personal loyalty from them. For example, for nineteen years he served with the highly peppery and irascible Peter V. Daniel of Virginia, a man mixed of equal parts of strong conviction, ego, and vinegar. These two lived together, worked together, and on occasion vacationed together. Taney, although a little older, had more stamina, and an evening hike along the ocean sands of Virginia when both men were in their sixties was likely to send Daniel back to his quarters considerably more tired than his Chief. Taney had a genuine personal solicitude for Daniel and his physical welfare; Daniel wrote almost pathetically to his daughter that the Chief would not let him leave his quarters until he had recovered from some little illness. This was matched by Daniel's pleasure when he could bring up from his farm in Virginia some delicacy to please the palate of his Chief.

This was the relationship of Taney with an essentially like-minded Justice. On the other hand, the wrangle of Taney, a Jacksonian Democrat and Southerner, with his colleague Curtis, a Websterian Whig and Northerner, was one of the most unseemly in the history of the Court. In the *Dred Scott* case, in which the Court involved itself deeply in the issue of slavery in the territories, Taney sustained the Southern and Curtis the Northern point of view. Passions rose so high that Taney took steps to bar Curtis from seeing the opinions of the other Justices, thus making it more difficult for Curtis to dissent effectively. The resulting correspondence reflects badly on Taney's judgment at the same time that it highlights his vigor.[9]

The turbulence of that moment had its direct effect on the efficiency of the Court. There were nine—count them, nine—separate opinions filed in the *Dred Scott* case. If ever there was a case in which the majority at least should have spoken with one voice, it was here. The discord stripped the Court of the Olympian quality which it needs particularly when delivering a judgment that will offend a large section of the country. Imagine the chaos that might have resulted if there had been nine separate opinions in the segregation cases, with each Justice, for varying reasons, coming to slightly or radically different conclusions, and one may sense the confusion that followed Dred Scott's case in 1857. One difference between a Warren in the segregation cases and a Taney in *Scott* is that Warren's personal qualities permit him to keep the Court generally happy even in cases that provoke sharp disagreement. Notably, he is temperate himself even when he dissents strongly.

Harmony may be helped along when the Chief influences the appointment of a Justice, but this is not always the case. Taft appointed Van Devanter, who became his favorite colleague when Taft himself was later appointed to the Court. After he became Chief, Taft strongly influenced the appointment of Pierce Butler, his sturdy ally. On the other

[9] Another instance of Taney's excessive partisanship occurred in *Bank of United States* v. *United States,* 2 How. 711 (1844). This case involved an episode that had occurred when Taney had been Attorney General almost ten years before, and he therefore very properly disqualified himself from passing on the case in the Supreme Court. Nonetheless, he felt so strongly on the subject that he proceeded to file in the appendix to the Supreme Court Reports an expression of the views he would have expressed if he had not been disqualified, an essay over twenty pages long. As he disagreed with the decision of the Court, this amounts to a dissent in a case in which he did not participate.

83

hand, Taft vigorously fought the confirmation of Brandeis, and no particular harm resulted; and Stone's support of the appointment of Frankfurter did not result in teamwork. The late Secretary of Interior Harold Ickes told me that he vigorously supported the appointment of Robert Jackson to the Court, and that he regarded this as the worst mistake of his life; doubtless Justices too can repent their enthusiasms.

Finally, the status of a Chief may depend much upon his own personal ability as a lawyer, as a thinker, as a writer, and as a judge. Before the Civil War the Chiefs stood head and shoulders over the other members of their own Courts. For the last hundred years this has not been the case, not because of a shrinkage in the quality of the Chiefs, but because of a strengthening of the other Justices. From Lincoln's day on, Presidents have appointed abler men to the Court. Stone may have made a poor Chief, but his immense abilities as a judge earned him a real eminence.

Any Chief is likely to be a mixture of qualities. In many respects one of the very weakest of the Chief Justices was Fuller, who served from 1888 to 1910. He assigned himself negligible opinions and occupied himself as Chief with many petty details. Take, for example, this note to the Court reporter:

> In *Mendenez* v. *Holt* (128 U.S. 514) the initials of the name of the English reporter, Johnson are given V.C.— 3rd line from top of page 522. I think but am not sure that they are H.V.C.
> P.S. They are H.R.V.[1]

Clearly a Chief who is worrying about the middle initial of someone whose full name is not of the slightest consequence could easily make a different, if not better, use of his

[1] This note is taken from King: *Melville Weston Fuller,* p. 142.

time. A stickler over nice details, Fuller thought the dignity of his office required him to decline to attend a dinner for any person who had not first called formally upon him. His colleague Holmes, a less sticky fellow, once concluded his invitation to a dinner in honor of a Japanese friend: "If you would honor us with your presence, he would come to meet you rather than you to meet him, on the general principles of gravitation. You would add greatly to our pleasure, and I don't think that the dignity of your office would be impaired." [2]

But though he may have been more a fuddy-duddy than a legal light, Fuller in one respect made a real contribution to the legal operation of the Court. He ran his conferences extremely well, and in his close attention to the management of the administrative side of the Court Fuller may have been one of its outstanding presiding officers. The stories of how Fuller stopped a quarrel that was developing between Harlan and Holmes; how he handled the unpleasant duty of persuading the senile Field to retire; how he dissuaded Holmes from using a certain word that might have annoyed the other Justices—all these incidents led Fuller's biographer to conclude that, though Fuller was not the greatest intellect ever to guide the Court, "he was an extraordinary Chief Justice in his relations with his colleagues." [3]

Twentieth-century examples also show that a Chief may be of uneven strength and is no more likely than other humans to satisfy everyone. Vinson brought extremely limited

[2] Ibid., p. 318. This touchiness as to dinner protocol was not peculiar to Fuller, and has been a commonplace small problem. In 1908 Fuller did not attend President Theodore Roosevelt's dinner for the Court because of a recent bereavement. This left Justice Harlan as the senior Associate, and it became his duty to escort Mrs. Roosevelt in to dinner. Speaker of the House Cannon refused to attend; he was willing to be outranked by Fuller but not by Harlan. Charles Henry Butler: *A Century at the Bar of the Supreme Court* (New York: G. P. Putman's Sons; 1942), pp. 124–5.

[3] King: *Melville Weston Fuller*, p. 336.

technical ability to the post and was quite incapable of leading his colleagues. In conversations with lawyers, Vinson concentrated on baseball, partly from a sense of the impropriety of talking law off the bench. But Vinson was also a likable and diplomatic fellow; and with these qualities he did much to end the excessive tensions of the Stone period. Certainly he was a friendly, unassuming man quite dedicated to his country's welfare. For all-around legal skill and superb administrative ability, I regard Charles Evan Hughes as the greatest Chief since Marshall. Yet some critics believe he ran the conference with excessive discipline.

It is too soon to make definitive judgments about the present Chief Justice. So far, it is clear that the country is greatly fortunate to have Earl Warren in the center chair. Under his leadership, *esprit* is good, quality is high, and quantity and efficiency are increasing. Of his individual contributions, history will have enough to say; but it will never need to say more than that he wrote the school-segregation opinion.

Chapter V

METHODS OF PERSUASION

One tradition is that the two greatest arguments in the history of the Supreme Court were the *Dartmouth College* case near the beginning of the nineteenth century and the *Income Tax* case near the end of it. The central question in the *College* case was whether the State of New Hampshire could revise the college charter, granted originally by the crown, to get one set of trustees off, and another on, its board. The college contended that the charter was a contract that could not be impaired. The case had everything—old college pride, a loyal alumnus as counsel, a state about to take the charter of the college, and, above all, the extraordinary talents of Daniel Webster. The classic description of the conclusion of that argument has been given by Beveridge, from whom I borrow it:

> "We had hoped, earnestly hoped," exclaimed Webster, "that the State Court would protect Dartmouth College. That hope has failed. It is here that those rights are to be maintained, or they are lost forever." He closed with a long Latin quotation, not a word of which Marshall understood, but which, delivered in Webster's sonorous tones and with Webster's histrionic power, must have been prodigiously impressive. . . .
> At length, addressing the Chief Justice, Webster delivered that famous peroration ending: "Sir, you may destroy this little institution. It is weak. It is in your

87

hands! I know it is one of the lesser lights in the literary horizon of the country. You may put it out. But if you do so, you must carry through your work. You must extinguish, one after another, all those great lights of science which, for more than a century, have thrown their radiance over our land.

"It is, Sir, as I have said, a small college and yet, there are those who love it. . . .

"Sir, I care not how others may feel," (glancing at the opponents of the College before him,) "but, for myself, when I see my Alma Mater surrounded, like Caesar in the senate-house, by those who are reiterating stab on stab, I would not, for this right hand, have her turn to me, and say, *et tu quoque, mi fili!*" [1]

In the *Income Tax* cases, the issue was whether, back in 1895, the government could constitutionally take two per cent of incomes over twenty thousand dollars. The Old Man Eloquent was Joseph Choate, surrounded on both sides with a galaxy of talent, and when Choate reached his climax with his denunciation of the Communistic, Socialistic, yea, Populistic trend of the times, it was said that the Court could never rise above the height of this great argument.

For purposes of present evaluation, the most conspicuous fact about each of those arguments is that they occurred in the last century. In recent years, oratory has been a dwindling and, indeed, usually impracticable and unwelcome courtroom art. By the 1930's the forensic leaders of the bar were two men who were already elderly and who were both very, very good. One was John W. Davis, and the other was George Wharton Pepper. With Mr. Pepper, still a leader of the bar as I write this, the talent lay not in old-style oratory but in a glowing fluency and dignity coupled with a shrewd instinct for the simple but right word. Take, for example,

[1] Albert J. Beveridge: *The Life of John Marshall* (Boston and New York: Houghton Mifflin Co.; 1919), Vol. IV, pp. 249, 250.

this passage from his successful argument following which the Court invalidated the first Agricultural Adjustment Act.

> If it is going to be possible for the Federal government to offer pecuniary reward to the farmer under conditions such that he cannot very well afford to decline, you get a situation in which he sells his freedom for this mess of pottage, and disavows his allegiance to that State which, under the Tenth Amendment, is entitled to control his production, and subjects himself to what is, in that sense, an alien scheme. I always distrust my capacity to put a perfect dilemma; but I suggest that in this case one of two things is true—either that control acquired by purchase is, if lawful, the supreme law of the land, or that a scheme of local regulation which it is within the power of the State to nullify is a scheme which Congress lacks the power to set up.

The most colorful argument heard within my own experience was the *Schneiderman* case in 1943.[2] The issue was whether Schneiderman, a Communist, could be denaturalized on the ground that he had defrauded the government when he obtained his citizenship by false allegations concerning his loyalty to the United States. Counsel for Schneiderman was Wendell Willkie, then but recently the Republican candidate for President of the United States, who was convinced that basic principles of the rights of immigrants were involved. Counsel for the government was Charles Fahy, then Solicitor General of the United States.

The courtroom was jammed. This room, to which the judges moved in the 1930's, is a far cry from the small chamber in the Capitol used for so many years. The new room, in the great marble palace across from the Capitol in which the Court is housed, has nothing of intimacy about it; it is a

[2] *Schneiderman* v. *United States,* 320 U.S. 118 (1943).

big, cold, richly hung and decorated chamber with the bench itself at one end raised somewhat from the floor. Behind the bench sit the Justices, each in a swivel chair of such height and design as is most compatible with his size and, perhaps, his sacroiliac. In front of the bench, at floor level, at each side of a speaker's stand are the tables for the lawyers arguing the case. On the tables are the traditional goose quills, placed there for the attorney who may wish to take a few notes and who has forgotten his twentieth-century pen and pencil in the excitement of the occasion. Their principal utility now is as souvenirs. Stretching behind counsel tables are the seats for other members of the bar, and then the seats of the public. When the case of Schneiderman was heard, the public cued up outside the courtroom door along the great marble entranceway that leads from the high steps and the outdoors into the courtroom itself.

Schneiderman's case presented a grave issue, and the distinction of counsel on both sides heightened interest. That Schneiderman's lawyer was Willkie, a Wall Street lawyer and a Republican, gave drama to the occasion. Mr. Fahy was also a distinguished American, had been Solicitor General longer than anyone else, and as such was counsel for the government before the Supreme Court. He was a quiet-spoken man, so far removed from the traditional orator as at times to be almost inaudible to any but the Justices. As they were the only audience toward which he was directing himself, this was of no consequence. This seemingly meek and mild man had a number-one record as an ace in World War I, and was on his way to a later career as chief counsel for the State Department and as judge on the United States Court of Appeals for the District of Columbia.

Mr. Willkie's conduct was colorful and unusual. Custom and courtesy dictate that when counsel for one side is speak-

ing, counsel for the other shall listen and take notes in perfect quiet, as unobtrusively as possible. Not Mr. Willkie.
Across his mobile features, underneath the falling lock of
hair that was his trademark, ran a constant rebuttal. After
the fashion of an indignant high-school debater, his mouth
would form into an almost audible "no" at some expression
of Fahy's with which he disagreed. At one point he rose to
his feet to remonstrate in the middle of Fahy's argument. In
his own time he was colorful, vigorous, emphatic, and really
very good. His bubbling demeanor was such that probably
no one but an ex-presidential candidate would have dared it.

Fahy's argument was in his personal grand style. He was
concise, he analyzed thoroughly the legal problems of the
case, he was immensely in earnest. He was a man not given
to gesture, and occasionally in moments of great earnestness
he would step away from the speaker's stand and emphasize
his point with a slight and slow up-and-down movement of
his clenched hands, a movement whose very restraint gave an
emphasis greater than if he had shouted and pounded the
table. No person hearing that argument could have doubted
that two distinguished Americans were doing their best to
persuade the Court in opposite directions on a matter of
consequence. Mr. Willkie prevailed, though there has been
some movement away from his position in recent years.

In the early years of the Court, when it was not busy, it
could indulge counsel in arguments of almost limitless
length. Each side might take days on a case, and the arguments themselves had an entertainment value for the ladies
of the Capitol, particularly when one of the greats was
speaking. Justice Daniel, a bit of a prude, was downright
shocked by the number of ladies who turned out to hear
Henry Clay, who in addition to his other attainments was a
notorious rake. In one case, argument was adjourned to give

the distinguished lawyer Luther Martin a chance to sober up, and in another case an argument was begun over again to give a lady a chance to hear some choice bits that she had missed. A good crowd gave the bench a sense of self-importance; the Justices themselves were sometimes stimulated to more active interest by the presence of an audience. There is obvious pride in Story's letter on one argument: "The audience was very large, especially as the cause advanced;—a large circle of ladies, of the highest fashion, and taste, and intelligence, numerous lawyers, and gentlemen of both houses of Congress, and towards the close, the foreign ministers, or at least some two or three of them." [3]

As the docket of the Court became more crowded, necessarily the time allowed for argument had to shrink. Under today's system the time is either a half-hour or an hour for each side, depending on the complexities of the case. This obviously precludes long introductions or eloquent perorations. Time is usually rigidly controlled; the legend is that Chief Justice Hughes once cut off an attorney in the middle of the word "if." If there are not too many interruptions, the hour is sufficient; lawyers must learn to be brief.

Throughout the argument the attention of the Court is usually good. Justice Woods in the 1880's was described by the distinguished Arkansas lawyer and Senator, A. H. Garland, as "the best and closest listener to arguments by counsel I ever appeared before." [4] This was not always so, particularly in days when extremely leisurely arguments exposed the Justices to the most excruciating boredom. Not all of the lengthy arguments were by Websters or Clays; all too

---

[3] Quoted in Charles Warren: *The Supreme Court in United States History* (Boston: Little, Brown & Co.; 1937 printing), Vol. I, p. 297.

[4] A. H. Garland: *Experience in the United States Supreme Court* (Washington: John Byrne & Co.; 1898), p. 26.

many were prolific excursions by people who had really
nothing to say. Garland describes the confusion in the late
nineteenth century which resulted because some of the Justices left the bench to take their lunch behind a curtain immediately to the rear of the bench. During the hungry hours,
argument had to proceed against the clatter of china.[5] That
problem is solved today; the Court sits from twelve to two
and then rises for a half-hour for lunch before coming back
again.

The most striking difference between the argument of the
nineteenth century and that of today is the difference in
the lawyers themselves. In the nineteenth century there was
a Supreme Court bar, a group of lawyers in or about Washington for at least portions of the year to whom other lawyers sent their cases in the same fashion that a New York
lawyer today might send a piece of San Francisco business
to a San Francisco lawyer. These lawyers could be, but were
not necessarily, Senators, who would be in Washington at
least for their own session. An example is one of the foremost
post-Civil War attorneys, Matt Carpenter of Wisconsin.
Justice Miller has left us an excellent description of this
man, who may well have been the most talented advocate ever
to appear in the Court with frequency:

> He was beyond any one whom I have known—in fact
> he is the only man whom I recall, to whom I would apply
> the old fashioned phrase—"a man of genius." Take his
> will, his manner, his command of language and his skill in
> argument. I think he is the foremost orator of his day. As
> a lawyer, he stood in the front rank deservedly. This was
> founded on all the elements which go to make up a great
> lawyer. In addition to his eloquence, his logic was close,
> his judgment sound, and his perception of the legal prin-

5 Ibid., p. 63.

ciples involved in a case both quick and accurate. With all this he spent as much labor on the case which he argued as if he had just entered the profession. . . .

He wanted some fixed purpose or aim. He sadly wanted dignity of demeanor, or sense of reverence or respect for himself, or for position in himself or in others. He delighted in the dress and swagger of the bar room. In his loftiest flight of eloquence, or closest train of logic, if a funny or ridiculous illustration struck him he would have it out then without regard to its fitness. He had the finest private library both legal and miscellaneous, of any man west of the Allegheny Mountains and he was familiar with its contents.[6]

The ease of modern transportation coupled with the desire of individual lawyers to have the experience of appearing in the Supreme Court have almost totally destroyed the system of a Supreme Court bar, so that today a very small number of appearances makes a man an unusually experienced Supreme Court practitioner. The number of lawyers under the age of sixty engaged solely in private practice who have appeared before the Court a substantial number of times could be quickly counted. Today the lawyer from Little Rock takes in his own case, whereas in 1880 he would have retained A. H. Garland, who as Attorney General and private counsel argued 130 cases. Jeremiah Sullivan Black presented sixteen cases between 1861 and 1865 and won thirteen, including eight reversals of lower courts. Today a very experienced private practitioner may have argued five cases in a lifetime.

This is not true on the government side, and a very large proportion of the cases do involve the government. The office of Solicitor General is in charge of all government litigation in the Supreme Court, and the Solicitor General can

[6] Quoted in Charles Fairman: *Mr. Justice Miller* (Cambridge: Harvard University Press; 1939), pp. 116–17.

either take the cases himself, parcel them out to his own small staff, or assign them to other government lawyers. This office has, from time to time, achieved considerable eminence. Among the great Solicitors General have been William Howard Taft, John W. Davis, and Thomas D. Thacher, to name only those long gone. As is the fate of government offices, it has also on occasion sunk to some amazing lows. Even at the lows, the office staff has usually been good. The citizen may be represented by a virtual novice in Supreme Court practice, the government by a pro who may do nothing else. As a result, the government has an immense edge in litigation.

This is true in the presentation of oral arguments, but it is even more true in the presentation of written briefs. In argument, the professional country bumpkin, than whom there is no slicker article, may quickly win the heart of the Court, which may be tired of the perpetual smoothness and finesse of the office of the Solicitor General. Once the Court begins sympathizing, it may also begin helping, and at that point alert Justices sometimes suggest by questions points that are better than those the counsel has brought with him.

In the briefs, which are the written detailed arguments of both sides submitted in advance of the oral argument, the difference can be enormous. In hundreds of cases each year the private litigant is represented by a lawyer whose brief reveals that he has no notion at all of the requisites of Supreme Court litigation or of what is and what is not persuasive to the Court to which the brief is addressed. These are the cases that never get to argument because by its preliminary order the Court disposes of them; and in such cases the government wins very frequently because of the weight of its experience. Nowhere is this more obvious than in the tax cases, where, if the private tax attorney is inexperienced in his field, only the government's side of the case will be effectively presented. The law clerks often read the government brief first, not because they have the faintest bias in favor of the government but because they want to get on to other business as quickly as they can and the government states the case more clearly than do most private counsel. The government from long experience has the advantage that comes from knowing the idiosyncrasies of the Justices. The benefit is illustrated in this advice from Justice Miller to a friend due to argue a case before Justice Swayne:

> An appropriate allusion to some anecdote or striking event, or remark in reference to any of the great jurists of England to whom you may have occasion to refer, or any remark of yours showing you have made yourself familiar with the history of these great names, and the general course of personal and legal history will not be lost on him.[7]

This is not to say that counsel inexperienced in the Supreme Court may not do a fine job. James A. Garfield, then an Ohio Congressman and later President, was not even admitted to the Supreme Court bar when Jeremiah Sullivan Black associated him in the great post-Civil War case of Milligan, involving the validity of military trials of civilians. According to Garfield's account,

> Black came to me, he had seen what I had said in Congress, and asked me if I was willing to say that in an argument in the Supreme Court. "Well," I said, "it depends upon your case altogether." He sent me the facts in the case—the record. I read it over and said, "I believe in that doctrine." Said he, "Young man, you know it is a perilous thing for a young Republican in Congress to say that, and I don't want you to injure yourself." Said I, "It don't make any difference. I believe in English liberty and English law. But," said I, "Mr. Black, I am not a practitioner

7 Ibid., pp. 233–4.

of the Supreme Court and I never tried a case in my life anywhere." Said he, "How long ago were you admitted to the bar?" "Just about six years ago." "That will do," said he. I had been admitted to the Supreme Court of my state enough years to come under the rule of the Supreme Court.

I was admitted to the Supreme Court and immediately entered upon this case. . . . The day before the trial was to come off in the court, all the counsel got together for consultation at Washington to determine upon the course of the case and when we got together Judge Black said, "Well, we will hear from the youngest member in the case first. What do you intend to do?"

Well, there were the very foremost lawyers in the land and I had to put myself forward before them and show my hand. I took my points and stated succinctly the line in my argument and when I got through, they said with one accord "Don't you change a line or word of that." The next day I went in and spoke two hours before the Supreme Court.[8]

The really basic question is: what difference does it make? What is the significance or consequence of the role of the lawyer in Supreme Court litigation?

The answer depends very heavily upon the class of case involved. If the case is in an area in which the Justices have marked opinions to start with, they may be unpersuadable, and in that situation the argument and briefs are unimportant. To take an extreme illustration, when Truman broke the post-World War II coal strike by seizing the coal mines, Chief Justice Vinson may have been so determined to uphold the President that, so far as he was personally concerned, the argument might as well not have been made. This was often the attitude of Justice Butler, as described in Chapter III. But the Court is a nine-man bench, and although in

8 William N. Brigance: *Jeremiah Sullivan Black* (Philadelphia: University of Pennsylvania Press; 1934), pp. 147–8.

many cases counsel may not have a hope of persuading one or another, he still may have a chance of persuading five; and that is enough.

In a second class of cases the argument may be immaterial if it is poor, but the case, for one reason or another, commends itself to the Justices so that they do their own work. For example, the cases of the farmer debtors under the Frazier-Lemke Act in the late 1930's and early 1940's were commonly presented with something less than legal magic, but the unhappy plight of the farmers was such that the Justices did independent work to find out what the answers ought to be. Again, in the cases of that period involving the sect of Jehovah's Witnesses the arguments were frequently a mish-mash of not very relevant religious lore, leaving the Court with the task of doing all the work itself. In each of these categories, if the decision had been made simply on the quality of what was presented by the attorneys, the side that prevailed would often not have done so.

On the other hand, in a very large number of cases the Justices are pursuing no special enthusiasms and invoking no sentiments. In those cases the function of counsel may be controlling. Take, for example, a routine piece of federal statutory construction. The lawyer who does the best job of finding the materials that show the meaning of the statute and the best job of presenting them may well win. Particularly where the matter, properly understood, is controlled by some obscure point, the lawyer who finds it has the edge.

The relative weight of the briefs and the oral arguments depend very much on the judge. The brief gives the detailed story of the case. The oral argument gives the high spots. One judge may make up his mind on the matter by considering every detail, another may be ready to decide when the talk is over, and a third may use one technique on one occasion and another in different circumstances. In theory, at least, the Court has thoroughly read the briefs before the argument begins, and this is very often so. On the other hand, the briefs cannot be exhausted without exploring some of the material cited in them, and one may doubt that this is regularly done in advance. Charles Evans Hughes expressed at least one point of view when he said: "I suppose that aside from cases of exceptional difficulty the impression that a judge has at the close of a full oral argument accords with the conviction which controls his final vote." [9]

In many notable instances the lawyer has contributed either the result or the means by which the Court gets there. Great successes in this regard were Daniel Webster and John Campbell. Many of Marshall's best points were drawn from Webster's arguments, but Webster's greatest achievement came in the twilight of his own life in connection with the rules on the powers of the state to regulate interstate commerce, when Marshall was long dead. In 1824 Webster, in a famous case, advanced to Marshall's Court the argument that state control of commerce should be subjected to a qualified limitation, and that the states should be barred from interfering with what he regarded as the "higher" or more important reaches of commerce. This point of view was explored by Marshall but never conclusively adopted by him. In the 1830's and 1840's, particularly after Marshall's death, the Court moved toward rejecting this approach altogether and holding that state burdens on commerce were a matter for Congress, rather than the Court, to attempt to control. In 1851, when an important case on that subject was pending, Justice Levi Woodbury unexpectedly died. This happened during the only Whig administration be-

---

[9] Charles Evans Hughes: *The Supreme Court of the United States* (New York: Columbia University Press; 1928), p. 61.

tween 1830 and 1860, and when Webster was at the height
of his influence. He suggested the appointment of Benjamin Curtis of Boston to the vacancy, and the appointment
was made. Curtis wrote the opinion in the case then before
the Court and adopted almost exactly the argument that
Webster had made more than twenty-five years earlier.

John Campbell, a Justice of the Supreme Court in the
1850's, resigned to go with the South during the Civil War.
As a practicing lawyer he came before the Court in the
Slaughterhouse cases in 1873 to interpret the Reconstruction constitutional amendments. The argument he made there
was adopted only by a minority of the Court, but it was ulti-
mately accepted and became the basis of the later conception
of due process of law.[1] In nonconstitutional areas, as in the
field of railroad or corporate reorganization and similar
technical subjects, much of the law is contributed to the
Court by the lawyers. There was sense in Matt Carpenter's
response to Senator Roscoe Conkling of New York when the
latter asked how Carpenter would handle a certain difficult
point. Carpenter said: "Employ a good lawyer." [2]

To sum it up, the role of the lawyer before the Supreme
Court is substantial but not conclusive. The best lawyers will
lose the case that cannot be won. Charles Evans Hughes as
an attorney was outstanding, and yet he lost a great many
cases; he was too expensive to be retained unless the case was
a difficult one. Over half of such cases are bound to be lost;
but the good man wins a larger proportion of them than the
poor one. Yet this distinction between the merit of the per-
formance and the result is sometimes a little sour. Chief Justice Waite sent William Allen Butler a note saying that Butler's presentation of a complicated set of facts was the best

[1] For discussion, see Benjamin Twiss: *Lawyers and the Constitution*
(Princeton: Princeton University Press; 1942), pp. 44-5.
[2] Garland: *Experience in the United States Supreme Court*, p. 27.

Waite had ever heard. Nonetheless, the Court decided against Butler, who observed that his pleasure at the compliment was hardly equal to his disappointment in the opinion.[3]

Sometimes the Court goes off in a direction suggested within itself and not even discussed by counsel, as in the 1957 case that invalidated certain inquiries by the Attorney General of New Hampshire into the conduct of a professor of the state university. The Court is extremely expert in the fields in which it works, and it is not strange that on occasion it should take hold of a matter altogether on its own.

Courtesy in the Court is the overwhelming rule. However, the judges may on occasion press counsel hard enough to create very difficult situations. Justice Roberts on the bench was usually the most benign of men, but once when he suspected an attorney might be involved in a fraud, he quizzed the lawyer until the man fainted in the courtroom. It may be noted that Roberts voted *with* the lawyer's position. Justice Miller was once termed with less than affection "that damned old hippopotamus," and he was not gentle with lawyers. Miller also caused a lawyer to faint. Many Justices blow up on occasion and give some lawyer a bad time. When a man has heard a thousand or so arguments, this is perhaps occasionally to be expected. Garland describes a rough morning when he moved the Court to reconsider an opinion it had handed down:

> . . . On motion call I arose and offered to present a motion for a rehearing of the case, and was about to proceed to make a few "brief remarks" when Justice Bradley started as if powder had exploded under his seat, and with much spirit said: "What is that?" I repeated what I was seeking to do, and then he turned somewhat pale and remonstrated with much spirit, and told how hard the

[3] Charles Henry Butler: *A Century at the Bar of the Supreme Court* (New York: G. P. Putnam's Sons; 1942), pp. 37, 38.

court labored at cases—how closely the judges consulted
—how wearied they were with these applications for rehearing after all their intense work to arrive at conclusions—how the House of Lords disposed of such things,
and growing warmer and warmer, how inappropriate it
was in lawyers to be asking the Court to travel over all this
work again, and many other things not well remembered,
as my mind just at these utterances was not as clear as
the often alluded to *noonday sun*. What astonished me
more was that Justice Bradley had not delivered the opinion of the Court, but Justice Miller had, and as I thought
the storm was lulling and almost lulled, Justice Miller
with his usual scratch over his right ear, when he was
getting ready to charge, came to Justice Bradley's aid,
and really it occurred to me it was superfluous as Justice
Bradley then needed no aid;—he was not the suffering
one;—then Justice Field, with more moderation gave me
a lecture upon the error of such a course, and I did wish
that night or Blucher would come. I looked in vain for a
friend at Court. The Chief Justice looked as if he would
say something consoling to me—sympathetic as it were,
but he had not been there very long and probably he did
not wish to appear too previous, and he did not say it. I
thought, too, Justice Harlan once looked like he would
help me, but he fell back and sent out a note to someone
else. I fought nobly I thought, but it was uphill and
against decided odds, and I was somewhat routed and
driven back almost in dismay, and the lawyers present did
enjoy it;—it did them good as it always does, notwith-
standing their so-called clannishness, to see the Court
pounce down upon and shake up a brother lawyer.[4]

Contemporary argument is closer in format to the quiz
programs on television than to the magnificent speeches of
a hundred years ago. Counsel plans his argument. If he has
an hour, he may prepare to use, say, forty minutes of it.

[4] Ibid., pp. 40, 41.

102

The remainder is left for questioning from the bench. Any Justice can interrupt at any time to ask a question on any point that interests him. Counsel sometimes may proceed with his argument as planned, but he must be adroit, because questioning may almost at once take him off in other directions.

The argument will be purely oral. The Court does not look kindly on graphic presentations, charts, or other displays; indeed, a certain stodginess in this regard cuts it off from some useful aids. Maps may be used, and on special occasions involving bulky patents, machinery has been set up outside the courtroom for the judges' inspection. In censorship cases, movies have been shown.[5] After the showing of *The Miracle*, Justice Minton was heard to observe in the hallway that if he had paid anything to see that film, it would have been too much. In February of 1958 the Court, in connection with an alleged violation of copyright by the television comedian Jack Benny, saw Charles Boyer and Ingrid Bergman in *Gaslight* and compared it with a showing of Benny and Barbara Stanwyck in *Auto Light*. The showing, which took place in the east conference room of the Court building, was accompanied by a few laughs from the judicial audience, but no audible comments.

Basically, the question-and-answer system is excellent. Hughes, speaking after his years of practice, put it this way: "Well prepared and experienced counsel . . . do not object to inquiries from the bench, if the time allowed for argument is not unduly curtailed, as they would much prefer to have the opportunity of knowing the difficulties in the minds of the Court and attempting to meet them rather

5 Robert Stern & Eugene Gressman: *Supreme Court Practice* (Washington, D.C.: B.N.A. Inc.; 1954), pp. 329–30.

than to have them concealed and presented in conference when counsel are not present. They prefer an open attack to the masked battery." [6]

But the Chief Justice is careful to say "if the time allowed for argument is not unduly curtailed." When the questions become so numerous as to make argument impossible, then a system intended to shed light may well succeed in blocking it out altogether. In one case when an hour was allotted to each side, the Court interpolated 153 questions or observations during the argument of government counsel and 84 during the argument of private counsel. Only four times after his brief opening did government counsel speak more than six consecutive sentences without interruption. 237 interpolations during 120 minutes of argument, an average of about two to a minute, turn what should be an argument into a conversation.

The Justices vary greatly in the skill with which they ask questions and in the extent to which they use the privilege. Great exponents of the system were Chief Justices Hughes and Stone, who had a way of grasping an argument that was wandering and bringing it back, and Justice Black, whose instinct enables him often to put his finger on *the* vital point of a case. On the other hand, some questions may not add much to the Court's useful knowledge. Argument of the *Schneiderman* case came not long after the battle of Stalingrad. Mr. Willkie, to give color to his argument, observed that his client had been born a certain number of miles from Stalingrad. Justice Murphy, who almost never asked a question, interrupted to inquire: "Just how many miles was that from Stalingrad, Mr. Willkie?"

A sometimes amusing operation of the system occurs when counsel is whipsawed between Justices. In this situation Jus-

tice A asks counsel a question that counsel is either unable
to answer or handles poorly. Justice B, who is sympathetic
to counsel's position, then asks a question that implies an
answer to the question asked by Justice A. Thus, Justice B's
question may begin: "Isn't it true that . . ." and then proceed to state the correct answer. Justice A then asks another
question aimed at the answer just supplied by Justice B,
and so on.

The greatest abuse of the system occurs when a judge
goes into some point which seems crucial to him, but which
does not seem of much importance either to counsel or to any
other judge. When, as it sometimes the case, this is accompanied by a hectoring manner, counsel is in the worst possible position. He is being pushed about on a matter that he
believes to be nonessential, his time is slipping away from
him so that he may not be able to make his important points,
and he may be feeling abused as well.

This can be terrible. It happens. Some Justices ask very
few questions—Justice Douglas, for instance. Others ask a
great many. In the case of the 237 interpolations and questions cited above, 93 were by Justice Frankfurter.

Any candid discussion of this problem requires mention
of that Justice, whose professorial background and whose
inclination to see angles in a case of more interest to him
than to many of his brothers (as demonstrated by his numerous separate concurring opinions) make for some real
difficulty. On occasion Justice Frankfurter appears to forget that the attorney before him is not a student in a seminar
who is privileged simply to abandon a position under force
of questioning. The attorney is hired to represent a point of
view, and he cannot throw it away. I once observed a friend
of the Justice, personally devoted to him, sit in the courtroom, his face in his hands and tears in his eyes, and heard

him mutter: "Why does he have to behave like that?" When these excursions occur, counsel is almost hopelessly caught, because a proper respect for the bench requires him to stick with the questioner and yet he wishes to get on with the case. The result is a series of devices for changing the subject in the hope of getting back to the main line of argument. Renowned for his dexterity in dealing ruthlessly with what is sometimes impiously called "the Felix problem" was the late Chief Justice Vanderbilt of New Jersey during his practicing days. Vanderbilt made cursory answers, brushed the questions aside, and by force of his powerful personality thrust on to other things.

Chapter VI

METHODS OF DECISION

The circumstances of life in pre-Civil War Washington gave the Justices an intimacy with one another never since quite achieved. A letter from Justice McLean to the widow of Justice Barbour, written only a day or so after Barbour's death in 1841, suggests something of this spirit. Barbour had died in Washington while his wife was at their home in Virginia.

McLean explained that, while he did not know Mrs. Barbour personally, he felt free to address her because of his intimacy with her husband; and this in itself is interesting because McLean and Barbour did not share the same views of public affairs. McLean reported that a fever had confined Barbour to his bed for a few days, and that for two subsequent weeks he had been kept to his room. Speculating that Barbour might not have mentioned the illness to his wife because of a desire not to worry her, McLean assured her that her husband, who lived in a house with several other Justices, had not been lonely: "His brother judges, too, prompted by a solicitude and friendship which each one felt for him called repeatedly on him every day."

By the day of his death, Barbour seemed to have recovered and had returned to work. He was in conference with the other judges on the night he died. "On that night as usual the judges were engaged in consultation until about 10:00. We had under consideration a most important case, and

Judge Barbour the evening before had given his opinion in the same case, which employed him about an hour." On the evening of his death Barbour listened to the comments of the other judges, and McLean observed: "I never saw him in higher and better spirits."

Continuing the sad report, McLean said: "The next morning the servant made the fire in his room as usual, but observed that the Judge did not speak to him as was his practice." The death was thus discovered, and the landlady informed McLean of it when he went into the dining-room for breakfast. McLean immediately went to Barbour's room and there found two or three other Justices. Barbour had died quietly in his sleep of heart trouble.

The circle around the body of their recent comrade was a group of men who were together all the time. They heard cases together, they took meals together at a common boardinghouse, they talked over the cases together in the evenings, they went to church together, they walked together; they *were* together.

During those years the Court terms were short, intensive working periods, with very little time for relaxation. During the 1847 term Justice Daniel went out socially only twice, except for his official calls on the wives of the Justices who had brought their families to Washington. On one occasion he dined with the President, and on the other he stopped for a few minutes, after the evening conference was over, at a ball given by the clerk of the Supreme Court. Daniel, anticipating the usual nightly labors, had sent a formal apology and gone to the conference. He found the other judges in a hooky-playing mood, and in a short time they adjourned the conference so that all could go to the party. Upon arriving there, he discovered that the only lady present he knew was the wife of Justice Catron, and in a letter to his daughter

Daniel noted: "She, however, is quite a civil and cheerful lady and seemed disposed to take me under her care, and I was very much indebted to her kindness." It was on this occasion that Daniel Webster was also present and, as mentioned earlier, Daniel reported: "My hand was actually contaminated by contact with his."

This tight-little-groupishness was even closer before the 1840's because in that decade the Jacksonian Democrats acquired control of the Court and proceeded to put the spoils system of their great President into action on the judicial front. The Court reporter for many years had been Richard Peters, a particularly close friend and intimate of Justice Story. While Story was ill in Massachusetts, a Democratic bloc of four Justices (Chief Justice Taney not being involved) proceeded to dismiss Peters and put General Howard in his place. Story was greatly embittered and never forgave his associates for this. There is no reported instance of any similar subsequent act. Indeed, Court employees commonly have life tenure, if they desire it; some of them begin in childhood as pages.

In 1847 Chief Justice Taney, Justices Wayne and Daniel, and Reporter Howard took a house for themselves on Pennsylvania Avenue. A housemaid, Sally, followed the judges to their new location. Daniel wrote his daughter: "We have not James for a waiter, but have a very civil and apparently well instructed manservant—the house is very clean, the furniture including beds, mattresses, and bed clothing also, and the food all good and served up." It was a working house: "No sound of the distracting gong throughout the house, nor running to and fro of servants, but perfect silence prevails throughout." [1]

[1] Peter V. Daniel to Elizabeth R. Daniel, December 18, 1847. The various Daniel quotations are from letters collected by the author from several unpublished sources.

From such quarters as these the Justices moved daily to the Court to hear argument, and to conferences every night of the week except Saturday.

Today things are very different, although they have moved back a little toward the close relationship of earlier years. The Justices usually maintain houses in the Washington area, but these are scattered from Maryland to Virginia and great distances often separate them. The Justices have a certain amount of formal social exchange but no more personal intimacy than happens to appeal directly to any of them—commonly not much. Prior to the construction of the present Court building, the Justices frequently worked at their homes. Stone, for example, built himself a virtual palace of a workshop; and upon seeing the plans for the new Court building, with separate lavatory facilities in the office of each Justice, Holmes is perhaps apocryphally said to have observed that the abandonment of a common men's room meant that off the bench he would no longer see his brothers at all. The present building arrangement, in which each Justice has a suite of three rooms for himself and his clerks, secretary, and messenger, brought the Justices back together again. While doing their work they can now visit from office to office as freely as personal taste dictates, and, when they wish, can also use a common lunchroom reserved for them.

The heart of the decision-making process has always been the conference. At the present time the Court hears cases for two weeks and then recesses for two weeks (except for one longer recess during the winter). During the two weeks of sittings, arguments are heard; during the two weeks of recess, opinions are prepared. At the end of each week of argument and at the end of the two-week recess, the judges gather to decide the matters that must be decided, to give final approval to opinions that have been generally agreed upon, and, in short, to transact the business of the Court. The conference is secret. No one other than the Justices is ever allowed in the room. A messenger sits outside the door, so that if some material is desired it can be sent for; and the junior Justice answers the door and receives from the messenger whatever he wishes to hand in. The Justices no longer confer in Washington boardinghouses, but meet in a grandly impressive room adjacent to the office of the Chief Justice, who presides at the head of a long table.

Because the conference is secret, very little is known about its operation. There have been some descriptions by Justices of its workings in a mechanical sense—for example, the manner in which cases are presented to the conference. Of some moment (whether for better or for worse) in this regard are Mason's biography of Chief Justice Stone and Bickel's publication of certain papers of Justice Brandeis. It has long been known that many Justices have kept copious notes. Both Mason and Bickel used some of these, and thus revealed what had hitherto been kept wholly secret. It happens that the revelations are of no great consequence. Nonetheless, if they should start a pattern, we may learn a great deal more than we have ever known about past events. But the free give-and-take of a secret conference may dry up if the Justices feel that what may be highly biased accounts by some of their brothers are going to find their way into the history books. The use of confidential notes may make it extremely unlikely that there will be any more confidential notes left around for biographers.

As was noted in the chapter on the Chief Justiceship, under Hughes the conference concentrated primarily on results. The business went speedily. While there was time for each Justice to express his views briefly on each case, there necessarily could not have been a great deal of debate, for the Court in four hours' time disposed of up to twenty applications for cases to be heard and ten cases that had been argued. A very well-informed and shrewd observer of the Court during the Hughes period has made this criticism:

> I am shocked by the decisional process in the Supreme Court of the United States as it proceeded under Hughes. The judges heard arguments throughout the week on cases that had been for the most part carefully selected as the sort of cases that required the judgment of our highest Court. Few of the judges made any extensive notes about the cases they had heard; few of them had made any careful study of the records or briefs of the cited authorities before they went to conference. Then in the space of four hours the Court decided not only the cases that it had heard, but also voted on the pending petitions for certiorari, jurisdictional statements, and other materials on the docket. This meant that the discussion in conference was perforce a statement of conclusions more than it was an exchange of mutually stimulating ideas. Some of the apparent unanimity in the Hughes Court derived, in my estimation, from the superficiality of the discussion which glossed over rather than illuminated difficulties in the past. If judging is as important a governmental task as we lawyers assert it to be, I am not at all inclined to say that extended conferences about the matters being judged should be viewed as a deficiency in a Court.[2]

Although the view just expressed is that of a very acute observer, I do not at all share it. It is true that in the nineteenth century the conferences were discussions of details. It will be recalled from the letter of Justice McLean quoted at the beginning of this chapter that on the night before his death Justice Barbour had spent a full hour expounding his own views on a particular case, and that the next evening

---

[2] Confidential communication to the author from someone in a position to observe the pre-1937 Court.

was spent in criticizing those views. This is discussion at its very fullest. But those were also days of a light docket. As the work load increases, the methods must be streamlined or else the work output will go down. Because Chief Justice Stone personally believed much more than did Hughes in a town-meeting approach to the conference, and because (if rumor is to be believed) one of Stone's Justices was extremely discursive, the conferences under Stone did become extremely lengthy. Tempers were inflamed, energies were used up, and the output of the Court went down, down, and down. While the general decline of the Court's output for the last fifteen years is undoubtedly attributable to many things other than the extension of the conference, that was probably one of the factors. Each man has only so many ergs of energy to give to his judiciary.

Chief Justice Warren has moved the conference back in the direction of the Hughes pattern, though his more amiable personality has eliminated much of the disciplined quality of the Hughes conference.

The question remains as to how the Justices individually make up their minds. As was noted elsewhere, this is largely a product of individual ways of thought. As his clerk, I was able to watch Justice Black. He usually prepared for cases by studying them in advance and at the close of oral argument usually wrote "affirm" or "reverse" in his own working notes. On the other hand, Stone did much studying after the arguments—although when a case comes at the end of the week, there must be very little time between the argument and the moment of decision, for very nearly all cases are decided in the week in which they are argued; sometimes the moment of decision may come the next day. Particularly on those unhappy occasions when a case has been both badly briefed and badly argued, this may require the Justices to

113

shoot from the hip. Yet the success of the system is repeatedly demonstrated by the absence of gross or glaring or wild errors in most opinions. Experience demonstrates that the Court is usually quite prepared to decide quickly.

The real work on detail comes at the opinion-writing stage, and here the care is often exquisite. The means of assigning the opinions was described in the chapter on the Chief Justices.

At this state there is a variety of techniques. The opinion may be a dash-off. Justice Holmes frequently went home and wrote his opinions over the week end, a flash of insight and a good phrase quickly illuminating the whole problem. On the other hand, a Justice like Brandeis may choose utterly to exhaust a subject. Justice Black on occasion has directed that books or articles broadly related to the subject of the opinion be collected in his own office so that he might read at large on the topic for some days before attempting to put a word to paper. In an admiralty case in which two Justices happened to be interested, they directed that a room be set aside in the Supreme Court building and that all the works in the Library of Congress on admiralty be assembled there, and they then had their law clerks extract from every one of those volumes anything that might possibly bear on the subject of the case in hand.

The extent of the poking about and roaming of the Court is suggested by some of their footnotes. For the 1956–7 term those notes include all of the conventional legal materials, a large share of which may have been taken from the briefs of the attorneys. However, it is a good guess that in many instances these materials were found by the Court itself, as, for example, quotations from debates in Congress, correspondence among government agencies, or Justice Frankfurter's very elaborate analysis of past jury cases that had come to the Supreme Court. Other 1956–7 items chosen at random which may or may not have come from the briefs: a reference to a 1937 study entitled *Personnel Practices Governing Factory and Office Administration;* a report from a Bar Association conference on delays of justice; a history of the operation of the Federal Employers' Liability Act; an address by Elihu Root to the American Bar Association in 1914; a report of a committee on tests for intoxication; miscellaneous reports on traffic safety; some historical materials on the number of automobiles in the United States; a handbook on fire protection; studies of comparative criminal procedure in England, France, and Italy; the *Encyclopaedia of Social Sciences* on railroad history; a whole series of works on the history of collective bargaining, developing the history of multi-employer labor negotiations.

On one occasion the Solicitor General caused one of the country's best legal historians to be assigned for a year to write a history of the law of treason for the Court. There has been some criticism of the fact that the Court in the segregation cases took advantage of the literature of psychology and sociology instead of restricting itself purely to "legal" materials. This misses the point that the Court for many years has felt free to acquire general knowledge wherever it can find it. In his own days as a practicing attorney, Louis Brandeis invented the device known as the "Brandeis Brief" for the purpose of bringing before the Court immense amounts of factual material, and this tradition has been liberally expanded.

Of necessity, much of this miscellaneous information is collected by the clerks of the Justices. The practice of providing clerks for the Justices began in the late nineteenth century. Thereafter, for many years, each Justice had one clerk. Chief Justice Stone took two, and after World War II most of the rest of the Court followed suit. The number for Chief Justice Vinson was raised to three, and now usually the Chief has three clerks and the others too, except Justice Douglas, who prefers one. These are almost always boys (or girls) recently out of law school who usually serve for one year, although some Justices have maintained permanent clerks. Justice Roberts, for example, had a husband-and-wife team as his permanent clerk and secretary. The selection of the clerks is the purely personal patronage of the Justices, who can make their choices on any basis. Harvard furnishes the clerks for Justice Frankfurter, Justice Black tries to get Southern boys—and tennis-players where possible—Justice Douglas chooses from the West Coast, and so on.

The tasks of the clerks are also very much the product of the whims of their Justices. In general, it is the job of the clerk to be eyes and legs for his judge, finding and bringing in useful materials. This can involve an immense amount of work, depending upon how curious the Justice is. It is a legend that Justice Brandeis once asked a clerk to look at every page of every volume of the United States Reports looking for a particular point. The clerks may also have semi-social duties, like those who visited with Holmes or took walks with Stone or played tennis with Black, or superintended the circulation of the guests at the Brandeis Sunday teas. All of this is in the spirit of an amiable relationship between a wise, elderly man and a young cub at the bar.

In respect to the more serious business of the Court, some of the Justices use their clerks to summarize the petitions for certiorari, or the applications to be heard. Other Justices prefer to do this themselves.

The function of the clerks in relation to the writing of the opinions also varies widely. In the early 1940's, at least,

Justice Black wrote the first draft of all his opinions, except that toward the end of the year he would let the youngster try his hand at one first draft of something extremely unimportant. In my own case, the day of glory came when I did the first draft of a lone dissent on a minor point of statutory construction, which the Justice then revised and which no one has ever noticed since. Sometimes a Justice writes the first draft of one opinion while the clerk writes the first draft of another, and the opinions are then exchanged and the clerk writes a second draft of his Justice's opinion while the Justice writes a second draft of the clerk's. Sometimes clerks are allowed to do the bulk of the serious writing for the Justice.

The latter condition requires a candid look. When the President of the United States appoints and the Senate of the United States confirms a Justice of the Supreme Court, the operation is not intended to result in turning over any serious responsibility to untried boys. The ghost writer may be a necessary evil in the White House, in the Senate, or in the cabinet, but nothing in the Court's situation requires the ghost to walk in that marble palace. The tradition is overwhelmingly against it.

The extent to which Justices use clerks as ghosts is largely unknown because of the traditional secrecy that surrounds each office. It is known that Justice Douglas gives his clerks next to nothing to do in this area, preferring to keep more of the office work in his own hands than does any other Justice. On the other hand, there were rumors that the excellent clerks of Justice Murphy did more of the office writing than was commonly thought proper; there is no corroboration of this, however, and the style of many Murphy opinions shows a consistency over the years indicating that they came from only one hand. The most notorious rumors concern Chief

Justice Vinson, who is said to have done all his "writing" with his hands in his pockets, outlining to his clerks generally what he wanted, and then criticizing this bit or that in a clerk's draft and making suggestions for revision. His successor, Warren, clearly does his own work; one of his clerks with an exceptionally able critical facility has told me that many of Warren's own first drafts are better than the finished product of some judges.

Even on those rare occasions when the clerk does the writing, the judge does the deciding. The ultimate matters of yes or no, affirm or reverse, the judges invariably keep in their own hands; while the clerks may on rare occasions persuade, their influence in this regard is not really significant. Some newspaper talk to the contrary in the summer of 1957 was so much foolishness; in my own year as a law clerk, my Justice made approximately one thousand decisions, and I had precisely no influence on any of them.

The writing problem (which excludes the making of the ultimate decision but may include the making of a whole series of important intermediate decisions on details) raises a serious difficulty in the future of the Court. The Justices are very frequently chosen from other public offices. The complexities of the rest of government are such that the men who hold the great offices—Secretary of the Treasury, Senator from New York, or the Presidency itself—must be men who can delegate every function except decision-making. The jobs have become so big that even the very largest details cannot be handled by the leaders. Abraham Lincoln wrote almost all of his important state papers. If Franklin D. Roosevelt had done anything of the kind, he would have had no time left for anything else. We live in the age of the staff researcher, the ghost writer, the first-draft man; most important public officials must make use of them. We

118

have developed a breed of men who work that way, and as a result we are filling the reservoir of public officials from which Supreme Court Justices are drawn with men who are able to handle broad responsibilities; Chief Justice Vinson, for example, was a superb holder of very important offices during the war. At the same time, we are developing men who are not at all cut out for traditional judicial responsibility.

Once the opinion is written, its author circulates a print to the other Justices for their reactions. This may result in a clear "I agree" or in an equally clear "I shall dissent." It may also result in suggestions, a Justice agreeing to go along if certain items are changed. Each Justice must face the practical question of how much time he wishes to devote to tinkering with another man's work. A very common attitude is that of Justice Bradley, to whom Chief Justice Waite once sent an opinion with a request for criticism. Bradley's note of response was: "Where I concur in the doctrine I am willing to trust the Chief Justice in the mode of expressing it." [3]

In cases of exceptionally fine work, the responsive notes may be very enthusiastic. On the other hand, a Justice may disagree with major details of an opinion, and the result may be considerable revision or sharpening as the opinion goes through draft after draft to accommodate all of the suggestions. The writing judge may make extensive concessions either to keep his majority or to get as close to unanimity as possible.

The final opinion is thus truly the opinion of the particular judge, but it is also truly an institutional product. By this process of refinement the comparative casualness with

[3] Bruce R. Trimble: *Chief Justice Waite* (Princeton: Princeton University Press; 1938), p. 263.

which the case was decided in conference is compensated for; indeed, cases are sometimes reversed in this process of circulation and criticism within the Court. This happens in two ways. Sometimes the writing Justice finds, as he digs in, that he is no longer persuaded of the rightness of his own original vote. He then turns the case back to the Chief for reassignment; and frequently the Chief suggests that the newly converted Justice circulate a new draft to see whether the rest of the Justices may also wish to change their minds.

The second type of change occurs when a Justice has circulated an opinion to which a dissent is also circulated. The remaining Justices may find the dissent more persuasive than the majority opinion. The majority may then shift, and what was a dissent may become the opinion of the Court. On rare instances a reader can pick out those cases, because the judges may not change their written opinions much after the conversion, and sometimes an "opinion of the Court" *reads* as though it had originally been a dissent. There are also rare occasions in which the Justice who has written the majority opinion is persuaded by the dissent, changes his mind, and withdraws his own earlier draft.

When the whole process is over, and each Justice has taken his stand, the opinion is ready to be announced. The time ranges from a week to six months or more, with an average of about six weeks after the argument. In rare instances the case must be reargued; and sometimes a case goes over from year to year. A famous case coming near the end of the administration of Chief Justice Marshall and the beginning of the administration of Chief Justice Taney took some six years for its disposition; and the segregation cases were also, by one delaying device or another, held up for a period of years before final determination. The interstate litigation between Wyoming and Colorado was argued in 1916, reargued in 1918, reargued again in 1922, and finally decided in the last-mentioned year. However, these extreme cases only emphasize the abnormality of delay.

The opinions are announced orally from the bench. This is a remarkable proceeding; a busy institution interrupts pressing work in order to tell a handful of persons in the courtroom what everyone else in the country necessarily learns by reading. On opinion days, which during the regular term are commonly three Mondays in each month, from thirty minutes to four hours may sometimes be taken in making these announcements. In the extreme case this means that as much as twenty per cent of the courtroom time for a week may go into these statements, all of which would be as effective if the Justices simply handed them to the official reporter.

Nonetheless, this ceremony is deeply gratifying to those who see it. Clearly it is expendable, but in the various adjustments to the pressures of time, it should be among the last to go. The tradition of announcing opinions orally is old, and while the announcements are sometimes a bore when a case is not particularly interesting or the opinion is poorly announced, they are sometimes lively and exciting. The Justices themselves sometimes control tedium by giving extremely short statements summarizing the holdings, but occasionally they respond to the inherent drama of the situation by giving the statements with some verve. Variances between the oral statements and the written statements occasionally provide color, although the variations are of no practical importance. Sometimes a Justice is carried away by his enthusiasm, as when Justice McReynolds is supposed to have said from the bench in a lugubrious dissent: "The Constitution is gone." In an earlier day lengthy oral statements sometimes misled the press. Reporters might have the impression that an opinion was going one way while a Justice examined one side of the argument, and then at a later stage he might reverse his field and come out the other way. Where major speculations were involved, this sometimes had unfortunate financial consequences; stocks fluctuated because of different impressions gained in the course of a long opinion. This very practical evil is avoided now by giving printed copies of the opinions to the press as a Justice begins his delivery so that the reporters can at once see how the story comes out.

Attorneys being admitted to the bar may be admitted by the Court on any day, but the attraction of the opinions tends to concentrate them on Mondays. Each applicant is moved for admission, frequently by some prominent person; it is a common whim for the applicant to wish his sponsor to be his Congressman or his Senator if either is a lawyer. This little ceremony takes only a few seconds for each person, but when there are many persons to be admitted, a busy legislator may be kept away from the halls of Congress for a considerable time. It was for many years a practice to take the admissions *after* the opinions, thus giving the Court a captive audience of prominence. As a Senator could not know in advance how long the opinions would take, if indeed there were to be any, he had to turn up in Court at noon and might sit for an hour or two before moving his constituent's admission. The ex-legislator members of the Court have been keenly aware of this nuisance, and when Chief Justice Vinson, an ex-Representative, joined Justice Black and Burton, ex-Senators, on the bench, the system was changed so that the admissions would come first. The Justices still have a respectfully full house on most opinion days.

In the beginning it was by no means foreordained that there should be an "opinion of the Court." The House of

Lords in England commonly received individual opinions in each case from each of the Law Lords, and the Supreme Court in the 1790's set out with the same system. For example in the principal case of the year 1796, *Ware* v. *Hilton*,[4] Justice Chase gave an extended opinion, and then everybody else had his own say. When Marshall became Chief Justice in 1801, he assumed the function of either writing the opinions or assigning them. The Court has abided by the assignment system, subject to some variations, ever since, despite President Jefferson's demands on Justice Johnson to attack the Marshall dominance of the Court by returning to the system of individual opinions. Johnson yielded to the extent of occasionally expressing his views independently of Marshall.

The single collective opinion of the Court is far superior to the individual system in three basic respects. First, the single opinion pools talents; it is the only means by which a busy Court can conceivably get its work done. Second, the single opinion has clarity and decisiveness which make it far more useful to lower courts than would be the case if those courts were asked to decide the case of the future on the basis of what had been said by Justice A, as modified by Justice B, as disagreed with by Justice C, and so on. Third, and perhaps most important of all, the single opinion gives maximum weight to the Court's expression and thus commands maximum respect from the country itself.

There remain, however, two other types of opinion, the concurrence and the dissent, which any Justice is free to use at any time he desires. The concurrence is simply a variation of the old series type of opinion of the 1790's. It means that an individual Justice is saying his say separate from the Court.

4 3 Dall. 199.

It is the general, but not the universal, view that concurrences ought to be saved for very substantial occasions and ought not be lightly used. In the year 1955–6 the Court handed down ninety-four opinions. There were twenty-one concurrences, fourteen of them by Justice Frankfurter, who is regularly the "concurringest" of the Justices.

There are bound to be occasions on which some Justices will get to the end result of "affirm" or "reverse" by pathways wholly different from those followed by other Justices. This sometimes leads to puzzling results. For example, in the *United Mine Workers* case arising from the coal strike immediately after World War II,[5] Chief Justice Vinson and Justices Reed and Burton found that the United Mine Workers and John L. Lewis should lose on each of two separate grounds. Justices Rutledge and Murphy dissented as to both grounds. Thus, these five Justices alone scored three for the United States and two for the Mine Workers. Justices Frankfurter and Jackson concurred with the Vinson opinion on one of the two grounds by which the result had been reached, but rejected it on the other. Justices Black and Douglas concurred with Vinson on the other ground, rejecting the ground that appealed to Frankfurter and Jackson. There were thus five Justices to support one reason for the result, a different alignment of five Justices to support a second reason for the result, and a total of four votes against each reason for the result.

In an even more remarkable case of this kind, involving again a double ground, there was a majority *against* each of the grounds for the result, but as a majority could be counted for the result itself, the case was decided for a party despite the fact that a majority of the Court rejected each

5 *United States* v. *United Mine Workers,* 330 U.S. 258 (1947).

individual reason as to why that party should prevail.[6] Of this rare kind of mix-up in connection with the Insular cases after the Spanish-American War, Mr. Dooley, the favorite wiseacre of the time, quipped: "Mr. Justice Brown delivered the opinion of the Court and only eight Justices dissented."

Such experiences are a near-breakdown of the normal conception of the judicial system. In these spectacular cases the conflicting concurrences earn no respect for the result, and the law loses the element most essential to its dignity: an atmosphere of rationality. On the other hand, a well-placed concurrence may be invaluable. Perhaps the most useful expression ever given by Justices Brandeis and Holmes on the topic of free speech was a concurrence that profoundly affected general thought. In some instances, important new ideas set out in concurrences may, after criticism by the bench and the bar, move on into majority positions. In 1957, upon the decision of the Court in the case of the West Coast Communists, Justices Black and Douglas concurred on the ground that, under the First Amendment, speech relating to public affairs is intended to be absolutely and completely free, subject to no restrictions; and they incorporated in their utterance the views expounded by the philosopher Alexander Meiklejohn in his recent volume *Freedom of Speech*. Such a concurrence gives substantial food for thought.

However good the uses of concurrences, they are contrary to the system established by Marshall and conflict directly with achieving as massive as possible an "opinion of the Court." They ought not to be used where differences are either minor or insignificant.

[6] *National Mutual Ins. Co.* v. *Tidewater Transfer Co., Inc.,* 337 U.S. 582 (1949).

Justice Frankfurter directly challenges the soundness of this view, by concurring extremely frequently. By now there has been sufficient experience with the technique of that Justice to permit serious doubt as to its wisdom. The use of judicial opinions can be analyzed by studying the extent to which they are later referred to and applied in subsequent cases or in scholarly writings. Usually it takes some little time for the sinking-in process to operate so that the opinions begin to be applied to other situations. An analysis of the Frankfurter concurrences for a period of two years, made after sufficient time had elapsed to give them an opportunity to be applied, showed that in almost no instance were the concurrences ever used by anyone. The lower courts in subsequent cases frequently applied the majority opinions with which Frankfurter had concurred, but they did not use the concurrences as well, or treat the main opinions as modified in any way by the concurrences. Much the same thing was true of the scholarly literature. The study of written evidence indicated that Justice Frankfurter had consumed a large portion of his energy and talent in essays which, for all practical purposes, might as well have been written on paper airplanes and thrown out a Supreme Court window.

The occasion for dissent is also a highly variable matter of judicial taste. Dissents are always colorful, and Justices Holmes and Brandeis gave the practice a glorious connotation because their dissents were usually so far superior to the majority opinions, and because so many of their dissents subsequently became the law. Stylewise, the dissent has a greater freedom and verve than majority opinions because the majority opinion has been through the institutional process of opinion, agreement, revision, conciliation, and so on, while the dissent need please only its author. Former Justice John Hessin Clarke once observed that Associate

Justices are remembered chiefly for their dissenting opinions,[7] an unduly modest point of view.

In other days dissents were usually saved for serious business. Hughes described them as "an appeal to the brooding spirit of the law, to the intelligence of a future day, when a later decision may possibly correct the error into which the dissenting judge believes the Court to have been betrayed."[8] It is commonly believed, for example, that if Hughes was outvoted, he usually joined the majority without further argument. Unfortunately, today dissents are as common as the snows of winter. There are functions for dissent, but overliberal dissent tends to cheapen the currency and reduce the value of the dissents that are really worth while. Dissent ought to be free always in constitutional cases, because by tradition constitutional decisions may be more freely reexamined by the Court itself than decisions that merely interpret statutes or declare other parts of the law. There is good reason for this: the amendment process is so difficult that in most instances only the Court can correct its own errors, while Congress can easily change mere statutory interpretations. Since constitutional questions are open to re-examination, Justices in disagreement should freely note their differences so that the bar can know whether to raise a topic again.

In the interpretation of statutes, dissent is occasionally useful. For example, the dissent may point up more clearly than the majority opinion the importance of changing a statute. Dissent may also be important in exceptional statutory cases where, for one reason or another, a judge will feel free to re-examine the same question if it comes back to

[7] Joseph E. McLean: *William Rufus Day* (Baltimore: Johns Hopkins University Press; 1946), p. 61.

[8] Charles Evans Hughes: *The Supreme Court of the United States* (New York, Columbia University Press; 1928), p. 68.

the Court. For example, the Sherman Anti-Trust Act is treated almost as if it were a constitutional mandate.

In the general run of cases, none of these things is true. Where differences are of minor significance, once a case is decided, the Court, including the dissenting Justices, will peacefully abide by the result. In such cases the dissent serves no useful purpose. Take, for example, a typical tax case such as a 1957 decision determining whether a particular system of sickness insurance by a private company was "health insurance" as that term is used within Section 22(b)(5) of the Internal Revenue Code.[9] Regardless of the answer, once the question is answered it seems scarcely worth mentioning that Justices Burton and Harlan disagreed; and this may be why they were very concise in doing so. As other illustrations of dubious dissents, the question of whether an injured handyman on a dredge in the Mississippi River was a "member of the crew" for the purposes of receiving the benefits of the Longshoremen's and Harbor Workers' Act invited a dissent from Justice Harlan and two other Justices.[1] Justices Frankfurter, Douglas, and Black dissented from a decision holding that the Stolen Car Act covered a car which was "embezzled" as well as one which was actually "stolen" as that term is commonly used in the technical law.[2]

These casual dissents do not unsettle the law; it is almost certain that in each of the cases mentioned, the law as declared by the majority will continue for the rest of time. But these dissents do use up judicial energy. In the instances mentioned, the effort may have been slight, but, whatever it was, it could have been given to something else.

9 *Haynes* v. *United States*, 353 U.S. 81 (1957).
1 *Senko* v. *LaCrosse Dredging Co.*, 352 U.S. 370 (1957).
2 *United States* v. *Turley*, 352 U.S. 407 (1957).

Of graver consequence, the constancy of dissent on little matters weakens the Court as an institution, robbing it of that oracular quality which it needs on the big cases. The impression that the "Court can't agree on anything" not only helps to drain dissents of their potency where they might matter a great deal, but also robs Supreme-Court-made law itself of much of its dignity.

To put the matter in a capsule, before Marshall everyone on the Court was free to give an opinion on every case. From Marshall's time until the death of Hughes, the Court gave single opinions, with rare concurrences and occasional dissents in matters of considerable substance. From Stone's time until the 1950's both concurrences and dissents have been common, Justices Frankfurter and Rutledge concurring very often, and most of the members of the Court dissenting freely.

Few members of the bar approve of this innovation. As Judge Learned Hand puts it: "[D]isunity cancels the impact of monolithic solidarity on which the authority of a bench of judges so largely depends." [3] As a matter of the Court's own public relations, no single thing has more depreciated the standing of the institution since the time of Hughes than the impression that it is overtalkative. Chief Justice Vinson set himself against the pattern of frequent dissents, but his was a lonely role.

[3] Learned Hand: *The Bill of Rights* (Cambridge: Harvard University Press; 1958), p. 72.

Chapter VII

THE LAW AS LITERATURE

There are more than 350 volumes of United States Supreme Court Reports, consisting of the best written work of which some ninety men have been capable over a period of almost one hundred and seventy years.

This mighty pile is, from the literary standpoint, explored approximately as much as Mount Everest. English-composition classes pass it by, not with a shudder, but with indifference. Anthologies of American writing, except for an occasional passage by Justice Holmes, include no product of these labors.

This is no enormous oversight by the compilers, no prodigious ignorance of the critics which can be corrected by sensational revelation of untold treasures. The critics are right. The treasures are rare. What appears to be a great literary wasteland is just that.

There are some exceptions, but the general style over the years is what might be called "legal lumpy."

Take, for example, Justice Shiras, who through the 1890's produced a large quantity of a standard brand of awkward English. There is nothing atrocious about it grammatically; it is simply not very pretty. The sentences are not so bad that *The New Yorker* would poke fun at them, but they are long, involved, and clumsy. Samples are contained in the appendix.

If the reader bothers to puzzle the appendix fragments out, he will find not that they are unintelligible, but that they are tedious. Extended over thousands of pages, they become a major affliction to those who work with them. The lengthy sentences, the endless parentheses reveal authors not concerned with readability. There are certain standard judicial styles that may themselves seem uninviting to the non-legal reader even though they may be highly esteemed by lawyers, but these passages are not very much esteemed by anyone.

One creditable style of legal writing which is not serviceable for anything else may be termed "legal massive." This style is a parade of propositions, each precisely supported by the authority that sustains it. At its worst, it results in long compilations of case names. At its best, it represents a solid presentation, although one that only a lawyer could love. The appendix example, a quotation from Justice Stone, illustrates it at its best.

There are changing styles of judicial prose just as there are changing styles in other forms of written expression. The Stone style as illustrated is now obsolete, having been replaced by a footnote method; the identical thought can be expressed in the identical words, but with the citations at the bottom of the page, the text is easier to read. The change is comparatively recent, and is probably an instance of the influence of legal magazines. Yet, for all of its awful cragginess, those whose eyes were trained to accept the style of Justice Stone still look at it with a certain nostalgia; the concluding chapter of this volume regrets for other reasons the coming of the footnote. The Stone method gave an impression of weighty truth. When it is taken out of the lawbooks, it is the most forbidding method of verbal expression known to man.

Judicial writing ought to be concise and lucid more often

than it is. Verbosity is a pervasive vice. The vice is not one of length, but of wordiness and of detours. Inevitably some topics will profit from lengthy treatment. The evils are rabbit-chasing—the business of going after irrelevancies— and overlong discussions. The Justices have an unlimited license to use the printing machine, with no restraint except their own sense of self-restraint, their own standards of verbal artistry, and such suggestions as their brothers may wish to give them. This leaves considerable room for personal taste. Only a few naturally write a lean prose. Some can boil out the fat on redraft; others do not really care to try.

Polar opposites in this respect are Justice Black and the late Justice Rutledge. Black has an impression that some people other than lawyers may actually read the Supreme Court Reports. When a paragraph is turned to his satisfaction, he has a way of saying with gusto: "Now they'll understand that," and "they" are some unidentifiable general readers. To reach "them," Black uses a simple and strong vocabulary, wrings out the water and deletes the superfluous word or citation or paragraph. He does not always achieve his goal; his 1957 opinion on state standards for bar admissions is not exactly the shortest distance between two points. Nonetheless, he hits the bull's-eye of lucid brevity as often as, or more often than, anyone else in the business. Heywood Broun once said of a Black opinion: "He recently wrote a dissent in English as plain and simple and clear as a good running story on the first page. Naturally, reporters take to those who speak their own language, and it is a far finer tongue than that invented by Mr. Blackstone."

Justices Rutledge and Black were of like mind on matters of policy. Rutledge was, however, less rapidly decisive, thinking longer before getting to the common result. This kindly and scrupulous man suffered from his own fair-mindedness.

All of his doubts, byways, and self-torturings cropped up in bulky opinions. Rutledge had a gift for phrase and his prose was extremely readable, but there was a lot of it.

Early in Rutledge's career he was assigned an opinion on a simple point. His clerk and I (then a clerk myself) agreed that a concise Justice would use two pages. We also agreed to give Rutledge a handicap. A dinner was wagered, the Rutledge clerk betting that his Justice could write the opinion in four pages. The Rutledge clerk paid for dinner.

All of which is to say that some Justices are more concise than others. In his opinion on the West Coast Communist case in 1957, Justice Harlan devoted nine pages to the meaning of the one word "organize." [1] A week later Justice Brennan polished off the entire subject of obscenity in American constitutional law in seventeen pages. [2]

Prolixity is conquerable at least in part by a judge who is sensitive to the problem. When Justice Burton came to the bench, his opinions were endless, with main points badly obscured by details. Perhaps perceiving that he was handicapping his own effectiveness, Burton gradually put a sharp rein on his own discursiveness. Some Justices, however, are beyond cure by criticism. These two perfectly accurate comments from the *New York Tribune* and the *Southern Literary Messenger* on Justice Wayne about 1850, for example, had no noticeable effect: "He has an ingenious, copious mind—fluent and rapid in expression, but lacks conciseness, lucid argument, and vigor"; and his style "is overloaded with words; scarcely any of his sentences convey a distinct idea; and some of them are quite beyond a pale of criticism." [3]

---

[1] *Yates* v. *United States*, 354 U.S. 298 (1957).
[2] *Roth* v. *United States*, 354 U.S. 476 (1957).
[3] Quoted in Alexander A. Lawrence: *James Moore Wayne* (Chapel Hill: University of North Carolina Press; 1943), pp. 91, 114.

Brevity is not always a value in itself. The short opinion and the long opinion are tools, and the wise Justice picks the spots for each. Chief Justice Warren affords excellent examples. In the segregation cases Warren turned out a very short opinion. His triumph of condensation was all the more remarkable because the parties gave the Court a mountain of material. Legal, historical, psychological, sociological, and anthropological references were stacked knee high. The Court concluded that the time had come for a great step; that the country was morally and spiritually ready for a new development in the law for which the Court itself had long been preparing the way. It also concluded that much talk would not improve matters. The eleven-page opinion is essentially a statement of conclusions.

On the other hand, in 1957 a Warren opinion greatly restricted the activities of the House Committee on Un-American Activities.[4] In this case the opinion is much more than a statement of conclusions; it is a fully reasoned and illustrated appeal to all who will read it, meant to carry conviction based on a study of American traditions of legislative investigation. There is a good deal to be said, and it is said for thirty-five pages.

For purposes of appraisal, the question is whether an opinion is as short as it can be and still do the job its author wishes for it. In that respect, the Court has never distinguished itself, and the current tendency is strong in the direction of more rather than less. In 1900 the Court wrote approximately twice as many opinions in the same number of pages that it uses today.

Sometimes ambiguity is a device rather than an accident. The Court must function as an institution, which means that

4 *Watkins* v. *United States,* 354 U.S. 178 (1957).

at least five Justices must commonly agree on a given statement. This may require use of terms that means one thing to one Justice and something else to another, thus getting rid of the case at hand and postponing the problem of precision to a future day that may never come. In this there is nothing peculiar to the Court; it arises whenever several men must be brought into agreement on a statement, and it accounts for much of the ambiguity in political-party platforms. Chief Justice Marshall was particularly dexterous at holding his Court solid by general wordings.

There are occasions when necessity results in ambiguity that approaches unintelligibility. A classic instance is the case of General Yamashita, the Japanese general in the Philippines, who was executed after a trial by the MacArthur forces. The Supreme Court reviewed the case. If General Yamashita was entitled to a trial with due process of law, he did not have it; any American judge would be outraged if a pickpocket charged with taking twenty cents were thus tried in an American court. For example, no effort was made to subject many of the witnesses against the General to cross-examination, or even to identify several of them; the remotest kind of investigative reports or rumors was used as evidence.

The resulting opinion by Chief Justice Stone has never been regarded as marking one of the better days in the Court's history.[5] The Court recognized the question of whether the General was entitled to due process. It held that the General might be executed. But the Court never did say what it thought about the constitutional question. A recent biography reveals that Stone, unable to hold his majority together with any one solution of that problem, finally took

5 *In re Yamashita*, 327 U. S. 1 (1946).

out the disputed portions of his draft opinion and put nothing in their place.[6] The story is more fully revealed in a letter to me by dissenting Justice Rutledge shortly after the opinion. Rutledge began by saying that this "was perhaps my hardest battle here from the very beginning, first to get a hearing, and then to get time to state my reasons for my views." He continued:

> First, and this will not be pleasant for you to read, it was only after three days of debate in conference and by the narrowest margin that we succeeded in getting a hearing. Second, there was no excuse whatsoever except necessity, and it was not necessity of time, for the Court's failure to treat the constitutional problem. They were not rushed into handing down an opinion without having time to answer the dissents. The rushing was the other way.
>
> Here are the facts: We voted on the case on Saturday after the argument. It was then understood that every effort would be made to get the case down three weeks from the following Monday. Murphy and I agreed to cooperate. Nothing could be done the first week because we had arguments going on. The Chief Justice was the general choice to write for the Court. I knew better than to start writing before I knew what he had to say and I had other things to do. He sent me about half of his opinion on Monday following the first week of recess. I could not tell where he was going from that—rather how he was going where I knew he would go. I received the first full draft of his opinion Tuesday noon. Then I put everything else aside and worked night and day until Saturday noon, finishing the first draft one minute before the conference bell. I was under the pressure of believing that the case might be sent down on the following Monday with leave to the dissenters to file opinions later. I was not going to do that.
>
> The printer is the real hero of the story. He got the last installment of my stuff a little after noon. He had it back

6 Alpheus T. Mason: *Harlan Fiske Stone* (New York: The Viking Press; 1956), pp. 666–71.

here by 3:30. I then had it circulated. The next day, Sunday, the Chief Justice undertook to deal in several pages with the constitutional argument for the first time. I got his typed additions at seven o'clock Sunday night. I worked practically all night to show up what they came to.

We met at ten o'clock Monday morning in conference to decide whether the case should go down. I knew it couldn't; I knew some would not accept his treatment. Then for the first time it dawned that speed was not the most important thing in this case. They decided not to send it down, but to take another week. The result was that after about four days the Chief Justice took out substantially all of his constitutional treatment. What was done on that phase was done deliberately. Neither more nor less could have been done without splitting the majority wide open. After he cut out most of his junk I cut much of mine and took the constitutional stuff in my opinion back into a separate section. During that week Murphy added his constitutional argument to what he had previously written on the charge. Then the case came down the next Monday. This is enough to give you a glimpse of all that went on behind the scenes. In my opinion the majority did the only thing it could do, namely, ignore the constitutional argument. I think they would have done better to ignore it altogether, as they did in the first place. But there are times when men seem unwilling to stand squarely up to what they are doing *and* to admit that is what they are doing. . . .

A dissenter of course is apt to exaggerate in his view of what the majority do. Maybe I do so here. Nevertheless in my honest, and I hope sober, judgment this case will outrank Dred Scott in the annals of the Court.[7]

An example of an intriguing style, usually completely clear, is that of Justice Frankfurter. Much criticized for the use of an ornate vocabulary, Frankfurter undoubtedly en-

[7] Wiley Rutledge to John P. Frank, February 22, 1946.

joys words that few writers would choose. Samples from the 1956–7 term of Court are: "to assume that the Kansas Courts construed the pleadings *sub silentio* as alleging monetary loss is to excogitate";[8] "a futile collocation of words";[9] a certain course of conduct brings "the result below the Plimsoll line of due process";[1] "the penultimate sentence of section 8(d)";[2] and, from the same case: "the Murdock view is an artifact; it is not a bit of quixotism to believe . . .";[3] or "the problems that are the respective preoccupations of anthropology, economics, law, psychology, sociology, and related areas of scholarship are merely departamentalized dealing, by way of manageable division of analysis, with interpenetrating aspects of holistic perplexities."[4]

But a Justice is free, if he wishes, to reject the notion that the opinions are written for Everyman, and he need not compromise with the standards of his own vocabulary. Moreover, Frankfurter's choices of words unfamiliar to his average reader are widely scattered. An exception to Frankfurter's usual clarity is his statement of what he described as the "governing constitutional principle" concerning the meaning of the contract clause of the federal Constitution. This "governing constitutional principle" is: "When a widely

[8] *Walker* v. *City of Hutchinson,* 352 U.S. 112 (1956).
[9] *Paoli* v. *United States,* 352 U.S. 232 (1957).
[1] *Fikes* v. *Alabama,* 352 U.S. 191 (1957).
Professor Richard H. Field of the Harvard Law School, in a good-natured poem titled "Frankfurter, J., Concurring," 71 *Harvard Law Review* 77 (1957), has suggested that the Justice may not himself have known what a Plimsoll line was. However, on the general matter of the Justice's vocabulary, Field observes:

> *We don't decry the vivid phrase,*
> *The erudite bravura,*
> *That gives Judicial mayonnaise*
> *A touch of Angostura.*

[2] *Labor Board* v. *Lion Oil Company,* 352 U.S. 282 (1957).
[3] *Rogers* v. *Missouri Pacific R. Co.,* 352 U.S. 500 (1957).
[4] *Sweezy* v. *New Hampshire,* 354 U.S. 234 (1957).

diffused public interest has become enmeshed in a network of multitudinous private arrangements, the authority of the State 'to safeguard the vital interests of its people,' [citation] is not to be gainsaid by abstracting one such arrangement from its public context and treating it as though it were an isolated private contract constitutionally immune from impairment." [5]

The passage just quoted has not helped all its readers to understand just when the state could and when it could not tinker with the obligations of a contract.

There is mystery as to why we lawyers commonly write a prose that varies from the uninteresting at best to the awful at worst. The appendix contains an example of rock-bottom contemporary. That the pages of the *Journal of Electrical Engineering* or the *Journal of the American Medical Association* should afford few samples intended for the shelf of the best American literature is not remarkable; the practitioners of those professions are destined to do deeds and not to write words. But lawyers are workers with words. Words are their tools, as wires or scalpels may be for electricians or doctors. They are the inheritors of the tradition of the village letter-writer, whose very function is to put down on paper agreements, letters, proposals, or conclusions that the other persons in the community cannot well express. Why are lawyers unable to use their tools to more glorious effect?

Contemporaneously, much of the blame rests on legal education. A lad goes to law school to sit before a professor who, if not brighter than he, is at least far better informed on the subject at hand. The method of instruction usually involves an exercise in which the professor leads the student into error and out again, quizzing him to explore what he has learned of his day's lesson. Whatever the student answers will speed-

[5] *East N.Y. Savings Bank* v. *Hahn*, 326 U.S. 230 (1945).

ily be shown by the professor to be wrong. This device is clean intellectual fun but embarrassing to the student, who quickly learns that a decisive answer will get him into more trouble than one which contains many "if" and "but" escape clauses. The habit of thinking and writing in terms of multiple qualifications is ingrained with final examinations. The student studies the writings of judges who in turn were educated by studying writings of judges.

Only the student who contributes to his school's legal publication enjoys a variation from this discipline. The student sections of these publications have developed a style of their own in which the process of revision after revision usually results in the driest stuff in the books.

The reasons just given may be speculative and shaky. They do not account for the judges of a century ago, before the days of law schools. The result, however, is generally clear: the legal profession vary rarely turns out written work that would be much admired by anyone outside it. The efforts by Professor Cavers of Harvard, an advisor of the Office of Price Administration during World War II, to convert the regulations of that agency into general comprehensibility resulted in such a radical improvement in their language as to dramatize how far below general intelligibility legal writing can fall.

Some of the Justices have consistently turned out work that was admirable at least to lawyers, and a few have been authors of passages that should commend themselves to anyone. Both Marshall and Hughes had a good, solid gift of expression. Both of them sometimes said more than they needed to; it has been speculated that this was particularly true of Hughes because he dictated with great fluency and perhaps ran on a little. Nonetheless, a student brought up on the prose of either would not suffer from it.

Passing the level of the merely good, Holmes and Cardozo have reasonable claim to be included in anybody's anthology. The endless parade of Holmes's books, the endless charm of the Holmes legend are partly the product of the brilliant military record, partly the product of the brave mustachios, partly the product of the saltiness—and partly the product of Holmes's ability to say well what he wanted to say. The appendix contains a sample. As Francis Biddle, a former Holmes clerk, put it: "[H]is clarity, his freshness, and his poet's touch clothed his ideas in a style that made them sound inevitable." [6]

In addition to the virtuosos who gave sustained performances throughout their lives, there are others who achieve occasional flashes either of wit or of eloquence. For the consistent capacity to turn a nice phrase, Justice Jackson has never been matched. For example, in the case of *Kristensen*, in which the issue was whether violation of the liquor tax amounted to moral turpitude, Jackson, dissenting, said: "I have never discovered that disregard of the Nation's liquor taxes excluded a citizen from our best society and I see no reason why it should banish an alien from our worst." On an occasion when he, as a member of the Court, voted to reverse a position that he himself had taken as Attorney General, Jackson expressed his regrets, and said: "If there are other ways of gracefully and good-naturedly surrendering former views to a better considered position, I invoke them all." [7] Regretting excessive publicity about a criminal case, he said: "The case presents one of the best examples of one of the worst menaces to American justice." [8] In a combination

6 Francis Biddle: "Oliver Wendell Holmes," in *Mr. Justice,* edited by Allison Dunham and Philip Kurland (Chicago: University of Chicago Press; 1956), p. 10.
7 *McGrath* v. *Kristensen,* 340 U.S. 162 (1950).
8 *Shepherd* v. *Florida,* 341 U.S. 50 (1951).

of cases in which, as he saw it, an organization was getting rights of due process and an individual was not, he said: "So far as I recall, this is the first time this Court has held rights of individuals subordinate and inferior to those of organized groups. I think that is an inverted view of the law—it is justice turned bottom side up." [9]

Jackson's longer passages are outstanding prose. His opinion in one of the Communist cases was republished as an article in *The New York Times Magazine*.[1] In one case the Patent Office disbarred an attorney for procuring a patent partly on the strength of an article by a person who purported to be independent but who in fact was hired by his client. Justice Jackson disapproved, saying:

> I should not like to be second to anyone on this Court in condemning the custom of putting up decoy authors to impress the guileless, a custom which as the Court below cruelly pointed out flourishes even in official circles in Washington. Nor do I contend that the lawyer's special adaptation of the prevailing custom comports with the highest candor. Ghost writing has debased the intellectual currency in circulation here and is a type of counterfeiting which invites no defense. Perhaps this Court renders a public service in treating phantom authors and ghost writers as legal frauds and disguised authorship as a deception. But has any man before [the Attorney] ever been disciplined or even reprimanded for it? And will any be hereafter? [2]

The foremost professional writer on the Court is Justice Douglas, whose books appear on the best-seller lists almost as regularly as he returns from abroad. He is the only Jus-

[9] *Joint Anti-Fascist Refugee Committee* v. *McGrath*, 341 U.S. 123 (1951).

[1] *American Communications Assn.* v. *Douds*, 339 U.S. 382 (1950); reprinted as "Justice Jackson on Communism in America," *The New York Times Magazine*, May 21, 1950, p. 12.

[2] *Kingsland* v. *Dorsey*, 338 U.S. 318 (1949).

tice in history who demonstrably could make his living as a professional writer on non-legal subjects. From him, as well as from other Justices, the problems of civil liberty which come to the Court occasionally evoke short passages of great eloquence. Regardless of one's views of the constitutionality of the basic statute relied on in prosecution of Communist leaders, probably no professional student of the English language would doubt that Douglas's dissent in that case, quoted in the appendix, ran circles of verbal skill around the majority opinion.

For another example, Justices Black and Douglas together presented a few words on the invalidity of the requirement that school children be compelled to salute the flag against their own religious objections:

> Neither our domestic tranquility in peace nor our martial effort in war depend on compelling little children to participate in a ceremony which ends in nothing for them but a fear of spiritual condemnation. If, as we think, their fears are groundless, time and reason are the proper antidotes for their errors. The ceremonial, when enforced against conscientious objectors more likely to defeat than to serve its high purpose, is a handy implement for disguised religious persecution. As such, it is inconsistent with our Constitution's plan and purpose.[3]

This recital necessarily overlooks much that is good. Justice Murphy published some magnificent passages, and Justice Brandeis handled the building-blocks of the law with a skill that on occasion rose to beauty.

In short, an anthology of very good things could be put together from the 350 volumes of the United States Supreme Court Reports—but the editor would probably have 348 volumes left over.

---

3 *West Virginia State Bd. of Educ.* v. *Barnette,* 319 U.S. 624 (1943).

Chapter VIII

THE COURT

AND DEMOCRATIC THEORY

On October 7, 1950, a Chesapeake & Ohio Railway worker prepared to go to the yard for his night's work. Before leaving home he had a bowel movement. He said to himself: "This won't do," and took a dose of salts, washed down with sweet cider. On arrival at the switching-yard, he had a second bowel movement at the roundhouse. He then took his engine out onto the track, and while waiting for an airbrake test he had a sudden urge to relieve himself again. He hopped out of his locomotive cab, but a long train of empties passed between him and a near-by toilet. He frantically climbed into a low-sided car loaded with steel plates. While he was relieving himself there, a yard crew switched two cars onto the same track. The two cars bumped the steel car, shifting its load and crushing the employee's right leg. In June 1957 the United States Supreme Court found that a jury rather than a judge should have decided the critical questions of fact concerning the possible liability of the railroad.[1]

As this case shows, the Supreme Court has more to do than to decide whether an act of Congress is unconstitutional, how a congressional committee can conduct its business, how a bank should be reorganized, what type of money the

[1] *Ringhiser* v. *Ches. & O. Ry. Co.,* 354 U.S. 901 (1957).

The Court and Democratic Theory

United States shall use, whether a given tax shall be paid. It must also decide cases about *people*, human beings with bowels, hearts, feelings, and very human problems. To those people the high reaches of policy may not be important; what matters to them is how the case affects their own lives.

A favorite example is a tale told by Walton Hamilton, onetime professor of Supreme Court studies at Yale. In 1934 the Supreme Court decided the great case of *Nebbia* v. *New York*,[2] which dealt with the powers of the several states to regulate business. The particular law involved forbade the sale of milk at less than a certain price, and Leo Nebbia, a storekeeper, had violated the law by giving a loaf of bread with each bottle of milk he sold.

Some years later when Professor Hamilton was in Rochester, New York, the home of Nebbia, he went to the store, desiring to meet the protagonist in such an important legal battle. After a pleasant visit, Professor Hamilton turned to go. As he did, the thought struck him that for sentiment's sake he might well make the same purchase. He bought a bottle of milk and picked up a loaf of bread. Turning to Nebbia, Hamilton said: "Will you toss this in, too?"

Leo Nebbia replied: "Never again."

Because litigation is also people, because a case, however great a precedent to the Court and the country, is a very real personal problem to the human beings immediately involved, there is a constant adjustment in the Court between the needs of human beings and the necessities of broad policy. These two needs, the needs of the law in general and of people in particular, may directly conflict.

For illustration, the law permits some cases to be brought *either* in a state court or in a federal court, according to the choice of the people involved. A typical example is an auto

[2] 291 U.S. 502.

145

accident involving two motorists from different states. However, some cases can be brought *only* in the state courts, and other cases can be brought *only* in the federal courts.

If a case is brought in a state court, in certain circumstances the defendant may have it removed to the federal court. If there is a mistake and a case is wrongly removed to the federal court, the federal court will simply send it back again.

But what happens if the mistake runs the other way and a person brings a case in a state court which can only be brought in a federal court? Suppose that such a case is brought, and that the defendant then attempts to remove it to the federal court where it belongs. The United States Supreme Court has repeatedly held that the federal court cannot keep the case, but must dismiss it, *even though it is exactly where it ought to be*. The legal theory behind this odd rule is that the only cases which can be removed to the federal courts are those which were properly in the state courts to start with, and as this case was never properly in the state court, it cannot enter the federal courthouse through the wrong door. Yet, by then it may be too late to start all over again in the federal court.

Some rule of law! A party loses because he has finally got to the right place, and is not allowed to proceed with his case because he is where he should be. Surely when the Court concocted that rule, it was focusing exclusively on legal theory and general principles; if individual needs had been considered, such a result could never have been reached.

Another instance of the same kind of thing is the tale of misfortune of the Spector Motor Service Company of Missouri. This is a trucking company that, among other activities, was hauling in Connecticut. It had a difference with the State of Connecticut over some $7,795.50 in taxes, which the Spector Company thought were an unconstitutional burden on interstate commerce and therefore need not be paid.

In 1942, with high hopes for a speedy determination of its taxes, the Spector Company filed a suit in the federal trial court. The case then went up to the United States Court of Appeals, and from there to the United States Supreme Court. In 1944 the Supreme Court decided that it could not decide; that before the question of constitutional law could be determined, there must first be a decision by the Connecticut courts that Spector was subject to the state tax. The Supreme Court directed the district court to have the parties bring another suit in the Connecticut courts to get the answer to the state-law question.

This was done. A suit brought in the trial court of the State of Connecticut eventually went to the Supreme Court of that state. The Supreme Court of Connecticut, playing Alphonse to the United States Supreme Court's Gaston, decided the state-law question, but declared that, in the circumstances, it could not decide the constitutional question. The case was then marched back to the federal district court in which it had originally begun, and started up the ladder again. After two arguments, the Supreme Court finally decided the case on March 26, 1951.[3] The Spector Company then learned that it did not need to pay $7,795.50 in taxes. The answer came nine years after the case began, and after the expenditure of many times the amount of the taxes in legal fees. A matter which, if the Supreme Court had decided it in the first place, could have been settled after a maximum of three court proceedings, took eight. Meanwhile, for almost a decade Connecticut did not know what it could and what it could not tax.

[3] *Spector Motor Service, Inc.* v. *O'Connor*, 340 U.S. 602 (1951).

As it happens, the two rules of law just described are two that I personally believe should be junked. The rightness or wrongness of the rules, however, are quite apart from the point under discussion. The point is that there is a constant struggle between the practical needs of an immediate situation on the one hand and the great policies of the Court on the other. People are not made for courts, but courts for people; and yet a court sitting at the top of a great ladder, deciding only a few cases a year chosen on the basis of their general importance, must keep its eye on the whole picture as well as on the particular case. The problem is one of striking a balance. If a court focuses only on the particular people before it, it may do justice in a particular case and yet make very poor general policy; and so it is often said that hard cases make bad law. On the other hand, if a court or judge concentrates overly much on little specialties of practice or procedure, then the court has become precious, or overly finicky, too much interested in *itself* to serve the general good.

This is a real problem. Particularly when Justices sit in Washington, concentrating in a little professional circle on a narrow range of problems year after year, they may become overinterested in the minutiae of the business and underinterested in the merits. They may be more interested in whether the parties come to the court through the right door than in what happens to them after they get there.

For illustration, in a gathering of a dozen or so people, I once heard a Supreme Court Justice upbraid and deride a distinguished judge of a state supreme court because that judge acknowledged that he did not know whether the Justices passed on petitions for certiorari separately and individually, or delegated them to some one or a committee of their number for disposition. To the Justice it seemed almost

148

incredible ignorance that this obscure fact should not be known. Yet, surely only a person grossly overimpressed by the importance of the details of what he was doing would regard as an ignoramus another man who did not happen to know those details.

Compare Justice Murphy, whose goal was always substantial justice no matter how technical the problems. In one criminal case there was a good technical legal reason why the Court should not be able to go into a particular matter. Said Murphy: "Legal technicalities doubtless afford justification for our pretense of ignoring plain facts before us, facts upon which a man's very life or liberty conceivably could depend. Moreover, there probably is legal warrant for our not remanding the case . . . to allow those facts to be incorporated in the formal record." However, Murphy said, the result "does not enhance the high traditions of the judicial process. In my view, when undisputed facts appear in the record before us in a case involving a man's life or liberty, they should not be ignored if justice demands their use." [4]

Of course, the desire to do substantial justice regardless of technical considerations is stronger in some Justices than in others. Chief Justice Waite once observed that his associate Davis "used frequently to say that when he was sure justice required a decision in a particular way, he could always find a good reason for doing so." [5] Justice Miller repeatedly took positions such as "If this is not due process of law it ought to be." [6]

How to keep Justices appointed for life themselves in tune with the throbbing life of the American people and

[4] *Carter* v. *Illinois*, 329 U.S. 173 (1946).

[5] Bruce R. Trimble: *Chief Justice Waite* (Princeton: Princeton University Press; 1943), p. 266.

[6] Charles Fairman: *Mr. Justice Miller* (Cambridge: Harvard University Press; 1939), p. 65.

to prevent their becoming remote high priests of a mysterious ritual has concerned some of the best minds in the country since 1790. The Justices in the beginning traveled about the country to sit as trial judges, a tradition that was stubbornly maintained at least in form until the present century. A great reason for that practice was the feeling that the judges must "get out amongst them" if they were adequately to perform their job in Washington. As late as 1869, Senator Edmunds of Vermont, a distinguished chairman of the Senate Judiciary Committee, expressed the fear that the Court would become a Star Chamber, or center of tyranny, if it were cut loose from the circuits.

The circuit-riding system could not survive the expansion of the appeals business. For as long as it lasted, it was a terrible burden. It did, however, keep the Justices thoroughly acquainted with the America that they served. As was mentioned in Chapter III, Justice Daniel had the Mississippi and Arkansas circuit for the 1840's and '50's, thanks to the spite of the Whigs. In 1843 Daniel wrote former President Van Buren from Jackson, Mississippi, saying: "I am here two thousand miles from home (calculating by the travel record) on the pilgrimage by an exposure to which, it was the calculation of sad malignity, that I had been driven from the bench. Justice to my friends, and a determination to defeat the machinations of mine and of their enemies have induced me to undergo the experiment, and I have done so at no small hazard, through the air of fever at Vicksburg and convulsive and autumnal fevers in this place and vicinity." [7] The next year he was out again on a five thousand-mile, three-month trip.

The Daniel trips illustrate that, whether for better or for worse, the travelers kept the common touch. On his 1851

[7] P. V. Daniel to Martin Van Buren, April 8, 1843.

150

excursion Daniel traveled from Washington to Baltimore and then set out for Pittsburgh. This latter leg of the journey took two nights and a day, during which time he could remove neither his clothes nor even his boots. The train from Baltimore to Holidaysburg crossed the Alleghenies at angles so steep that it was difficult to stand. It took one night to cover thirty-six miles. From Johnstown, Pennsylvania, to Pittsburgh he went by canalboat for a day and a night, a thoroughly unpleasant excursion: "The discomfort of being about in immediate contact with all sorts of people, some of the most vulgar and filthy in the world, women more disgusting if possible by their want of cleanliness than the men; with squalling children and being required to use in common, two tin basins encrusted with filth, and one long towel for the whole male establishment, is a misery beyond which my imagination can scarcely picture any earthly evil. My washing therefore was limited to wiping my eyes and mouth with my linen handkerchief, but I neither took off my clothes nor slept during this purgatory." [8]

Ten days later Daniel reached Napoleon, at the mouth of the Arkansas River. Here the hotel was an abandoned steamboat that had been pulled up on the shore, the staterooms being to let. They were shared by the Justice and a large number of fleas. After handling his Arkansas business, which took only a few days, he moved on to Mississippi and then headed for his home in Richmond, Virginia. The return trip was outright hazardous. The steamer in which he ascended the Mississippi was snagged by a large tree that carried away a part of the wheel and the wheelhouse. For a night the party was pinned in the river while the workmen sawed out the snag. Shortly thereafter cholera hit the boat, and

[8] P. V. Daniel to Elizabeth Randolph Daniel, April 8, 1851, from the Grimes deposit of unpublished Daniel MSS. in the University of Virginia Library, Charlottesville, Virginia.

there were five deaths before Daniel abandoned ship in Cincinnati. To escape the cholera he traveled the full length of Ohio to Cleveland and there took a boat to Buffalo. He found the train north through Ohio "rougher than any travelling by horse, stage, or wagon that I have ever experienced. It is a wonder that the cars are kept on the track at all."

Not all of the trip was unpleasant. The townspeople he met were hospitable almost to a fault. Once or twice he was "made unwell by partaking (though as slightly as possible), to avoid singularity, of late suppers prepared principally for my entertainment." Upon his return home it took him some time to unwind: "The feeling of hurry is still upon me so strongly that between sleeping and waking this morning I found myself starting up to be in time for the boat or the cars." [9]

In the twentieth century the Justices have only a nominal connection by way of assignment to a particular region of the country. Today the problem of maintaining the common touch becomes entirely a matter of the taste of each Justice, a product of his own habits and customs. There are numerous invitations to public functions, usually of a ceremonial nature; Chief Justice Warren, for example, had a well-traveled summer in 1957, including participation in the dedication of the Truman Library in Missouri and an appearance at a meeting of the American Bar Association in London. Justice Douglas knocks about the world in his off time, and other Justices come and go to the extent that they please. Many of them participate a little in legal education, principally by sitting as judges for practice arguments of law students. Justice Holmes is said to have avoided the newspapers and

9 P. V. Daniel to Elizabeth Randolph Daniel, June 6, 1851.

concentrated on literature and philosophy. Brandeis read economics. Black reads history.

The best protection against an excessively rarefied atmosphere in the Supreme Court is the diversity of backgrounds among the Justices themselves. It is the other Justices with whom, in the winter season at least, a Justice spends most of his time. The hearings and the conferences consume many hours, and create an opportunity for interchange among the members. The mixture of a Wall Street lawyer, a Western politician, an ex-mayor of a large city, a schoolteacher, a Southern practicing lawyer and politician, and so on, may not be what Doctor Gallup would call a cross-section of the American people, but it is not bad. As Dean Griswold of Harvard has said after reviewing the various backgrounds of the Justices: "It is naturally a diverse group. And in that diversity there is strength. That this does not lead to unanimity of opinion on hard cases is expectable, and, by and large, not very important. The one thing which they should have in common is, as Judge Learned Hand has said, 'a bias against bias.' " [1]

For illustration, a number of years ago a lawyer was on the verge of disbarment for extreme negligence in failing to answer communications from the Court about one of his cases. One of the Justices revolted. "I know that this fellow has been pretty bad," he said. "All the same, some of those other judges from big offices don't understand about these things. Lawyers in small towns are careless with their correspondence. A fellow doesn't necessarily mean to be impertinent to this Court because he lets his mail pile up on his desk as lawyers in small towns always have done. Just because

---

[1] Erwin N. Griswold: "The Function of the Supreme Court," Address, Cleveland, Ohio, December 7, 1957.

that fellow behaved as small-town lawyers do, I am not going to vote to see his name plastered all over his home-town paper under the heading 'John Jones Disbarred by U. S. Supreme Court.' " The man was not disbarred.

The great problem of the relationship of the Court to American democratic theory arises from the very existence of this island in the middle of a democracy in which the holders of power are not responsible to the democracy at all. Here are men appointed for life. They may never have been elected to anything, and a good many of them could not have been. For one moment they are tossed into the balance of democratic review, when they are chosen by a President and confirmed by the Senate. Thereafter, perhaps for twenty or more years, they make decisions for the whole community. How can a community that believes in choosing its leaders by free elections justify a system in which these leaders are not the product of elections?

This question becomes dramatic when a Court is altogether out of accord with the dominant thought of its time. An extreme example is the conflict between the Court of the 1930's and the New Deal. In the 1936 decision holding unconstitutional the New York minimum-wage law, the vote was five to four. The five Justices included a man appointed in 1910 from a Western state whose total population at the time of his election was less than that of one good-sized New York election district at the time of this decision. A second had been appointed in 1914. Two others had been appointed in the early '20's by President Harding, and the fifth by Hoover. At the moment of decision, the country was deeply dedicated to a philosophy of life radically different from that of this majority, and was shortly to give to the Roosevelt administration the most overwhelming election victory in over a hundred years.

154

There were three answers to this obvious conflict with democratic theory.

The first is that the country does not purport to be a pure democracy or a pure republic, and never did. The country is organized on a system of checks and balances, and courts are among those checks and those balances.

The second answer is a pseudo answer. It is to deny that the Court is exercising a policy-making function and to assume that it is simply declaring law, as if it were running a large slot machine from which preordained results roll when it pulls the handle. This view avoids the necessity to justify the exercise of a policy-making function by judges in a democracy.

Sometimes this view is taken; it may even be the view of law held by many non-lawyers. Sometimes Justices themselves talk as though they were only so many mechanics. For example, Justice Roberts in his opinion holding the Agricultural Adjustment Act unconstitutional in 1936, said: "When an act of Congress is appropriately challenged in the courts as not conforming to the constitutional mandate, the judicial branch of the government has only one duty; to lay the article of the Constitution which is invoked beside the statute which is challenged and to decide whether the latter squares with the former." [2]

Justice Roberts was talking figuratively. He was far too wise a judge to suppose that all that is needed to decide a case is a copy of the Constitution, a copy of a statute, and a legal T-square. It is true that in some simple cases the results are automatic, so that one can fairly readily find "the law." In the cases of greater difficulty there is no foreordained answer, and no amount of searching will find one; these are cases in which something new has to be done. In

[2] *United States* v. *Butler,* 297 U.S. 1 (1936).

deciding these cases, all judges make policy—not as members of a legislature make policy, but as judges make it, within the limits of the legal system. Paul Freund begins his book on the Supreme Court with a quotation from Jeremiah Smith, of the New Hampshire Supreme Court, who, to the question "Do judges make law?" said: "Course they do. Made some myself." [3]

The Supreme Court docket is loaded with these hard cases. The Court's jurisdiction is discretionary, and if the answer were obvious, there would have been no reason for the Court to hear the case in the first place. It is when, let us say, the federal court of New York answers a question Yes and the federal court of San Francisco answers the same question No that the Supreme Court must resolve the difference; and if those two competent courts cannot agree, then the problem is almost certainly beyond the resources of a T-square and a dictionary.

A concrete but simple example is provided by a 1957 case [4] concerning a railroad employee who was injured while operating a gas-driven motor track car in maintenance work. On the occasion of his injury, the motor track car was pulling a heavily loaded handcar, which had no brakes. Five Justices held that this kind of vehicle, operated in this manner, was covered by a Federal law known as the Safety Appliance Act, and Justice Clark wrote an opinion to this effect. Four Justices dissented. The majority found that the Act covered "all trains, locomotives, tenders, cars, and similar vehicles." The dissenters thought that a maintenance vehicle such as this one was neither a "locomotive" nor a "car," and was therefore not covered by the statute.

There is no clear answer. Congress, in passing the law, did

[3] Paul A. Freund: *On Understanding the Supreme Court* (Boston: Little, Brown & Co.; 1949), p. 3.
[4] *Baltimore & Ohio Ry. Co.* v. *Jackson,* 353 U.S. 325 (1957).

not mean either to include or exclude this kind of vehicle; it simply did not think about it. Doubtless the device had not been invented at the time. If the job of the Court were merely to determine what Congress meant, it could decide nothing because Congress had no intention. When all the talk is over, when all the precedents have been examined and their language has been analyzed, the Court must supply a meaning of its own. In these circumstances the judges have no choice but to consult their sense of what is right and practical. The majority of five thought that Congress intended by the Act to secure "the protection of employees and others by requiring the use of safe equipment," and therefore it resolved the doubts in favor of compelling the use of safer equipment. The minority thought this result wholly impractical because added brakes would make the car so bulky that in an emergency it could not be lifted off the tracks by small crews; also, if power brakes were used, they might throw men out at sudden stops.

In these hard cases the judges draw upon their total knowledge of law and of life to make matters come out as fairly, as reasonably, and as justly as they can. There is no mechanical answer, no slot machine in the Court basement to give forth a card saying "affirmed" or "reversed." The question of justifying this limited duty of the Justices in a democracy cannot be ducked by pretending the problem is not there.

The real answer is that the Court serves not as a barrier to the democratic will, but as a gyroscope that helps to keep the democratic machine in balance and to prevent it from running off wildly in one direction or another. A hundred and seventy years of experience demonstrates that in law, as in other things, what the people really want, earnestly and for a long time, they get. Because of the longevity of the

Justices, a Court may at a given moment be out of relation to the will of the community, but in the long run it adjusts. Courts are replaced, and the wheels turn, though slowly. A total conflict, as in 1936 and '37, very rarely occurs. The Marshall Court was in conflict with much of the country, but the Taney Court modified the extreme Marshall positions. In the dwindling days of Taney's own time, some Justices, if allowed to go their way, would have greatly handicapped the prosecution of the Civil War. But this did not happen; Lincoln had enough opportunities for new appointments to carry his policies through.

This process of revision is extremely gradual, and is perceived in retrospect much more easily than when it is happening. It now appears to virtually every American who has considered it that the protection of business from regulation was carried to great excesses by the Court in the 1920's; but this course did not conflict with the majority attitudes of the 1920's. The law—and the attitudes—have been greatly modified since.

Beginning in the late 1930's, the country itself began to drift into one of its cyclical binges of repression of minorities and restriction of radicalism; this whole cyclical development is discussed in more detail in Chapter X. The Court was then and for some years thereafter inclined to be protective of civil rights. By the post-war period, however, the tendency of the country had become a landslide, symbolized by the concept of "McCarthyism," and the shifting personnel of the Court made no real resistance to this trend.

By the mid-1950's the country itself had begun to recover from its bender. McCarthy faded into obscurity, and there was a general relaxing of tensions. Under Chief Justice Warren, the Court began to attack the restrictions that had been tolerated in the intervening years. As the Court gingerly moved back from the right to the center, there was a torrent of abuse from, for example, the Senator from Mississippi, the chairman of the House Committee on Un-American Activities, and their numerous journalistic supporters. On the other hand, there was applause from *The New York Times*, from the *Washington Post* and *Times-Herald*, from the *St. Louis Post-Dispatch*, from the *Arizona Daily Star*, and elsewhere. The Court was again slowly helping the country respond to the better angels of our nature.

The principal irony of this latter shift is that the voices so violently denouncing the Court in 1957 were in many instances the very persons or papers who in 1937 had taken the stand that it was morally wrong to denounce the Court, un-American to bean the umpire. As a *New York Times* columnist has observed, "Leaders of the bar have opposed the Butler-Jenner legislation, but there has been no public outcry comparable to the court-packing fight of 1937." [5] A salient exception was a symposium held at Notre Dame University Law School in April 1958 by its Dean, Joseph O'Meara, in which education and bar leaders supported the Court's jurisdiction.

In this peculiar institution which Americans have created, a small body appointed for life with great influence in a democracy, there is a check to democratic impulsiveness, but no bar to sustained democratic will. Perhaps on occasion the interpretation of a statute is not in accord with the congressional wish; but Congress can always change it. In interpreting the Constitution, Justice Stone once said that the only check upon the Court's exercise of power is "our own sense of self-restraint." Usually, so far as the temper of the people is concerned at any given moment, this has been enough.

5 Anthony Lewis, *New York Times*, May 4, 1958, p. 10 E.

Chapter IX

SPECIAL FUNCTIONS

OF THE COURT

1. THE GOVERNMENTAL

FUNCTION

On and off between 1768 and 1775, troops were on the move in that sector of Pennsylvania around Wilkes-Barre known as the Wyoming Valley. These troops were Americans against Americans, forces from what is now Pennsylvania fighting forces from what is now Connecticut for the control of the land. At the battle of Rampart Rock on Christmas Day in 1775 the Yankees won, and the Connecticut legislature established the area as Westmoreland County, Connecticut.

But proximity was with Philadelphia, not with Hartford, and after the Revolution a new battle broke out known as the Second Pennamite-Yankee War. The matter was finally compromised by giving political sovereignty of the area to Pennsylvania while confirming the title to the land in the Yankee invaders.

The greatest single accomplishment of the United States Supreme Court is that the lesson symbolized in the Pennamite-Yankee Wars has by now been forgotten by almost every American. Today it almost never occurs to Americans that our forty-eight states could be, but for the Court and the Constitution, forty-eight separate countries, capable of all the conflicts of the Germans and French, or the little Italian states of the mid-nineteenth century, or the Dutch and Flemish in an earlier age.

Quarrels among neighbors are almost inevitable. Such controversies can be adjusted by diplomacy, by war, or by judicial decision of some sort. Since 1787 the American people have resorted to internal war only once. With the exception of the great North-South struggle, the states have adjusted their differences either by diplomacy—their "treaties" being called "compacts" in our system—or by decision of the United States Supreme Court.

In pre-constitutional times clumsy systems existed for settling disputes among the colonies. So long as England ruled, her Privy Council could decide such matters. English courts determined the great controversy between William Penn and Lord Baltimore over Pennsylvania and Maryland lands. After the Revolution the weak Confederate Congress was left to feebler arbitrations. The Court was the instrument chosen to fill the vacuum created by the withdrawal of the English courts. Alexander Hamilton explained this to the voters when he urged them to accept the Constitution. He said: "History gives us a horrid picture of the dissensions and private wars which distracted and desolated Germany prior to the institution of the Imperial Chamber of Maximilian, towards the close of the Fifteenth Century; and informs us, at the same time, of the vast influence of that institution in appeasing the disorders and establishing the tranquility of the empire. This was a court invested with authority to decide finally all differences among the members of the Germanic body." And so, continued Hamilton, the task of settling those "bickerings and animosities" which may "spring up among the members of the union" was assigned to the Court.[1]

Thus, the Court has always been the final arbiter among the states. As this volume is written, an appointee of the Court is taking evidence on a controversy over the waters of the Colorado River among the states of Arizona, California, New Mexico, Nevada, and Utah, as well as the United States. The Court itself has recently considered a conflict between Texas and New Mexico over the Rio Grande, and has entered a new order in the endless differences between Wyoming and Colorado over the Laramie River.

These disputes are frequent. When the Constitutional Convention met in 1787, there were pending disputes involving ten of the thirteen states over water, land, or boundaries. Since that day, interstate disputes have ranged wide, as when New Jersey sought to enjoin New York from injuring its shad fisheries by diverting into the Hudson waters that would otherwise go to the Delaware; and when Missouri attempted to stop Illinois and the City of Chicago from running sewerage into the Mississippi; and when Virginia and West Virginia settled the obligations of West Virginia on the public debt of Virginia after the western state pulled away from its parent during the Civil War. Sometimes the suits are brought by a state against a resident of another state, as when Georgia applied to the Supreme Court to restrain a Tennessee copper company from emitting sulphuric-acid fumes that crossed the border and destroyed the vegetation in Georgia.

The established system of settlement is the most leisurely on the books. First the states must persuade the Court that their case is an appropriate one for the Court to hear. If they prevail in this, the Court appoints as its proxy to take

1 *The Federalist*, No. 80.

the evidence a Special Master, usually a distinguished lawyer who has affairs of his own to worry about and therefore takes the evidence in bits and bites over the years. A good interstate lawsuit may last ten or fifteen years from beginning to end. The *Arizona Daily Star* has observed that interstate cases "should be speeded, so that the generation that sued or was sued could learn in its own lifetime how things were going to come out." [2] In this respect the Court, whether deliberately or not, has fallen into some danger of pricing itself out of the field by making interstate litigation so expensive that only a wealthy state can afford it. The maintenance of a battery of counsel and staff for a period of years could very nearly bankrupt a small state. In seeking to keep his state *out* of an interstate lawsuit, Mr. George Guy, then Attorney General of Wyoming, said:

> I will say to the Special Master and say in all sincerity that my state has found in these matters that discretion is the better part of valor. We learned that in the Nebraska litigation. We expended about $300,000.00 over a period of some ten years and we finally got a decree but it was a pretty expensive experience and my state has come to the conclusion that in the future we should rather heed the admonitions of the Supreme Court in that matter to the effect that these states should try to get together and settle these things rather than battling them out. . . . We think we have demonstrated that we can settle these things when we have anything really to settle by sitting down with our neighbors and working out compacts and saving long and expensive and sometimes frustrating lawsuits. [3]

As a result of its very cumbersomeness, the interstate practice does have the result, described by Attorney General

[2] April 21, 1958, p. 8 B.
[3] Argument of George Guy before Special Master George I. Haight, *Arizona* v. *California,* 306, 311, April 14, 1955.

163

Guy, of inducing the states to try to settle their disputes amiably. Yet when otherwise insoluble problems arise, the Court fully recognizes its duty. As Justice Douglas said in one of these cases, there is "a clash of interests which between sovereign powers could be traditionally settled only by diplomacy or war. The original jurisdiction of this Court is one of the alternative methods provided by the framers of our Constitution." [4]

The first great housekeeping job of the Court is to prevent wars among the states by deciding their controversies for them. There could also be "wars" of a sort between Congress and the President or between either of them and the judiciary, and one task of the Court is to keep the peace among the three rings of the federal circus.

Here the Court could easily bite off more than it could chew. Parties to a controversy may be asking the judges to do the impossible.

Illustration: During World War II, a Chicago Negro sued the Selective Service officials and President Roosevelt to enjoin his being drafted on the ground that it was unconstitutional to put him into a segregated army. An astonished United States marshal, receiving the summons and complaint to serve, had no idea what to do. Should he mail it on to his opposite number in Washington, D.C., sending the District of Columbia marshal over to the White House to serve the President? Visions of entanglements with the White House guards so appalled the marshal that he wired the Department of Justice for instructions. The Department, keenly aware of the political implications of such a suit and of the scene that would be created if a process-server attempted to lay a hand on F.D.R., applied to the federal

[4] *Nebraska* v. *Wyoming*, 325 U.S. 589 (1945).

district court in Chicago to dismiss the claim against the President.

The Department's contention was that courts have no jurisdiction over the President, who is the third department of government. Anyone dissatisfied with his acts has two choices: he can either wait until next election and vote for someone else, or he can try to persuade the Congress to impeach the President. The Court may strike down what a President has done—as in its invalidation of President Truman's steel-seizure—but it will not attempt to control the President himself. This view prevailed in Chicago, the claim against the President was dismissed, and it never became necessary for the marshal to try to edge his way past the Secret Service.

In the beginning, when the Court was not yet well established, it had to fight for its rights in relation to the other two, more powerful, departments. In the famous case of *Marbury* v. *Madison,*[5] in which Chief Justice Marshall established the power of the Court to hold acts of Congress unconstitutional, the suit itself was a claim by Marbury against Secretary of State Madison to compel Madison to give Marbury his commission for a federal position. The decision immensely exercised the Americans of that day, not because they were surprised or excited about the power of the Court to invalidate an act of Congress, but because the Jefferson faction was outraged that John Marshall should attempt to tell James Madison what to do.

By now the Supreme Court has won this war, and can control many of the actions of high government officers. The special immunity of the President is peculiar to him, and the Court has decided cases against Secretaries Stimson, Knox, and Ickes, among others. As the President cannot ef-

5 1 Cranch 137 (1803).

fectively function except through subordinates, this means that the special deference to him as an individual is more tactical than practical.

The Court has also had to determine the extent to which the President can control his own subordinates. Many a governor has no effective control over anything, surrounded as he is by elected officials who are quite free to thumb their noses at him. The federal government has no such system; all positions are appointive. If the President wishes to change the policy of the Department of Justice or the Federal Communications Commission, he need not wait for a new Attorney General or a new Federal Communications Commissioner to be elected; he has only to fill a vacancy.

Can the President make his vacancies, discharging an unsatisfactory Attorney General or unsatisfactory Federal Communications Commissioner at will? This question greatly perplexed the Supreme Court, and Chief Justice Taft gave some of the greatest labor of his life to determining it. The practical upshot has been to split the difference; officials such as the Attorney General, who serve for no fixed term, can be removed at the Presidential will even though it takes the advice and consent of the Senate to put them in office. On the other hand, officials such as the Commissioners, who serve for a fixed period of years and have some "legislative" duties, must usually finish their terms before they can be replaced.

Suppose the situation runs the other way; instead of the President seeking to remove an employee, the Congress wishes to remove someone with whom the President is satisfied. Can Congress point its finger and say that this man may no longer be employed?

Undoubtedly Congress can do the job by giant indirection, burning the whole barn to roast the pig. For example, if it wished to be rid of an Attorney General, it could, theoretically, refuse to appropriate any money for the Department of Justice, and the Attorney General would depart in the resultant confusion. Moreover, it need not cut off a department—it can clip off a mere division at a time. On the other hand, the Court has held that the Congress may not put a government employee on a black list by name, singling out one person or a group of named persons who are not to be employed.

Sometimes the conflicts to be settled are within the executive department itself. The great, rambling department, with its endless activities and its millions of employees, can only fictitiously be regarded as a single entity under the head of a guiding President; as everyone knows, inter-office wars are endless and bloody. Sometimes they break out into litigation, and when they do, usually the Department of Justice can settle them. The Attorney General is the normal representative in court for all agencies, and if an agency takes a position distasteful to the Department of Justice, that Department can simply refuse to present it.

This system does not always work. Some other agencies have direct access to the courts themselves, and then the Attorney General may be reduced to the position of just a litigant against a different government agency. The Attorneys General, not unreasonably, seldom like this prospect, and do their best to persuade the Congress not to pass laws that would permit it. Usually, but not always, this persuasion is successful.

The most spectacular conflicts have involved transportation, because the Interstate Commerce Commission has been considerably more tolerant of discrimination against Negro passengers than the Department of Justice. In 1937, Arthur W. Mitchell, a Negro resident of Chicago and a mem-

ber of the House of Representatives, left Chicago for Hot
Springs, Arkansas. When he reached Arkansas, he was refused the Pullman service he had bought and paid for in
Chicago, and instead was put into a coach without wash-
basins, soap, towels, or running water. According to him, it
was "filthy and foul smelling."

When Mitchell came home, he brought an appropriate
action to test whether he might legally be thus treated. The
Interstate Commerce Commission, five members dissenting,
upheld the railroad. Mitchell carried his case to the Supreme
Court, with the United States Department of Justice on his
side and the Interstate Commerce Commission against him.
The Court adopted the view of the government (Department
of Justice) and rejected the views of the government (Interstate Commerce Commission) in holding that the treatment
given Mitchell was discrimination "palpably unjust and forbidden." [6]

Fifteen years later the same two branches of the government were still opposed on much the same question. A Negro
passenger named Henderson on the Southern Railway in
Virginia got no dinner under a segregation system being
used by that railroad in its diner. The practice of the diner
was in accordance with an Interstate Commerce Commission
regulation. The brief of the government (Department of
Justice) said: "The railroad's dining car regulations, approved by the Interstate Commerce Commission, are unlaw-
ful because they subject passengers to discrimination and
inequality of treatment, solely on grounds of race or color."
The brief of the government (Interstate Commerce Commission) said that the Interstate Commerce Commission
regulation "reasonably provides substantial equality of
treatment for colored passengers." The Court adopted the

[6] *Mitchell* v. *United States,* 313 U.S. 80 (1941).

view of the government (Justice) and rejected the view of the government (I.C.C.) without commenting on the fact that Uncle Sam had managed to get himself on both sides of the same lawsuit.[7] These cases, in which Uncle Sam attempts to hit himself with one hand while guarding himself with the other, are rare enough to be merely curious, but it is a question whether they should be allowed to occur at all.

In deciding conflicts within the federal system the Court constantly considers the relations of the federal government to the states. In the famous case of *Gibbons* v. *Ogden* in 1824, involving the power of the State of New York to regulate commerce on the Hudson, Mr. Oakley, the attorney for New York, began his argument by reminding the Court of some general principles. By signing the Declaration of Independence, he said, the states became "free and independent" and "thus became sovereign."

In the opinion of the Court, Chief Justice Marshall turned at once to these remarks, referring to the discussion of "the political situation of these states" before the Constitution. He said:

> It has been said that they were sovereign, were completely independent, and were connected with each other only by a league. This is true. But when these allied sovereigns converted their league into a government, when they converted their Congress of Ambassadors, deputed to deliberate on their common concerns, and to recommend measure of general utility, into a legislature, empowered to enact laws on the most interesting subjects, the whole character in which the states appear, underwent a change, *the extent of which must be determined by a fair consideration of the instrument by which that change was effected.*[8]

7 *Henderson* v. *United States*, 339 U.S. 816 (1950).
8 *Gibbons* v. *Ogden*, 9 Wheat. 1 (1824) (emphasis added).

The Court determines the extent of that change. In making its decisions, it has, at various times, been more and less mindful of "the purpose of preservation of each government, within its own sphere, of the freedom to carry on those affairs committed to it by the Constitution, without undue interference by the other." [9] It has declared that "scrupulous regard must be had for the rightful independence of state governments and a remedy infringing that independence which might otherwise be given should be withheld if sought on slight or inconsequential grounds." [1]

The Court has gone through three basic periods in its dealing with the federal-state problem. The period prior to the Civil War may be termed the age of religiosity, when convictions, one way or another, about the relation between the states and the federal government burned with a bright flame, and the entire political atmosphere was illumined by its intensity. Second was the period of nationalism, when the federal power became accepted and dominant, and the states began to recede in significance. The third is our own age of casualness, when lesser problems of federal-state relationships remain, but when the public presumes federal dominance to such an extent that the zip has gone out of the fight. If a single date had to be chosen for the point of transition from the age of religiosity to the age of nationalism, it might be the Conference of the Governors at Altoona, Pennsylvania, in September 1863. The northern governors gathered there to deliberate on emancipation and the conduct of the war. President Lincoln issued the Emancipation Proclamation just as they were about to act, and completely stole their show. [2] From that day to this, in any struggle between

---

[9] *Educational Films Corp.* v. *Ward,* 282 U.S. 379 (1931).

[1] *Beal* v. *Missouri Pacific Railroad Corp.,* 312 U.S. 45 (1941).

[2] William B. Hesseltine: *Lincoln and the War Governors* (New York: Alfred A. Knopf, Inc.; 1948), Chapter XIII.

The Governmental Function

the President and the governors for national power, the advantage has been with the President. The country moved from the second to the third age with the Supreme Court opinion upholding the National Labor Relations Act in April 1937.[3]

In our own day, when it is regularly assumed that Washington will provide, we forget that in another day men died, literally and physically, for the principle of state sovereignty. John Marshall's nationalist decisions aroused bitter resentment. Of a case concerning Pennsylvania, a local paper there said: "The Federal courts prostrated the sovereignty of Pennsylvania at its feet by a sophistical construction of the Constitution."[4] In another case the Pennsylvania legislature directed its governor "to protect the just rights of the state from any process issued out of any Federal court." Marshall met this threat head on, saying: "If the legislatures of the several states may, at will, annul the judgments of the courts of the United States, and destroy the rights acquired under those judgments, the Constitution itself becomes a solemn mockery, and the nation is deprived of the means of enforcing its laws by the instrumentality of its own tribunals."[5] The United States marshal attempting to carry out the order was met by state troops, and there was very nearly open war between the United States and the State of Pennsylvania in the year 1809 before the state retreated.

In 1814, Virginia revolted. The United States Supreme Court reversed a Virginia Supreme Court decision and held unconstitutional certain acts of the Virginia state legislature confiscating English lands within the state. Virginia

[3] *National Labor Relations Bd.* v. *Jones and Laughlin Steel Corp.*, 301 U.S. 1 (1937).
[4] Charles Warren: *The Supreme Court in United States History* (Boston: Little, Brown & Co.; 1937), Vol. I, p. 370.
[5] Ibid., pp. 375, 376.

refused to obey, declaring unconstitutional the power of the Supreme Court to review its decisions. Spencer Roane, a stout Jeffersonian on the Virginia bench, said "no calamity would be more to be deplored by the American people, than a vortex in the general government, which would ingulph and sweep away every vestige of the state constitutions." [6] Once again the federal position finally prevailed.

Charles Warren in his splendid history of the Supreme Court catches this early-nineteenth-century spirit with his chapter headings: "Pennsylvania and Georgia against the Court"; "Virginia against the Court"; "Slavery and State Defiance." These titles suggest a mood and an era in which for sixty years the Court was at the heart of a constant struggle between the states and the federal government for the power to govern.

The same controversy—relative power of state and national governments—affected every other part of the government, bobbing up in every controversy. It was involved in the dispute over the power of the post office to mail abolitionist pamphlets into Southern states, and in the dispute over the right to petition Congress for the abolition of slavery in the District of Columbia. "States' rights" was the symbol in the battle over whether Congress or the states should improve the rivers and build the roads; it was the chief point of debate in the struggle between South Carolina and Andrew Jackson over the power of the state to nullify a tariff.

There are two important lessons to be learned from this early experience. First, the Court in dealing with federal-state relations was caught up in a general nationwide problem not peculiar to it. It was not isolated at a lone point on a firing-line, but was part of a general front. As a result, when the firing receded elsewhere, it receded for the Court too.

6 Ibid., p. 448.

Second, the fight over nationalism was only in one sense a matter of principle, a fight over basic political-science concepts of the situs of the power to govern. The struggle over the location of power always involved some independently important substantive issue. States'-rightism was a principle, but it was also a means to an end; South Carolina stood for states' rights, but it also stood for low tariffs, and the economic drive for low tariffs precipitated the raising of the banner of nullification by the state. From the 1830's on, the principles of states' rights were also the principles of slavery, and the political abstractions protected the slave system. As objectives shifted, theories sometimes did too. Webster, as the great New England nationalist, represented the area that at the time of the Hartford Convention during the War of 1812 was prepared to secede. John C. Calhoun, the great exponent of states' rights in the 1830's and 1840's, was the same John C. Calhoun who had been a nationalist in 1816. In his own state, South Carolina, there had been a shift of interest in the meantime.

The pre-Civil War Court itself was a composite of three separate strains. One was the high-church nationalists, lawyers and judges representing the forces of commercial business expansion, as distinguished from agricultural expansion. Marshall and Story are examples. These men upheld the power of the federal government to create a national bank, limited the powers of the states to interfere with that bank, cracked down on state interference with private contracts, and sought to restrain state burdens on commerce. They contributed the law needed for the creation of a widespread national corporate system, with corporation headquarters in one state doing business all over the union. They were, in short, consistently serving both the national and the business interests. They did not have to restrict federal power because that power was not being used in any fashion burdensome to the business community.

A polar opposite was Peter V. Daniel of Virginia, who represented the no-compromise school of states'-rightism. He came to his intellectual maturity in the years soon after the Virginia and Kentucky resolutions of 1798 declaring the limits on the federal powers in connection with the Alien and Sedition laws. He was a "states'-righter" not merely in terms of immediate advantage but also in terms of long-range principle, so that the doctrine was with him a true ideology. Emotionally committed to agriculturalism as a way of life, he regarded his own place, Spring Farm near Richmond, as the symbol of all that was good in the American economy, and the banks as the symbol of all that was bad. Daniel to the day of his death in 1860 was still dissenting from the proposition that a mere corporation might sue or be sued in the federal courts, and his will provided that none of the (pathetically small) funds left by him should ever be entrusted to "the stocks or bonds of banks, railroads, or corporations or joint stock companies of any kind." In any possible conflict of federal versus state power, Daniel invariably was on the state side.

Chief Justice Taney held the intermediate position. Taney was a states'-righter and an anti-businessman, but with sophisticated restraint. His own experience in the world of affairs had left him no illusion that America could be a bank-free, corporation-free community of cotton and grain growers and shippers. Taney was able to split differences, retracting a little from the extremes of the Marshall years without going as far in the direction of states' rights as Daniel.

The Civil War cut most of the heart out of this contro-

174

versy. The war excluded from the processes of government
for seventeen years part of all of that area of the union most
committed to the states'-rights approach. An ex-Confederate
general with the magnificent name of Lucius Quintus Cin-
cinnatus Lamar, appointed by President Cleveland in 1887,
was the first Southerner (excluding one carpetbagger) put
on the bench after 1852—thirty-five years without a Southern appointment. Meanwhile, the country as a whole lost its
passion for states' rights, and almost all of the Justices appointed represented the financial philosophy of the Republican Party. The Court approved a steadily increasing restriction on state powers to tax or burden commerce, and created
due process of law as a restriction on state regulation of
business.[7]

In this post-Civil War era the Court again was part of a
general national tide. The Court's economic conservatism,
coinciding with the economic expansion of the country, required restrictions on the states in favor of the businesses
within them. The Court was not put to the test of its nationalist pretensions until the 1890's, when the federal government itself began to exercise its own powers to regulate
the economy. Then came a switching of chairs as the representatives of the business community perceived that their old
adversary, states' rights, could be extremely useful. Between 1895 and the 1920's there followed a constitutional
recurrence of the old doctrine. For example, the Court
sharply contracted the Sherman Anti-Trust Act with the
reminder that the recognition of state power "is essential
to the preservation of the economy of the states as required by
our dual form of government, and acknowledged evils, however grave and urgent they may appear to be, had better

7 These economic problems are less casually treated in Chapter XII.

be borne, than the risk be run, in the effort to suppress them, of more serious consequences by resort to expedience of even doubtful constitutionality." [8]

To put it bluntly, the states'-rights doctrine was largely on the shelf from the 1860's to the 1890's except as the resistance to Reconstruction and to the establishment of Negro rights brought it back into play again. After the 1890's there was again a substantial commercial utility in the doctrine, and it was called upon from time to time.

The matter came to its final issue in 1937. The Roosevelt administration set out to deal with national problems in a thoroughly national way. In 1935 and 1936 the country divided in a great debate as to whether this should be done. In November 1936 the question was settled by an overwhelming victory for Roosevelt at the polls. In 1937, as the aftermath of Roosevelt's struggle with the Court in that year, the Court upheld the constitutionality of the National Labor Relations Act, and in 1942 the federal power reached its apogee when the Court upheld the power of Congress to regulate the production of grain on a farm even though the grain was never intended to go any farther from the field than the farmer's own barn, there to be fed to his own stock. [9] In the resulting press on Washington, the states have fallen to a low province.

The Court continues to receive cases involving the relations of the states with the federal government, but, there being nothing of immense consequence left to preserve in the states, these cases are embroidery around the edges of the important. The splendid issues of yesterday are dead. To contrast with nineteenth-century examples given earlier, it is no longer practically conceivable that a state would turn

[8] *United States* v. *E. C. Knight,* 156 U.S. 1 (1895).
[9] *Wickard* v. *Filburn,* 317 U.S. 111 (1942).

out its militia to resist the enforcement of a direct and pointed federal court order,[1] or that a state would use force to resist a tax-collection, or that a national monopoly of sugar-refining interests would be held free of federal supervision. Indeed the tide runs so strong the other way that a few years ago the Court held that refiners could be restrained under the Sherman Act from monopolizing the sale of sugar beets even within one state.[2]

In the labor-relations field, Congress has rendered the states powerless even in some areas in which the National Labor Relations Board does *not* assert jurisdiction. Justice Burton, dissenting, did say that "due regard for our federal systems suggests that all doubts on this score should be resolved in favor of a conclusion that would not leave the states powerless when the federal agency declines to exercise its jurisdiction," [3] but there was no real heart in it; imagine for a moment what Justice Daniel would have had to say on this subject. More important, in the case just quoted, two Justices upheld state powers where the federal government had power but chose not to use it; if the federal government had affirmatively used its power in the particular case, then the states would not even have challenged the federal supremacy. Justice Frankfurter is the Justice who most frequently reminds us of the necessity for due regard for the rightful independence of state governments, and in the decision in May 1957 in which the Court reviewed a California bar admission, Justices Harlan and Clark dissented in part on the

---

1 This sentence was written in 1957, shortly before Governor Faubus of Arkansas called out the National Guard at Little Rock. I let it stand in part as a monument to my own error, an admonition to humility in judgment. The Arkansas incident also highlights the point: when the court order was made explicit, the Governor did withdraw his troops just in time to see the President strip him of all further power over them.

2 *Mandeville Island Farms* v. *American Crystal Sugar Co.,* 334 U.S. 219 (1948).

3 *Guss* v. *Utah Labor Board,* 353 U.S. 1 (1957).

ground that this case "involved an area of federal-state relations—the right of states to establish and administer standards for admission to their Bars—into which this Court
should be especially reluctant and slow to enter." [4] But
while some believe that the states should not be required to
accord due process to applicants for bar admission, the
situation is far different from that of a hundred years before in another California case when the Supreme Court of
that state refused to tolerate any review by the United States
Supreme Court.[5]

To sum it up, for one hundred and fifty years the Court
has concerned itself with working out federal-state relationships. At times the Court has very materially affected that
relationship. The nationalism of Marshall, in particular, undoubtedly contributed in a major way to turning a mere
confederation into a living and real federal nation. However, the really stupendous alterations in federal-state relationships have been largely the product of forces that the
Court could neither direct nor control: a great civil war and
an awesome depression. The former remade the Constitution,
the country, and the Court. The latter unleashed forces to
which the Court could only somewhat belatedly yield. Short
of these cosmic alterations in the nature of things, the Court
has often had a definitive say on the rights of the two
branches of government in respect to taxation, the regulation
of commerce, and criminal administration. Even where the
Court has not controlled the final outcome of events, it has
affected them substantially for a period of years.

There is one last housekeeping function of the Court to
be mentioned, and that is the settlement of disputes between
people. The principal duty of courts is to decide cases. The

4 *Koenigsberg* v. *State Bar of California,* 353 U.S. 252 (1957).
5 *Johnson* v. *Gordon,* 4 Cal. 368 (1864).

trial court in anybody's home county is a useful institution, worth paying taxes to support, because it puts criminals in jail, thus preserving the peace of the community; decides disputes between businessmen so that they can take their profit or loss and get on to something else; distributes the responsibility and the costs for accidents; gives divorces; and settles estates.

This dispute-settling function is obviously no longer a job for the Supreme Court. Dispute-settling is a quantity job, and the Supreme Court cannot possibly handle a large number of cases. In suits between private individuals over accidents or contracts, for example, it cannot even provide any effective leadership. Its function here is limited to the issuance of general rules for the conduct of such disputes, known variously as Rules of Civil or Criminal Procedure; and as this volume is written, the Court appears to be on the verge of handing over even this rule-making function to the lower courts. The Court can lay out broad principles on large questions of general public concern. Apart from the Rules, it does not and cannot even attempt to make any serious contribution to determining the general run of comparatively humdrum disputes that must be settled as a convenience to society.

Chapter X

SPECIAL FUNCTIONS

OF THE COURT

2. THE LIBERTIES OF THE

AMERICAN CITIZEN

(SPEECH AND PRESS)

One great difference between the Americans and the English is that Americans have never learned to take their politics even a little calmly. By some remarkable trick of fate, every four years presents us with the gravest emergency that has ever confronted our country, and the crisis is always now. President John Adams was a tyrant bent on enslaving the people. His successor, Thomas Jefferson, was a miserable tool of the French seeking to betray us altogether to that power. Abraham Lincoln, in addition to being a gorilla, aspired to the destruction of every liberty of the citizen. Franklin D. Roosevelt was insane, and should have been in an asylum.

This is the hyperbole of our boisterous democracy. Along with it goes a recurrent compulsion to imprison, deport, or otherwise penalize the person who does not share the speaker's point of view. Those desiring to punish their adversaries

180

at any given instant always recognize that the American tradition is one of liberty and freedom to disagree, but *now* is always different. *This* is the moment of exception when, for the sake of the very existence of the country, we must abate the freedom under which we have so long prospered so that it may be preserved for future generations; and so on, through the familiar recitative of him who wishes to put his enemy in jail.

This "let's put 'em in jail" spirit always exists to some extent on the American scene. Usually it is a minority attitude. Sometimes it bubbles over and achieves greater general approval. When this occurs, the country experiences what may be called a repression. Repressions are to the spirit what depressions are to the economy. There is always a little repression in the air, just as there is always a little unemployment. The break-throughs are sporadic.

The first and, at least until very recent times, the extremest of the repressions was in the latter portion of the Adams administration when those statutes known as the Alien and Sedition Acts were passed.

The Alien and Sedition laws were chock-full of constitutional questions that might have, but never did, come before the Supreme Court, because the Jeffersonians won the election of 1800 and repealed the statutes before the Supreme Court had a chance to review them. Hence, in a history of American liberty, that incident bulks large; but in a history of the Supreme Court the only significant fact is that there is nothing significant to report. Some of the judges dealt with the Acts in their trial capacity, but not as an appeals bench. In what is commonly regarded as our history's most spectacular instance of menace to individual liberty, the Supreme Court had no role to play.

Between 1800 and 1860 the country fought two wars in

which it was bitterly divided, and yet in neither was national legislation to insure solidarity and loyalty adopted or even seriously proposed. The War of 1812 was largely unwelcome to the New England states, which went to the point of threatening secession to oppose it. In the 1840's the Mexican War, which from the standpoint of sheer conquest is the most stupendous of American military victories, was opposed by a very large block of American opinion, including an obscure Illinois Congressman of the day named Abraham Lincoln. Again, no effort was made to legislate loyalty. Hence, in neither of those crises in American life did the Supreme Court have a function to perform in respect to the right to disagree over war policy.

This does not mean that the pre-Civil War period was devoid of repression. One movement of the time was antimasonry, an odd political surge that arose from a murder in the 1820's in northwestern New York and spread into a general attack on the Masonic order. In the aftermath, a new political party was founded which gained great prominence in Pennsylvania and New York and gave political starts to such later leaders as Thurlow Weed and Thaddeus Stevens. Antimasonry was contemporaneous with and was followed by the movement known as nativism, which emerged as the Know Nothing Party of the early 1850's, although its maximum dominion within the states was earlier. A pillar of nativism was Samuel F. B. Morse, who believed that the Pope was the center of a great international conspiracy as ardently as he believed in his own telegraph.

But the Supreme Court was not involved; and as it was not yet in the habit of inspecting state conduct, there was nothing for it to consider. The nativist movement broke its back against such figures as Governor Seward of New York in the 1840's and Lincoln, who in the 1850's owned a German newspaper of his own and made active alliance with German Catholics. If one's notion of American history were based only on the two-volume history of the Supreme Court by Charles Warren, he would scarcely know that there were any great problems of human liberty in America other than slavery before the Civil War, and this is no reflection on Mr. Warren. The judicial business simply was not there. John Quincy Adams, upholding in the House of Representatives the right of individuals to petition Congress freely on the abolition of slavery, had more to say on the subject of free speech than the entire Supreme Court bar in all cases together before the Civil War; and such speech and press restrictions as existed during the Civil War did not come before the Court.

The next great American repression came in relation to the anarchist scare of the late 1880's and 1890's, followed by the I.W.W. scare and the laws against criminal syndicalism about the turn of the century. After the Haymarket riot in Chicago, where a bomb was thrown, a group of anarchists were tried. Some were executed and others given long sentences. Those tried and executed for the bombing almost certainly had nothing to do with it, and the survivors were pardoned in an act of extraordinary political fortitude by Illinois's Governor John P. Altgeld a few years later. Again, the Supreme Court did not affect the matter. It fobbed off the anarchists' case on technical grounds.[1]

In short, before the twentieth century the Supreme Court had no effect on American political liberties; its treatment of speech, press, and religion [2] was negligible. Beginning

---

[1] 123 U.S. 131 (1887).

[2] In a volume of this sort, many intriguing topics are necessarily omitted altogether, and freedom of religion is one of these. Freedom of religion involves avoidance of both interference with religious freedom and favoritism toward one sect or another, or favoritism to all as against the non-religious. The Court has had a moderately active function in both areas, particularly

about 1917, two events turned the Court into a continuing seminar on the meaning of personal freedom. First, Congress (as distinguished from various states) undertook for the first time since Adams's day to restrict freedom of speech and press. Second, as recently as the early 1920's the Court began to review not merely federal but also state interference with basic liberties.

The Espionage Act of 1917, extensively amended in 1918, was the first sedition act passed in this country since the ill-fated statutes of the Adams regime. The federal Act, coupled with state acts passed in reaction to the Bolshevik revolution, introduced the next great American repression, which began about 1918 and faded away some ten years later. The 1917 and 1918 legislation sought to enforce uniformity of opinion when very nearly perfect uniformity existed without it. In four previous wars—the Revolution, the War of 1812, the Mexican War, and the Civil War—the nation had been badly divided and yet it had survived each of them without any attempt to legislate adherence to the war policy. In World War I only a few complainers and the pacifist wing of the Socialist Party were anti-war; the pro-war party included over ninety per cent of the country.

Nonetheless, the desire for unanimous ardor led to such federal prosecutions as that against three elderly German Americans in Cincinnati who had grumbled about the war in the back room of one of them and had been overheard only by means of an electrical device. This private conversation was supposed to have discouraged men from military service despite the fact that only an electrical wizard who was also a busybody could have known of its occurrence. An-

in the last twenty-five years, the largest problems involving the separation of church and state. Notable controversies have involved use of public funds for the benefit of religious education, as by subsidized textbooks or transportation, or the use of public school buildings for religious education.

other episode was the remarkably titled case *The United
States* v. *The Spirit of '76*, this *Spirit* being a motion picture depicting British atrocities during the American Revolution which was seized because the judge believed it might
make us a little slack in loyalty to our allies. State prosecutions were also common, such as that of the man who went to
jail for expressing doubt as to the efficiency of the Red
Cross. He had the temerity to say of the knitting of some
good lady: "No soldier ever sees those socks." [3]

The Espionage Act, among other things, forbade anyone
to utter abusive language about the United States or its government, or even language intended to bring either the flag
or the uniform into disrepute. Numerous prosecutions were
brought under the Act, usually for more serious matters than
these, and several of them reached the Supreme Court. The
Court was then required, for the first time, to consider the
meaning of freedom of speech and of the press in the United
States. The First Amendment to the Constitution provides
that "Congress shall make no law . . . abridging the freedom of speech, or of the press." The Espionage Act clearly
abridged the freedom of both, and the initial question therefore was whether the Court would interpret the Constitution
literally, barring any limitation on the exercise of freedom
of speech, or whether it would permit exceptions.

This was an immense crisis in the history of human liberty.
When the Bill of Rights was offered to the American people
by James Madison in 1789, he had said:

Independent tribunals of justice will consider themselves
in a peculiar manner the guardians of those rights; they
will be an impenetrable bulwark against every assumption

[3] The best review of this subject, including the cases mentioned and
many more, is Zechariah Chafee: *Free Speech in the United States* (Cambridge: Harvard University Press; 1941), enlarging his 1920 work on the
subject.

of power in the Legislative or Executive; they will be naturally led to resist every encroachment upon rights stipulated for in the Constitution by the Declaration of Rights.[4]

One hundred and thirty years later, confronted with this problem, the Court consistently took an extremely narrow view of the rights whose protection Madison had assigned to it. The initial opinion was written by Justice Holmes, who declared that, despite the Amendment, some limitations on speech were permissible. Holmes said:

> The question in every case is whether the words used are used in such circumstances and are of such a nature as to create a clear and present danger that they will bring about the substantive evils that congress has a right to prevent. It is a question of proximity and degree. When a nation is at war many things that might be said in time of peace are such a hindrance to its effort that their utterance will not be endured so long as men fight, and that no court could regard them as protected by any constitutional right.[5]

Holmes quickly discovered that he had unleashed the whirlwind. Once he had declared that speech might be limited where there was a "clear and present danger" of something dreadful, he found the Court quick to see such a danger everywhere. Having announced the rule, Holmes and Brandeis with him rapidly became dissenters to its application. In 1919 Holmes and Brandeis, in a deeply meditated and philosophic opinion, announced their basic credo of freedom of speech: speech could be restrained only where some emergency made it "immediately dangerous to leave the correction of evil counsels to time." [6] But these were dissenting views,

4 1st Cong., 1st Sess., June 8, 1789.
5 *Schenck* v. *United States,* 249 U.S. 47 (1919).
6 *Abrams* v. *United States,* 250 U.S. 616 (1919).

and the Court itself allowed the Act to run its course unchecked.

World War II presented the same problems but to a different Court and also to a different Attorney General. Francis Biddle, a onetime Holmes law clerk who presided over federal law-enforcement throughout the war, was determined not to suppress freedom of speech as in World War I. That the war was so largely fought without recourse to weapons of repression is Mr. Biddle's monument. The Department of Justice did bring one case up to the Supreme Court, and this time a majority of the Court set such high requirements of proof as to gut the statute, leaving it of no further practical effect.[7]

Meanwhile, during the 1920's the states began to prosecute Communists. The years 1920 to 1924, in particular, were the nadir of repression, with mass deportations, the *Sacco-Vanzetti* case, and numerous state sedition trials. In this period the New York legislature barred Socialists from its membership, and for that met the rebuke of then former Justice Charles Evans Hughes. The Hughes objections to the repression of that time were an omen of what was to come when he rejoined the Court in the 1930's as Chief Justice.

In 1925 the Court greatly extended its jurisdiction. When New York prosecuted a local Communist leader, the defendant appealed from his state conviction to the United States Supreme Court. The first question presented was whether the guarantee of freedom of speech and press in the federal Constitution applied to the states as well as to the federal government. The Court found that freedom of speech and of the press was protected by the federal Constitution from state as well as federal impairment, and that the Su-

[7] *Hartzel* v. *United States,* 322 U.S. 680 (1944).

preme Court had the duty of reviewing the state courts in
this field. This stupendous conclusion opened up for review
the entire subject of state restriction of civil rights.[8]

But the Court, having fired, fell back. In the 1925 case
it did hold that it could review what the state had done, but
it held also that there was no objection to the state course
of action. Over a most eloquent dissent by Holmes, the majority declared that the state could punish "utterances inimical to the public welfare."

Thus, between 1918 and 1930 the Court for the first time
moved into the area of protection of freedom of speech and
press, but in the great basic decisions of the time it upheld
not the freedom, but the restraint of the freedom. The result was that the repression of 1918–28 wore itself out without the Supreme Court's help.

The decisions of this period were those of a divided Court,
two leading supporters of restriction on freedom of speech
and of the press being Chief Justice Taft and Justice Sanford. In 1930 those Justices were replaced by Chief Justice
Hughes and Justice Roberts, men who took a very different
view of human liberty. Between 1930 and 1945 the Court
for the first time began to give some actual protection to
freedom of speech and the press. Significantly, during this
period the country as a whole was sympathetic to those freedoms. The financially desperate 1930's were an age of experimentation in every way, including experimentation with
ideas; almost all Americans regretted the excesses of the
previous decade, and many took a resolve not to repeat them.
It was not until the very end of the decade that the House
Committee on Un-American Activities (the Dies Committee)
succeeded in reopening the old wars.

8 *Gitlow* v. *New York,* 268 U.S. 652 (1925).

During the 1930's the Court built bulwarks around the First Amendment. The "clear and present danger" test, as Holmes had apparently intended it, was resuscitated, and the New Deal appointees expanded the judicial protection of liberty until about 1945. Justices Black, Douglas, Murphy, and Rutledge were the four stoutest exponents of individual liberty ever to sit on the bench.

In the late 1940's the Court began to abdicate the field it had just begun to occupy. About 1938 a new repression, spurred by the Dies Committee, began. Wartime preoccupation with more serious things, plus the circumstance that our alliance with Russia made it awkward to chase those suspected of Russian sympathies at home, worked a brief suspension of the activity. However, Russia's post-war hostility to America eliminated the latter obstacle, and the most extreme repression the country has ever known soon broke out. The inauguration of an enormous loyalty and security program, as a large portion of this activity was euphemistically termed, spread into private industry from the government. Millions of Americans became subject to scrutiny, not, usually, for actual misdeeds but for what they had thought or said ten or twenty years before. The deportation mania recurred, and active criminal prosecutions, particularly of Communists, got under way. The whole program was given a superfrenetic atmosphere by Congressional investigating committees that began to substitute for the normal objective of legislation the objectives of "exposure" and of "getting the witness for perjury."

This spasm of what might be called impassioned repression grew from about 1948 to approximately 1955. A book I published in 1952 estimated that "the years 1948–52 may prove to be the most extreme period of this repression, at least if direct war with Russia does not come." [9] I quote the prediction because in retrospect it seems about right.

In these post-war years the Court again experienced a shift of personnel, Chief Justice Vinson taking the place of Chief Justice Stone, and Justices Burton, Clark, and Minton succeeding Justices Roberts, Murphy, and Rutledge. The result, with rare exceptions on the part of Justice Burton and even rarer ones on the part of Justice Clark, was to remake the bench into a body that exhibited no real objection to the trend of the times and certainly had no intention of doing anything about it. The deaths in 1949 of the strong civil-libertarians Rutledge and Murphy ensured that there would be no judicial objection to the course of events. At the first session of the fall term after their death, Chief Justice Vinson concluded his memorial remarks with the words: "Saddened by our losses but inspired by the examples of devotion to duty which Mr. Justice Murphy and Mr. Justice Rutledge have provided for us, we turn to the work before us." Within six weeks the country knew that the "work before us" consisted in large part of rejecting the civil-rights views of the late Justices.

In this period the Court managed for the most part to avoid considering the government employee-control program at all. It upheld the deportation program in its widest range, approving such grotesque extremes as the deportation of a man who had been expelled from the Communist Party twenty years before for disagreeing with it. It reverted almost entirely to those doctrines of restriction of free speech from which Holmes and Brandeis had dissented in the 1920's. The majorities were heavy; as Professor Ralph Brown puts it, "of the majority that had exalted the free-

[9] *Cases on Constitutional Law* (Chicago: Callaghan & Co.; revised edition, 1952), p. 885.

doms of the First Amendment death had removed three (Stone, Murphy, and Rutledge), time had modified the convictions of two (Frankfurter and Jackson); only Justices Black and Douglas pursued an unswerving course." [1]

Recently the country has appeared to be recovering from its binge. The downfall of Senator McCarthy well before his death would scarcely have occurred if the country had not tired of him, and there has been evidence of increasing weariness with the so-called internal-security program and of a sense of excess in its applications. Once again the shifting temper of the country has coincided with an adjustment of Court personnel, Vinson being replaced by Warren, whose keenness for individual liberty is in total contrast to Vinson's indifference to it. The addition to the bench of Justices Brennan and Harlan has made a perceptible difference.

In consequence, the Court has begun in a gingerly and modest way to recapture some of the ground that the country, the Constitution, and it had lost. In the spring of 1957 it lowered the boom squarely on the House Committee on un-American Activities. That body had for some years been functioning essentially as a court, trying persons of whom it disapproved and passing judgment upon them. The Supreme Court, in a profoundly searching opinion by Chief Justice Warren on legislative investigations, concluded that Congress had never given this committee any authority to do what it was doing, and expressed considerable doubt that Congress had such power to give.[2] The Court also, in an opinion by Justice Harlan, put a check on the prosecution of some of the lower-echelon Communist Party members for their points of view, as distinguished from their acts.[3]

1 Ralph Brown: *Loyalty and Security* (New Haven: Yale University Press; 1958), p. 21.
2 *Watkins* v. *United States,* 354 U.S. 178 (1957).
3 *Yates* v. *United States,* 354 U.S. 298 (1957).

The Court was essentially following a middle-of-the-road program back toward sanity. The Communist trial case is a good illustration. Here there were fifteen defendants. The Court divided into three blocs. The majority, through Justice Harlan, held that the case must be dismissed as to six of the fifteen but that the other nine could be retried with proper directions to the jury. Justice Clark, at the right end of the spectrum, wished to affirm the convictions of all fifteen. Justices Black and Douglas, at the opposite pole, believed that the defendants were being prosecuted for what they said and wrote rather than for any direct act against the country and that American doctrines should prevail by force of reason rather than by force of imprisonment; these two wished to invalidate the statute. The weight of the Court was set upon an extremely moderate course.

A specimen of the relation of the Court to the declining repression was the case of *Jencks*,[4] who was charged with perjury for having sworn falsely that he was not a member of the Communist Party. The principal witnesses against him were two Communist Party members paid by the F.B.I. to make written reports of Communist activities. For the purpose of proving that Jencks was a liar, one of the two witnesses testified that he had attended Communist meetings at which Jencks was present, and the other testified that he had had private conversations with Jencks which revealed him as a Communist.

For purposes of cross-examining these two witnesses, the defense counsel asked to see reports that the witnesses had made to the F.B.I. about those meetings and conversations. Justice Brennan for the Court held that the defense attorneys, to cross-examine intelligently, were entitled to these reports so that they might compare the testimony with earlier

4 *Jencks* v. *United States,* 353 U.S. 657 (1957).

statements. As Justice Brennan said, "Every experienced trial judge and trial lawyer knows the value for impeaching purposes of statements of the witness recording the events before time dulls treacherous memory." The possibility that the witnesses might be lying was perfectly reasonable; one of them had recently been proved to be such a complete perjurer that the government had abandoned a conviction based on his testimony. The problem was the usual one of paid informers; the temptation to stay on the payroll by improving the information given is always present, and can be partially guarded against by comparing what is said later with what was said earlier.

As a result, Justice Brennan ruled that the defense was entitled to inspect the reports of these witnesses "written and, when orally made, as recorded by the F.B.I., touching the events and activities as to which they testified at the trial." This ruling seems to many lawyers and judges to state the obvious. To take extreme but perfectly possible instances, suppose that the witness in his original reports of the meetings had named everyone who was present and had not named the defendant Jencks, or that the witness reporting conversations with Jencks had earlier made very different reports of those same conversations. It would be tyrannical to convict a man without giving his jury an opportunity to know that the story being told against him had changed radically in the telling. It is difficult to conceive of any American who would doubt this if the atmosphere were calm and unemotional.

And yet, listening to the complaints of Senator Eastland, or Congressman Walter, or Senator Jenner, or columnist David Lawrence, one would suppose that this conventional principle of criminal justice could only lead to a Muscovite in the White House. The Court itself became subject to wild vituperation, particularly from quarters that, when President Roosevelt had criticized the Court so severely in 1937, had taken the high ground that criticism of the Court over disagreements was unpatriotic, immoral, and bad taste to boot. The ruling of the Court was grossly misstated, editorials were written on the false assumption that the Court had turned the keys to the F.B.I. files over to the enemy, and the talk of "ransacking" the F.B.I. files implied that J. Edgar Hoover was to be allowed to keep no secrets at all. As Wisconsin Supreme Court Justice George R. Currie blandly observed: "It is very apparent that most of these critics had not taken the time to read the decision itself." [5]

Immediately there was acute pressure for legislation to change the rule and to provide that American citizens could be convicted of crimes—not merely on political charges but on all charges of whatever sort—without giving them any opportunity to compare the earlier with the later stories of witnesses against them. Senator Cooper of Kentucky particularly warned the Senate that the *Jencks* rule affected not only those accused of subversion, but everyone. "One trouble about the interpretation of the *Jencks* case," he said, "has been that many think it applies only to F.B.I. documents, or only to Communist cases. It applies to any document which the United States Government might hold and to any criminal case." [6]

And then, as quickly as the storm blew up, it began to abate. Senator O'Mahoney offered legislation not to change the rule but to avoid any misinterpretation of it. Senator Ervin of North Carolina, respected conservative stalwart in the Senate, told his brothers that "The decision as I construe

[5] George R. Currie: "The United States Supreme Court, Protector of the Constitution," October 1957 *Wisconsin Bar Bulletin,* p. 25.

[6] *Congressional Record,* August 23, 1957, p. 14,403.

Speech and Press

it, is essential to the proper administration of justice." [7]
He joined O'Mahoney in endorsing legislation that would
preserve it, not alter it. That preservative legislation, in support of the opinion and not against it, became law.

The *Jencks* incident is a comparatively minor episode concerning a minor rule of law. Nonetheless, the forces of extreme reaction chose this moment and this incident on which
to make their fight, and they lost it. When we are far enough
removed from the post-World War II repression to write its
history, the *Jencks* incident may prove to be a bench mark,
an instance in which the Court chose to exercise leadership
on the way back from the repression and was sustained. As
this book has illustrated, the Court rarely moves far from
substantial public opinion. The discovery that it has been
sustained may give it renewed confidence.

Another illustration to the same effect is the cool reception
being accorded the bill by Senator Jenner to eliminate much
Supreme Court review, leaving as final the decisions of the
lower courts on many matters of civil liberty. This bill began
to make headway in a Senate judiciary committee, but adroit
maneuvering by Senator Hennings of Missouri routed it
back into committee for further hearings. The further hearings have brought striking condemnation of the proposal
from, among others, the American Bar Association. The
elimination of many of the most extreme features of the bill
by the Senate Judiciary Committee and the improbability of
the passage of the remainder are significant developments.

What has been said shows that the role of the Court in
preserving the basic American liberties of freedom of speech
and of the press has been slight. Its entry into the field on
any terms is barely thirty years old, and it has served more
as a ratifying than as a restraining body.

[7] Ibid., p. 14,400.

A Taft and a Vinson have been considerably balanced by a Hughes and a Warren, but in the hours of greatest urgency the Court existed only to approve. The entire "clear and present danger" doctrine of freedom of speech has failed tragically as a device for restraining legislative interference with fundamental freedoms because, the event proves, the passions of any given moment are such that danger is always present and always seems clear.

And so in the sense of restraining us from the madness of our own passions at their peak, the Court has not served us well. Perhaps it is too much to expect that it would. To face down a country that is in a frenzy is a great deal to ask of a handful of men; a Hughes might do it, but Hughes is not the common mold even for great Justices. When Jefferson contemplatively reviewed the failure of his own ideals as illustrated by the adoption of the Alien and Sedition Acts, he wondered how such a thing could have happened in a country that had a written Constitution. He concluded: "It is still certain that tho' written constitutions may be violated in moments of passion or delusion, yet they furnish a text to which those who are watchful may again rally and recall the people; they fix too for the people principles for their political creed." [8] Perhaps we can ask no more of the Court than that it be the first to rally.

On the basis of the two experiences the country has had— the 1920's and the turn of the 1950's—we must conclude that we cannot expect the Court to prevent our excesses. What we can expect, or at least what we can hope for, is that there will at least be a voice of dissent, a Holmes or a Brandeis as in the '20's, or a Black or a Douglas as in more recent times, to recall us to first principles. As Justice Black

[8] Jefferson to Dr. Priestly, June 19, 1802, quoted in Edmund Cahn; ed.: *Supreme Court and Supreme Law* (Bloomington: Indiana University Press; 1954), p. 131.

said in one of the principal Communist cases of recent years, "Public opinion being what it now is, few will protest the conviction of these Communist petitioners. There is hope, however, that in calmer times, when present pressures, passions and fears subside, this or some later Court will restore the First Amendment liberties to the high preferred place where they belong in a free society." [9]

Because of the recency of the entry of the Court into this whole area, it is still experimenting. If the Court is going to play a significant role in guarding American political liberty, it can do these things:

First, it can expand the area of cases it is willing to review. A certain technical doctrine of "political questions," under which the Court concludes not to decide certain matters, needs a thorough re-examination. When the government comes down on someone's head, the questions presented should be decided.

Second, the Court should abandon its doctrine of "standing," under which people who are obviously *about* to be in trouble cannot test their rights because they are not *yet* in the trouble. By the time they are, it is too late. A clear and present danger of trouble ought to be enough.

Third, the Court ought to apply a general rule that any interference with the basic rights of Americans as set forth in the Bill of Rights is wrong. The Court is accustomed to paying what it calls "great deference to the judgment of the legislature." When the legislature has decided to restrict someone's basic liberties, that deference ought to vanish.[1]

Fourth, the Court should keep the Bill of Rights abreast of the times, and it should recognize realities. Ingenious

9 *Dennis* v. *United States*, 341 U.S. 494 (1951).
1 For an opposite point of view from a highly distinguished source, see Learned Hand: *The Bill of Rights* (Cambridge: Harvard University Press; 1958), pp. 53–5.

people have had more than a century and a half to think up methods of oppressing their fellow citizens which never occurred to Jefferson or Madison. The Bill of Rights does not deal specifically, for example, with trial by legislative committee, with its "penalty" of exposure, humiliation and degradation. As a result, there are no constitutional standards of fair play in the field except as individual congressional committees choose to put them there. There is, for example, no right of cross-examination of hostile witnesses or, indeed, much of any other right. Partly the problem as presented is far beyond the Supreme Court powers; responsible Congressmen also have a sense of constitutional fairness and can make their own rules. And yet there is a little the Court can do despite the fact that the problem is novel; and during the Warren period the Court has begun to do it.

Another instance of the need to keep abreast relates to aliens. Because deportation is not technically a "punishment" for a "crime," but is something else, it has been held that the normal standards of fair play which would be required in a criminal matter that does result in "punishment" do not apply to deportation. It would unquestionably be unconstitutional to adopt a law today punishing a person with a five-dollar fine for having jay-walked yesterday; this would be an "ex post facto" law, or a change of the law after the offense. On the other hand, because deportation, which is infinitely more drastic than any fine, is technically not a "punishment," a law may be passed which makes conduct that was perfectly legal when done illegal retroactively— for an alien. The alien may be deported even though by now he may have children and grandchildren in this country, though he may have totally forgotten the language of the country of his birth, and though that country itself may have

198

disappeared in the shifting world. This the Supreme Court has condoned.

For a final example, the entire loyalty and security program in relation to government employees has run its course without any serious constitutional check, in part on the theory that to disgrace a man and deprive him of his job is not a "punishment." Former highly placed government officials may end up as truck-drivers or file clerks, if they are lucky enough to get any employment at all, after "trials" of their loyalty which would be unquestionably unconstitutional if used to impose a traffic ticket.

If the Court is to have a role of consequence in protecting basic liberties, it cannot turn its back on every form of repression which has been invented lately. "The Supreme Court of this country cannot be fettered with an interpretation of the Constitution which places it in the eighteenth century. The problems to be solved are those which never entered the minds of the men who drafted the Constitution and its Amendments." [2]

Fifth, if judicial protection of freedom of speech is to amount to anything at all, the doctrine must be re-thought from scratch. Alexander Meiklejohn has proposed that we recur to the express language of the Constitution, forbidding *any* restriction of speech or press at least in the field of public affairs, and Justice Black and Douglas have adopted this view. As Justice Douglas puts it in a recent book: "The First Amendment does not say that there is freedom of expression provided the talk is not 'dangerous.' It does not say that there is freedom of expression provided the utterance has no tendency to subvert. . . . All notions of regula-

[2] Justice Fred C. Struckmeyer, Jr.: "The Function of the Supreme Court Today," *The Arizona Weekly Gazette,* April 1958.

tion or restraint by government are absent from the First Amendment. For it says in words that are unambiguous, 'Congress shall make no law . . . abridging the freedom of speech, or of the press. . . .' " [3] Perhaps a virile program of civil liberty could be built on this foundation.

Nothing can make up for the ten years of lost judicial opportunity which ended about 1955. Now only the most profound statesmanship could bring the country back to the traditions of Madison and Jefferson—if, indeed, this could ever be done. Yet the program just outlined must be balanced with two words of caution. First, the Court must never get so far out of line with deep national convictions as to lose all communication with the people. Second, the criminal law must be enforced so effectively that the country can rest confident that those who do perform overt *acts* against it— whether of espionage, sabotage, or revolution—will feel the full force of the law. A law that deals sternly with real traitors affords a foundation of strength for tolerance of mere dissent.

---

[3] William O. Douglas: *The Right of the People* (Garden City: Doubleday & Company; 1958), p. 21.

Chapter XI

SPECIAL FUNCTIONS

OF THE COURT

2. THE LIBERTIES OF THE

AMERICAN CITIZEN

(COLOR AND CRIME)

The overlay of blue and gray, the resonance of the rebel yell, the somber aura of the bearded President, and almost a hundred years of romanticism sometimes obscure the fact that the Civil War was a revolution of the most stupendous kind. It was followed not by a re-establishment of previously existing conditions, but by a radically different America. Smashing changes hit the American economy, the American way of individual life, the American government. The America of 1870 differed from the America of 1860 as much as could any country without an actual overthrow of its government or a foreign conquest.

Most violent of all the revolutionary changes were those affecting the colored population of the country. In 1860 slavery was solidly entrenched in the United States. In five years with machine-gun rapidity came: the freeing of slaves used for military purposes by the Army; the prohibition against returning slaves who crossed Union lines; the termination of slavery in the District of Columbia; the abandonment of fugitive-slave laws; the Emancipation Proclamation; the first equal-rights laws for the District of Columbia; the establishment of schools for all in the District; the admission of Negroes into the military forces; the elimination of restrictions against Negroes carrying the mails; the establishment of Negro rights to transportation at least in the District of Columbia; and, finally, the Thirteenth Amendment declaring an end to slavery.

For five years the Negro needed a daily paper to keep track of what was happening to him. Shortly after the war came the formal establishment of citizenship, the adoption of civil-rights acts, the legal declaration of equality, and the Fifteenth Amendment giving the right to vote. Then, almost as suddenly, the trend began to reverse. There followed a counterrevolution, a vigorous movement to deprive the Negro of many of the very rights that had just been given him. Southern society had regained its strength and poise and had resolved to yield as little as possible to its former slaves.

Unlike the controversies over freedom of speech, in which the Supreme Court was at the edge of the field until recent years, the extent of Negro rights has been on the Supreme Court docket from the very beginning.[1] Some pre-Civil War cases involved the slave trade, perhaps the most famous being that of the *Amistad*, argued for the slaves by former

---

[1] Color once had a special significance in the Supreme Court. At a Washington dinner for Charles Evans Hughes shortly after 1910, Hughes asked his host what "the color line" meant as applied to the Court. His host replied: "That was when Justices Gray, Brown, and White sat in a row; but as only Justice White is left, there is no color now."

"Oh, no," observed the hostess, "the Court is all Hughes now."

Charles Henry Butler: *Forty Years at the Bar of the Supreme Court* (New York: G. P. Putnam's Sons; 1942), p. 167.

President John Quincy Adams. The Court held that slaves on a Spanish slave-trader's vessel who revolted and murdered the officers and were then picked up by an American war ship and brought to this country need not be returned to their Spanish owners.[2] Other slave cases involved commerce in slaves and the operation of state and federal fugitive-slave laws. The final and unhappiest step was the 1857 determination in the case of *Dred Scott* that Congress could not prohibit slavery in the territories.[3]

All of these cases can be put aside as historical curios except for two general observations. First, as has been said, the Court has been habituated to dealing with problems of Negro rights from the very beginning. Second, before the Civil War the Court had learned a stiff lesson about its own limitations in dominating an impassioned country. In the *Dred Scott* case the judges had the wholly erroneous impression that by their fiat they could set at rest the most disturbing problem in the country; the Court overestimated its own capacities. As late as February 15, 1857, the judges were resolved to decide that case on a narrow technical ground which would avoid the major controversy of the day. Justice Wayne then became persuaded that in one great utterance the Court could settle the question for the country. Justice Catron took the step, astonishing by twentieth-century standards of propriety, of requesting incoming President Buchanan to ask Justice Grier "to settle the agitation by an affirmative decision of the Supreme Court." This Buchanan did. As Charles Warren has put it, many "seemed to have a fatuous confidence in the Court's power thus to settle the slavery issue." [4] The case successfully settled nothing, helped

2 *United States* v. *Schooner Amistad,* 15 Pet. 518 (1840).
3 *Scott* v. *Sandford,* 19 How. 393 (1857).
4 Charles Warren: *The Supreme Court in United States History* (Boston: Little, Brown & Co.; 1937), Vol. I, p. 302.

to bring on the war, and put the Court itself in a more difficult situation with the public than it had ever known.

Subsequent generations have never forgotten this profound failure by the Court to use its strength wisely, and the Court in its constant consideration of Negro problems particularly since World War I has always been mindful of the limits of the practical.

For a very brief period following the Civil War, the Court itself entered into the spirit of reform. Shortly after the close of the war, Senator Sumner of Massachusetts, the country's leading abolitionist, moved the admission to the Supreme Court bar of a Negro. The acceptance of this member of the bar was widely taken as a quiet overruling of the *Dred Scott* decision; for that case had held that Negroes were not citizens, and this bar applicant could not have been admitted unless he was a citizen. Justice Wayne of the *Dred Scott* majority stayed off the bench on this admission day. Also in 1873, in the case of *Railroad Company* v. *Brown*,[5] the Court for the first time faced the subject of segregation.

Mrs. Brown, a Negro charwoman attendant in the room for lady visitors to the Senate, decided one day to go to Alexandria, Virginia, and bought a ticket on the Alexandria & Washington Railway. The then applicable law provided that "no person shall be excluded from the cars on account of color." The A. & W. had two connected cars for the Alexandria run, using one for white passengers and the other for colored. The cars were as identical as any two could be, and, indeed, their function was reversed at opposite ends of the line so that the "white" car on the way over to Alexandria was the "colored" car on the way back.

Mrs. Brown attempted to sit in the "white" car, and when she declined to move to the "colored" car, she was violently

5 17 Wall. 445 (1873).

ejected from the train. A United States Senate committee held a hearing in the shanty in which she lived, and concluded that Mrs. Brown should sue for damages. The railroad defended the damage action on the ground that these cars, which were separate but otherwise wholly equal, were "reasonable and legal." The Supreme Court altogether rejected the company's position as "an ingenious attempt to evade a compliance with the obvious meaning" of the law. The Court held, in an opinion by Justice David Davis, that the law required that "the colored and white race, in the use of the cars, be placed on an equality." Mrs. Brown was entitled to recover.

It is a commonplace in the aftermath of war that if the victors do not speedily wreak their will, they may never get around to it. The reforming zeal very rapidly wore out in both the country and the Court, leaving the Civil War constitutional amendments as a legal outcropping marking the highspot of a revolution. After 1877 the North resigned itself to allowing the white South to re-establish much of its dominance over the Negro. The Negro rights so optimistically established by the abolitionist surge withered away. As Professor Swisher puts it, "Other than Negroes and their faithful friends, the people were tired of giving special protection to the former slaves. It was felt to be time for the return to power of the dominant factions in the several communities." [6]

The Court as an institution swung with the pendulum of the revolution and counterrevolution in the country at large. In cases coming before the Court construing the war amendments, the Court regularly gave them a narrow interpretation. One of its most ardent Southern admirers has said that

[6] Carl Brent Swisher: "Dred Scott One Hundred Years After," *The Journal of Politics*, May 1957, pp. 167, 174.

the Court's decisions between the close of Reconstruction and the end of the nineteenth century "marked the practical overthrow of the Congressional ideal for the Fourteenth Amendment within seven years after its victorious adoption. The Supreme Court thus at the outset practically annulled section five of the Amendment and reduced the Bill of Rights section one to distant potentialities." [7]

The Court invalidated the civil-rights legislation passed by the Reconstruction Congress, radically contracted the power of Congress to legislate protection for any Negro rights, and finally, without mentioning the case of Mrs. Brown, for all practical purposes overruled it and upheld the legality of so-called "separate but equal" or segregated transportation. To this entire course of events over a twenty-year period, the one consistent dissenter was the first Justice Harlan, grandfather of the present Justice, whose famous phrase "The Constitution is color-blind" went onto the banner of another day.

In short, the Civil War abolished slavery; but society is not necessarily divided into only two classes, the slave and the free. There is the possibility of other, intermediate classes that have status somewhere between slavery and freedom. Schuyler Colfax of Indiana, Speaker of the House of Representatives immediately after the Civil War, told Congress that the Negroes were "free men, not freedmen"; but, despite this abolitionist aspiration, it was not so. The nineteenth century left the Negroes freed, but not free as white Americans conceive this status for themselves. For this profound failure to realize the potential of the Civil War amendments; the Supreme Court deserves some credit or some responsibility, depending upon the point of view; but

[7] Charles Wallace Collins: *The Fourteenth Amendment and the States* (Boston: Little, Brown & Co.; 1912), pp. 22–3.

not an enormous amount either way. National sentiment had abandoned the Negro population, and even if the powers of Congress had been upheld, they would not have been exercised or enforced; and if segregation had been declared illegal, the ruling would surely have been ignored. Samuel Shellabarger, a prominent member of Congress, observed in the memorial exercises for Chief Justice Waite that when the Reconstruction decisions came down, "many of the framers of those amendments received information concerning their intentions which was new." [8] Nonetheless, the Court was only accentuating the trend of the times, not manufacturing it.

The twentieth century tells a radically different story. From approximately 1920 to the present, the Court with almost unrelenting firmness has carried the banner of racial equality. Technically informed readers will know of certain deviations from this in the '20's, but in retrospect they are submerged in the general trend. The new course began with a 1917 decision unanimously holding unconstitutional an ordinance of the city of Louisville intended to require Negroes to live in one part of the town and whites in another.[9] As the Court somewhat gingerly put it, "That there exists a serious and difficult problem arising from a feeling of race hostility which the law is powerless to control, and to which it must give a measure of consideration, may be freely admitted. But its solution cannot be promoted by depriving citizens of their constitutional rights and privileges." The Court faced its obstacles squarely, saying: "It is urged that this proposed segregation will promote the public peace by preventing race conflicts. Desirable as this is, and important as is the preservation of the public peace, this aim cannot be

8 126 U.S. 596, 600 (1888).
9 *Buchanan* v. *Warley*, 245 U.S. 60 (1917).

accomplished by laws or ordinances which deny rights created or protected by the Federal Constitution."

During the 1920's the Court tolerated private arrangements that did approximately what the Louisville ordinance had attempted to do by law. It does not take a city ordinance to make New York's Harlem for all practical purposes a largely segregated area. Nonetheless, a corner had been turned, and when Chief Justice Hughes took office in 1930 the Court began a march in a new direction. By this date it was widely believed that the constitutional guarantee of equal protection of the laws required only that facilities be "separate but equal," which assumed that the Negro and white populations were separated but otherwise were treated with equality. This was the concept that had been rejected in the early decision concerning the ladies'-room attendant Catherine Brown, but by 1930 it was standard practice.

A considerable flaw in the maxim was that the separate "equality" proved to be utterly unequal in fact. Negro schools were inferior, Negro transportation was inferior, all of the services offered the Negroes were inferior. As a practical matter, separate-but-equal often entitled Negroes to the dubious benefits of no education, miserable transportation, and the highest tuberculosis rate in the nation. Hughes met this condition by insisting, without admitting the validity of segregation, that even the separate-but-equal maxim required true physical equality. In leading cases he held that if railroads were going to segregate Negro passengers, they had to give the Negro transportation as good as the white passenger's even though it meant putting a Pullman car on a train for one individual Negro; that if the states were going to segregate higher education, they had to furnish separate schools for Negroes at the university level even if it meant creating a law school for one student.

Color and Crime

Prejudice comes high. Hughes, by insisting that equality meant at least honest physical equality, put the price higher than many were willing to go. The Hughes Court contributed to a growing national awareness that the country, under a happy misapprehension that it was merely separating itself from its largest minority, was affirmatively discriminating against that minority.

In the 1940's the Court hit hammer blows at discrimination. Far and away the most important practical step was the decision that "white primaries" were unconstitutional. The Fifteenth Amendment guarantees the right to vote, but by convenient circumlocutions a pattern had grown up whereby Negroes might vote in the general election but not in the party primary. This ingenious sophistry had the workaday consequence of barring Negroes from any significant voting role in the area in which, for all practical purposes, the Democratic primary was the election. Since the Supreme Court's decision on the white primary, though many Negroes are still kept from the polls, several hundred thousand more Negroes have been voting than hitherto. Particularly in the border states the Negro has become a regular voter, and much of the favorable reaction to the segregation decision in those areas is attributable to his voting emancipation. The white-primary opinion, written by Justice Reed, fearlessly overruled an earlier case and thereby changed the political face of the land as have few judicial pronouncements.[1]

Another Reed opinion foreshadowing the end of all segregation involved interstate transportation. The device used on buses moving from the North to the South had been to let passengers sit wherever they wished in the bus when, for example, it left New York City. At the border of a Southern

[1] *Smith* v. *Allwright*, 321 U.S. 649 (1944).

state, the bus stopped and the passengers were reseated according to local segregation practices, with the white passengers in front and Negroes in the rear. If a white and a colored passenger were traveling together, they said good-by at the Virginia border. When this case came to the Supreme Court, the National Association for the Advancement of Colored People was not yet ready to risk everything by attacking segregation as such. Rather, as if to feel its way, it attacked the requirement solely on the ground that it unconstitutionally impeded interstate commerce by stopping interstate buses while the passengers were reshuffled.

At this point in its history, the Court was dealing with the legality of state regulation of commerce by balancing the burden imposed by the state against the benefit that resulted, and coming to a conclusion as to whether, from the standpoint of the general welfare, the benefit outweighed the burden. For example, when South Carolina restricted trucks to a certain width, the Court found that this immense burden on the New York–Miami trucking traffic was more than balanced by the safety factors in South Carolina, the conditions of their roads, and so on. Applying this benefit-burden approach to the Negro seating arrangement, the burden on commerce is as small as a burden can be—when a bus passes from one region of the country to another, it stops for a moment and some passengers move to other seats. That is all. It would take longer for a child to stop at a restroom. In holding that this was an undue burden on commerce, the Court necessarily concluded that there was *no* legally recognizable benefit in requiring segregated seating. The burden, though negligible, was greater than the benefit, which was nonexistent.[2]

An opinion, by Chief Justice Vinson, struck down the sys-

2 *Morgan* v. *Virginia,* 328 U.S. 373 (1946).

tem of private arrangements restricting Negroes to living in particular parts of communities. As was noted earlier, the ordinance by which the city of Louisville had attempted to require this separation had been invalidated in 1920. Almost thirty years later the Court held that the courts would not assist to achieve the same result by enforcing private contracts which restricted the sale of property to persons of one race or another.[3]

The immediate forerunner of the grade-school segregation cases was a decision on segregation at the University of Texas Law School. In response to the earlier decision requiring that Negroes be offered legal education within their own states, the State of Texas attempted to set up a Negro law school. This school, which was supposed to be "separate but equal," had four faculty members, all highly inexperienced; the state's white law schools had twenty-eight, including some of the outstanding men of the country. The libraries, the courses, and many aspects of the educational program were similarly disproportionate. A committee of one hundred and fifty law professors, of whom I was one, filed a brief in the Supreme Court contending, first, that the Constitution did not condone segregation at all, but, second, that in any case segregated legal education could never be "equal." Stressing that it was impossible to create overnight a Negro law school which would equal an established state university, we also emphasized that part of education is the interchange among students themselves, the understanding of character and of human behavior based on a true cross-section of the community. We concluded:

Every branch of the government, in its own way, has the duty of meeting a challenge of our times that Democracy is unreal, a promise without fulfillment. This requires

[3] *Shelley* v. *Kraemer,* 334 U.S. 1 (1948).

more than words. It requires that we bring our practices up to our pretensions. The account by General Bedell Smith of his experiences as Ambassador to Russia, as reprinted in the *New York Times*, dealt at some length with the publication *Amerika*, which our country distributes in Russia. In the *Times* General Smith reprinted two pictures from *Amerika* as samples of our message to Moscow. One of those pictures was of an unsegregated schoolroom. Is this *really* our message to the world, or must we send a postscript that there is a special exception for the young men studying the Constitution of the United States in the State of Texas? The Texas Legislature has no authority to answer that question for the rest of America. The equal protection clause has answered it.

The Supreme Court, through Chief Justice Vinson, took the position, in essence, that legal education could never be both separate and equal, that the inequality was inherent in the very act of separation itself.[4]

The final step was the unanimous opinion by Chief Justice Warren holding segregation in the grade schools unconstitutional.[5] After a concise review of the authorities, the Chief Justice said: "We conclude that in the field of public education the doctrine of 'separate but equal' has no place. Separate educational facilities are inherently unequal." In a related case decided at the same time, the Chief Justice said: "Classifications based solely upon race must be scrutinized with particular care, since they are contrary to our traditions, and hence constitutionally suspect. . . . Segregation in public education is not reasonably related to any proper governmental objective."

Because we are considering the Court as an institution rather than the details of its decisions, it is unnecessary to

---

4 *Sweatt* v. *Painter*, 339 U.S. 629 (1950).
5 *Brown* v. *Board of Education*, 347 U.S. 483 (1954).

mention the numerous other cases in this crowded field. Those mentioned are sufficient to focus on two points.

First, the Court has led the country without getting too far ahead of it. From 1920 to the present time, the Court, in the person of thirty or more different Justices, has moved consistently in the direction of real racial equality. At the same time, the march of judicial doctrine has been accompanied by a march of thought elsewhere, the combined effects of which have contributed to public receptivity to reform. The progress of Negroes, particularly in the entertainment industry, has given some humility in the remainder of the population. To give an instance, the spectacular act of Secretary Ickes in holding a public concert by Marian Anderson on the grounds of the Lincoln Memorial when she had been barred from the use of Constitution Hall gave a tremendous emotional release to hundreds of thousands, if not millions, of people. Advanced work in both psychology and sociology began to educate the leaders of the community to the everlasting hurtfulness of segregation. The mounting sense in the religious denominations of responsibility for equality made an immense difference, and the unceasing pressure of the National Association for the Advancement of Colored People and its able counsel, Thurgood Marshall, at the forefront of the battle swept countless others along in the rear. The widespread realization that our harsh domestic policy toward our colored population was throwing the rest of the colored world open to Communist infiltration affected the thought of many. All of these factors, merely suggested here, coupled with the slow but steady pressure of the Court itself, made the final decision almost a relief.

Thus, the Court was in part the creature of public opinion, while in part it acted upon that which was affecting it. Both the collapse of reform in the late nineteenth century and the cycle of the last forty years have kept pace with popular thought. Throughout, the Court has been both the object and the molder of public opinion, never very far removed from the dominant community response to the great problem.

Next in significance is the recognition of what the Court has been able to do, and what it could not do, for this bears on what may be expected of it. No decision in a marble palace in Washington, unanimous or not, has been able to wipe out segregation in the schools or even come very close to doing so. What the Court has been able to do is to give leadership to pre-existing local forces that were already champing at segregation. (For statistics on the first four years after the desegregation opinion, see Chapter II.) The sporadic violence and disorder have been extraordinarily modest in volume. In the District of Columbia, parts of Delaware, Kansas, and parts of Missouri, segregation has been abandoned altogether. Progress has been made in Maryland, West Virginia, Kentucky, and Tennessee. An imaginative school leader, Omer Carmichael, Superintendent of Education in Louisville, has made desegregation a reality in that city. On Memorial Day 1957 a fourteen-year-old Negro boy served as chairman of the graduation exercises at the Longfellow Junior High School in San Antonio, Texas, a school with 450 white and 4 Negro students. The lad was also the first Negro class president in any newly integrated school. There was a little strain at the University of Arkansas Law School when a few Negro students began their work, though the discovery that one of them could hit a baseball a country mile helped to ease the tension. On the other hand, it took federal troops to control the disorder fomented by the Governor of Arkansas at Little Rock.

Meanwhile, in the so-called "hard-core South"—the states

of South Carolina, Georgia, Alabama, and Mississippi—absolutely nothing happened by way of integration, and in Virginia and Florida, while there are signs of change in the wind, they are still only signs.

Accomplishment, yes; millennium, no. Law, like politics, is often the science of the possible.

A wholly separate area of the Court's responsibility for the liberty of the individual is its maintenance of efficient operation of the criminal law without sacrifice of the rights of the individual citizen. This has been a primary duty of the Court for as long as there have been criminal prosecutions under federal laws; and since the decision of the 1920's in which the Court also undertook to review some state aspects of fair play, the Court has also reviewed some state convictions.

In this field of justice and jails, one matter stands ahead of all others, and here the Court has been consistently effective. Of all of the rights of any free people, the most important and the most basic is the right to the writ of habeas corpus. This ancient and venerable writ enables judges to insist that no person shall be imprisoned except by due course of law, on charges properly made, subject to trials before judges and juries as the law requires. The writ is the tool with which the courts summon the jailer before the judge to account for the detention of the prisoner.

If every other individual liberty were to go, including the right even to freedom of speech or of religion, and this one were to remain, there would be something left. Without this right, all others would be lost. If a man could be tapped on the shoulder in the streets and hauled away to a prison for indefinite detention, without any charges at all, because someone in authority was dissatisfied with something he had said, the right of speech would become meaningless. The existence of the writ is the most basic distinction between a free people and a tyranny. If, prior to the French Revolution, Louis XVI, for any reason, good or bad or sheer whim, wanted to put someone in the Bastille, he had only to issue his *lettre de cachet*, and in the man went, where he might be altogether forgotten. The Nazis had and the Communists have similar conveniences for their own secret police. In America a man may disappear from the streets for a day or so, but when his friends or family find him the writ can always bring him out again if he deserves to be free.

Immediately related to the writ is martial law, the system by which the Army takes control of civilians and tries them in its own way for the offenses of the moment. Too often someone in authority concludes that it would be best to suspend courts, judges, juries, and all the other niceties of fair play and let the generals administer the law.

In this respect the Supreme Court has maintained a clean line. In 1866 it handed down what may well be the profoundest adjudication ever to come from the judges when, in the case of Milligan, a Civil War traitor in Indiana who was seized by the military, tried by them, and condemned to death, the Court held that the military could render no such judgments.[6] The main opinion, by Justice David Davis, said: "The Constitution of the United States is the law for rulers and people, equally in war and in peace, and covers with the shield of its protection all classes of men, at all times, and under all circumstances."

If such a person as Milligan could be prosecuted in military courts, then "Republican government is a failure," and Davis added: "Martial law can never exist where the courts are open, and in the proper and unobstructed exercise of

[6] *Ex parte Milligan,* 4 Wall. 2 (1866).

216

their jurisdiction." The Constitution permits the suspension of the writ of habeas corpus in times of great emergency, the opinion held, but even during a period of suspension our citizens should not be tried under martial law except in the extremest necessity. The civil courts may review the extent of that necessity.

There has been some occasional criticism of the *Milligan* rule. Professor Charles Fairman of the Harvard Law School, the country's best authority on military law, has said that "it by no means follows that what appeared a salutary restraint upon the tyranny of the Stuarts is today an appropriate limit on the power of both executive and legislature in a highly responsible national government." [7] And even Attorney General Biddle, a prosecutor with a rare sympathy for individual liberty, in the case of the Nazi saboteurs captured early in World War II asked the Court to modify the *Milligan* rule. But this the Court has never done. In the saboteur case President Roosevelt had issued a proclamation to the effect that the courts were barred from reviewing the disposition of the saboteurs. The Court totally rejected this limitation.

The government imposed a complete military rule over the Hawaiian Islands immediately after Pearl Harbor, including military trials of civilians on charges that had nothing at all to do with the war. Exceptionally courageous federal district judges in Hawaii proceeded to take jurisdiction of cases, ignoring the suspension, but by the time the cases reached the Supreme Court, the war was over and the government had already abandoned its suspension of the writ. However, there was still the question of whether the military trials of civilians had been effective.

[7] Charles Fairman: *The Law of Martial Rule* (Chicago: Callaghan & Co.; 1943 ed.), p. 163.

The Supreme Court invalidated those military trials. The majority opinion of Justice Black reminded its readers that "people of many ages and countries have feared and un-flinchingly opposed this kind of subordination of executive, legislative and judicial authorities to complete military rule. . . ." [8] Justice Murphy, concurring, added that "those who founded this nation knew full well that the arbitrary power of conviction and punishment for pretended offenses is the hallmark of despotism." He thought it the duty of the Court to preserve this tradition "at all times, that it may be handed down untarnished to future generations." Referring to criticism of the *Milligan* rule which maintains that total freedom from military trial has become old-hat and obsolete, Murphy said that "the argument thus advanced is as untenable today as it was when cast in the language of the Plantagenets, the Tudors and the Stuarts. It is a rank appeal to abandon the fate of all our liberties to the reasonableness of the judgment of those who are trained primarily for war. It seeks to justify military usurpation of civilian authority to punish crime without regard to the potency of the Bill of Rights. It deserves repudiation."

In 1957 the Court took another look at the *Milligan* problem. This time the issue was not military trials within the United States, but the legality of military trials of American civilians abroad, in connection with our armed forces. With American troops scattered all over the world, there are attendant on the troops a host of civilians—the wives of the servicemen, civilian employees of contractors, and many others. An Act of Congress permitted "all persons serving with, employed by, or accompanying the armed forces without the continental limits of the United States" to be tried by military commissions for any alleged crimes. This, the

[8] *Duncan* v. *Kahanamoku*, 327 U.S. 304 (1946).

Court declared, was unconstitutional; Congress, said the majority opinion by Justice Black, could not deprive citizens "of trial in civilian courts, under civilian laws and procedures and with all the safeguards of the Bill of Rights." To the contention that it would be awkward or difficult or expensive to provide real civilian courts for trials of Americans abroad, the Court quoted in response the statement of Senator Carpenter of Wisconsin in a Senate debate in 1881 on the subject of special, extra-legal American courts in China. Senator Carpenter said: "If we are too mean as a nation to pay the expense of upholding the Constitution in China, then let us give up our concessions in China and come back to as much of the Constitution as we can afford to carry out." Justice Black referred to the *Milligan* decision as "one of the great landmarks in this Court's history" and said that such cases "recognized and manifested the deeply rooted and ancient opposition in this country to the extension of military control over civilians." [9]

The cases mentioned justify the statement that the Court has repeatedly maintained the rights of American civilians to civil trials accompanied by all of the guarantees of individual liberty contained in the Constitution. There have been moments in American history when civilians have been subjected to arbitrary arrest, or have been held without charges, or have been subjected to military trials. The Civil War period and Hawaii during 1941–4 come to mind. Yet the rarity of such instances and their geographical confinement give a record of individual freedom to which not even that of England is superior, and with which no other important country in the world can compare.

On other procedural liberties, the Court's record has been spotty. Federal criminal justice is on the whole fair, with

[9] *Reid* v. *Covert*, 354 U.S. 1 (1957).

the right to counsel scrupulously preserved, and with fair trials and fair procedures. The number of instances in which the Court has been caught up in some momentary hysteria and fallen short of its own ideals of fair play is extremely small. Only in its tolerance of searches and seizures of private homes or places of business by the police has the Court seemed to many unduly lax, and its willingness to tolerate the use of prying electrical devices to spy on the citizenry has profoundly depressed some who have felt that the Court is not as alert to protect against new methods of invasion of personal liberty as it is to prevent old ones. The Court's tolerance, for example, of convictions based on statements picked up by concealed walkie-talkies is frighteningly reminiscent of the Nazi days when German citizens could not have the most innocent conversations in their own homes for fear of a secret "bug," and suggests Orwell's anticipation of 1984 with its screen in every home from which a Communist Big Brother monitors not only the deeds but also the thoughts of the inhabitants. These are not fanciful hazards to individual liberty, and the Court is by no means in the vanguard in meeting them. Yet in more conventional matters it is very alert.

Where state criminal justice is concerned, the Court has balanced one foot forward with one foot back. The grosser types of forced confessions, for example, have been repudiated by the Court, as when in a Mississippi case Negro defendants were taken by the police into the forest, tied to trees, and beaten to a pulp; or the cases in which defendants have been detained incommunicado for many days subject to prolonged interrogation under bright lights, without friends or counsel, without food, and usually without sleep. Yet these abuses are the inevitable concomitance of any secret detention and interrogation, for the rubber hose is always the lazy man's substitute for first-class detection; it is probably not accidental that the F.B.I. is almost never charged with these abuses, perhaps because the talents of its members make rubber hoses unnecessary. The Court has largely failed to afford a clear-cut constitutional rule for the states to follow—e.g., that persons seized by state police shall not be held and questioned without the filing of formal charges.

The tendency of the Court when reviewing state criminal cases is to make distinctions so fine that the general run of state trial courts can be expected to pay little attention to them. Examples are the fields of right to counsel and of illegal searches. The Court has held that anyone charged in a state court with an offense for which the punishment may be death or life imprisonment is entitled to a lawyer, and the state must appoint one for him if he has none of his own and desires one. However, the Court has denied the right to counsel in the case of some of the lesser crimes, even though very long prison sentences may be involved. For example, it upheld the conviction of an illiterate farmhand charged in the state of Maryland with robbery, though the man appeared in court without a lawyer solely because he could not afford one.[1] To this there has been vigorous dissent by Justices Black, Douglas, and Murphy, and indeed it seems almost incredible that anyone can condone the practice of tossing ignorant persons to the courthouse wolves with no help simply because they are poor. Let any reader of these lines challenge himself for a moment as to whether, in such a crisis, he would know how to make proper motions and objections, how to examine witnesses, how to develop his own case, and in general how to plead his cause. The most bloodthirsty Ro-

[1] *Betts* v. *Brady,* 316 U.S. 455 (1942).

man would have thought it unsporting to send a Christian
to the lions with as little protection as this.

The decision in *Wolf* v. *Colorado* [2] is another example of
the troubles of the Court in supervising state justice. In
Wolf, Colorado police had seized evidence without a warrant. Under federal law, evidence which is wrongfully seized
is inadmissible, so that if this had been a federal criminal
case, then without any question the seized materials could
not have been used against the defendant. What is to happen
in a state prosecution? The Court, in an opinion by Justice
Frankfurter, first marched up the field to hold that the seizure was forbidden by the federal Constitution, and then
turned around and marched back again by holding that it
was admissible in evidence anyway. Said Justice Frankfurter for the Court: "The security of one's privacy against
arbitrary intrusion by the police—which is at the core of the
Fourth Amendment—is basic to a free society." Justice
Murphy, dissenting, said in pained surprise: "It is difficult
for me to understand how the Court can go this far and yet
be unwilling to take the step which can give some meaning
to the pronouncements it utters." And yet, "even more important, perhaps, it must have tragic effect upon public respect for our judiciary. For the Court now allows what is
indeed shabby business: lawlessness by officers of the law."

There has been no serious over-all appraisal of the practical consequences of Supreme Court supervision of state
criminal justice in the last twenty-five years. A prodigious
job of fact-gathering and analysis would be necessary to
form any thoughtful opinion as to whether or not the Court
has made a substantial contribution in this field. There is
grave room for doubt. The Court can handle only an infini-
tesimal number of all the cases in the country, and where it

[2] 338 U.S. 25 (1949).

fails to draw sharp, clean lines, it may as well, for national-leadership purposes, throw in the sponge. There is no area on the civil-rights horizon in which the lines of Court policy are more fuzzy and unclear than in this one.

Chapter XII

SPECIAL FUNCTIONS

OF THE COURT

3. A FLOURISHING ECONOMY

As Calvin Coolidge accurately said, "The business of America is business." Since the first colonists came to Virginia in 1607 as part of a planned business venture, Americans have been a people getting ahead. It is both legend and truth that America's eminence has been in the acquisitive arts; as a handful of people grew in number and spread across the continent, they concentrated on both the production and the accumulation of wealth.

Every American institution relates to this urge. The Supreme Court's day-to-day work has always related to the people's push for a living, good or splendid. The Court is an integrated and not an isolated institution, a part of the whole American scene. The Court's role in economic history therefore equates generally to the economic history of the country, with some raggedness at the edges of what would otherwise be a perfect parallel because lifetime appointments permit members of the Court sometimes to outlast their own generations.

The economic legal history of the country in all of its institutions—executive and legislative as well as judicial—

A Flourishing Economy

has two dominating threads. The first is the impulse to encourage the getting of wealth, the second, the impulse to regulate or control it in order to prevent excesses by the wealthy. Prior to 1873 the dominating American drive was encouragement of wealth-getting, with negligible and ineffective regulation. From about 1873 the mood of the country was both to encourage and regulate, with regulation a subordinate but nonetheless constantly present and pressing force. Since about 1930 the goal has again been both encouragement and regulation, but the more conspicuous activities of government have been on the regulatory front.

The early Congresses and state legislatures were really chambers of commerce in legislative halls assembled. The most important early federal economic legislation was that for the assumption and financing of the debt, the inauguration of a protective tariff, the establishment of the United States Bank, the encouragement of land companies in the development and exploitation of the continent, the granting of special corporate charters for banks and railroads.

Problems arising from the growing concentration of wealth after the Civil War led to the drive by the Grangers and the Populists for economic regulation and resulted in legislative concessions such as railroad rate regulation, warehouse regulation, the Sherman Anti-Trust Act, and, under Theodore Roosevelt and Woodrow Wilson after the turn of the twentieth century, a whole parade of regulatory statutes. Nonetheless, government was still encouraging rather than restraining business; even in the Wilson administration a leading piece of legislation was the Federal Reserve Act, banking legislation enacted as much to convenience as to restrict the business community. After 1930 came the New Deal with both massive regulations and a new type of economic legislation, legislation aimed at improving the economic status of the bottom reaches of society by way of social security, farm relief, and so on. Encouragement of business continued, but different classes in the community had become the primary object of the solicitude of government. Even in the more recent Republican years, government has been widely regarded as more of a restraining hand than an unleashing force, at least for larger business; although this is perhaps no longer the balance.

The Court has had three basic functions in relation to these trends. First is that of creative lawmaking for the convenience of the business community; second, protecting or immunizing the business community from the regulatory efforts of other institutions of government; and, third, the Court's function as a partner in regulation.

The Court has created useful legal institutions and formulated major rules of law in aid of business. Take, for example, the history of the corporation in the United States. When the Constitution was adopted, there was only a negligible number of these bodies; the small commercial business of the country was carried on largely by individual owners or partnerships. As a result, the Constitution as drafted had almost as little relation to the corporate form of business enterprise as it did to the jet age. It fell to the Court to make necessary adjustments.

A typical adjustment was the determination that corporations should have the right to sue and be sued in the federal courts. The Constitution gives the federal courts jurisdiction "between Citizens of different States," and a corporation is an artificial person, not a citizen. The Constitution was drafted on the assumption that lawsuits would exist between Mr. Jones of South Carolina and Mr. Smith of New York, and for them the federal courts would be open. If there were to be more than one party on each side, it was assumed that each side would be all from one state, as *Jones and Peters* (South Carolina) v. *Smith and Hopkins* (New York). The possibility that giant corporations, each with citizen shareholders in every state, might one day battle never dawned on the Constitutional Convention. Yet this problem reached the Court in the age of encouragement before the Civil War. Early in the nineteenth century John Marshall had to decide whether the Bank of the United States, a corporation with which Marshall was most sympathetic, could sue in federal courts; and so Marshall, wholly in the obliging spirit of the time, declared that corporations should be regarded as aggregations of their shareholders, and that corporations should be allowed in the federal courts by treating them as if they were citizens of the state in which their shareholders lived.[1] Thirty years later the Court revised this rule to cover the situation of a corporation with shareholders living everywhere by treating a corporation as if it were a citizen of the state of its incorporation.

The rule illustrated the Court's creativeness on behalf of the business community in the age of encouragement. America's corporations had a problem, and, with ingenuity and daring, the Court solved it for them. In a very few decisions it set the rule for hundreds of thousands of cases in the lower courts. There was opposition within the Court. The country itself was divided over the growth of corporations, and there were strong anti-charter movements, as they were called, in many of the states. There were also anti-charter Justices; Justice Daniel, for example, still dissented from giving corporations this privilege when he died in 1860. Nonetheless, the job was done.

Infinitely more important was the decision as to whether the national corporation could exist at all. Citizens move

[1] *Bank of United States* v. *Deveaux*, 5 Cr. 61 (1809).

freely from one state to another. Mr. Smith, citizen, with an office in New York, can operate a second office in Los Angeles if he desires. But corporations are not citizens and do not necessarily have the same privileges; they are creations of a state. By getting a corporate charter in Delaware authorizing him to run a railroad or engage in banking or sell real estate or operate a grocery store in that state, can a man thereby have the privilege also of banking or railroading or otherwise operating in the other forty-seven states? Or must there be a new and independent corporation in every state?

This question has largely been answered, with many restrictions and limitations, in favor of the existence of national corporations. One can buy a pair of trousers or a bicycle from the great chains in every state without dealing with a separate corporation each time. The Court, in its most creative mood, made that development possible. After hearing the profound arguments from Daniel Webster, Chief Justice Taney in 1839 held that, in effect, a bank incorporated in Georgia could validly accept a check endorsed over to it in Alabama, and enforce that endorsement despite the fact that it was not also incorporated in Alabama. As Taney said, this was a question "of a very grave character" because "a multitude of corporations for various purposes have been chartered by the several states; a large portion of certain branches of business have been transacted by incorporated companies, or through their agencies; and contracts to a very large amount have undoubtedly been made by different corporations out of the jurisdiction of the particular state by which they were created. In deciding the case before us, we in effect determine whether these numerous contracts are valid or not."

The Court held that a corporation chartered in one state might make valid contracts in another state at least until that second state took some steps to forbid it. A contrary decision would have killed the national corporation. Justice McKinley dissented—the matter might have gone the other way.[2] As Justice Story observed in a private letter, McKinley's view "has frightened half of the lawyers and all the corporations of the country out of their proprieties." The anti-bank people, including many prominent Democrats, were of the McKinley persuasion. While a conservative newspaper observed accurately that "the decision will give great satisfaction to the business community at large," others denounced as a "deadly blow to the rights of the states" the decision "by this august tribunal, of the vandal overrunning by these paper corporations of the policy and laws and constitutions of the sovereign States." [3]

This legal creativeness reached its apogee toward the turn of the century when the Court, peopled by lawyers of much schooling in large corporate affairs, created the (dubiously just) system of corporate receiverships and corporate reorganizations by which corporations crippled by stock-watering or overexpansion might shake off their creditors and still continue to operate.

This imaginativeness exists today, though in a markedly different degree. The opinion by Justice Douglas in 1939 on the remedy of claimants in bankruptcy, for example, is a leading case in a great tradition.[4] However, today the creative urge of the Court is usually in other directions. Just as, after 1930, legislative and executive attention turned to the control of abuses and the extension of prosperity to the general public, so these areas also have been the business

2 *Bank of Augusta* v. *Earle,* 13 Pet. 519 (1839).
3 The story is well told in, and these quotations are taken from, Charles Warren: *The Supreme Court in United States History* (Boston: Little, Brown & Co.; 1937), Vol. II, pp. 50–62.
4 *Case* v. *Los Angeles Lumber Company,* 308 U.S. 106 (1939).

of the Court. In recent years the Court's principal assist to big business has not been by the creation of a whole new legal machinery for economic aggrandizement, but rather (and more negatively) by watering down regulation through occasional "soft" judicial enforcement.

From early times the Court has reviewed and interpreted the controls imposed on business by other branches of government. While prior to the Civil War most economic legislation was of the business-sponsoring variety and not truly regulatory, even in sponsorship there were conflicts within the business community itself. Any business community is bound to have old and new rights, some bustling newcomers and some staid old-timers. Such an intra-class conflict was the pre-Civil War controversy between national and local banking. In this bitter battle the Court put its whole weight on the side of the national bank.

The two constitutional devices developed before the Civil War for business-protective purposes were the contract and commerce clauses of the federal Constitution. The contract clause provides that no state may impair the obligation of contracts, a conception which if pushed to its logical extreme would render social legislation altogether impossible. For example, if the government is wholly incapable of regulating contracts, then an employer who makes a contract with an employee to work for twenty-five cents an hour would forever be immune from legislation requiring that the minimum wage be a dollar.

However, before the Civil War the contract problem involved not contracts between individuals, but contracts of the state itself. To what extent can the state modify its own commitments? Suppose, for example, that a state granted an utterly improvident charter to a corporation to do particular business; could the state ever change its mind? In a leading—and extreme—case a spectacular gang of crooks descended upon the Georgia legislature and bribed it into giving the group prodigious quantities of public land for a song. A United States Senator from Georgia resigned his seat and ran for the state legislature to redeem the name of his state; an indignant electorate turned out the scoundrels who had sold their patrimony. The very next legislature repealed the sale, and public feeling in the state was so keen that the original statute was taken into the public square and there burned with a magnifying glass concentrating the sun's rays so that God's own power might be said to have avenged the crime.

The Supreme Court held the repealer ineffective, rescuing the first Act from God's flame. Stressing the assertion that the crooks had speedily passed off the land to innocent hands, Marshall held that the state could not impair its original contract. In still another major opinion he held that the charters granted by the state to corporations—banks, insurance companies, colleges, or any others—could not be altered once the states had given them.

The Marshall rule meant that a legislature had only to be bribed once; and this was a day when bribery was common. In a more profound sense, the Marshall rule undoubtedly lent great stability to capital investment in the United States. The usual case was not that of the bribed legislature or the excessive charter. Even assuming that crooks were to be involved, they might besiege the legislature as much when attempting to change an Act as when it passed the first time; virtue is not always the last to appear on the stage.

And yet the Marshall rules pushed to their logical extreme would have put the country in an economic strait jacket. The critical conflict between the old and the new came in connection with a charter for a bridge across the Charles

River near Boston. This bridge, a toll affair, outlived its usefulness before it outlived its charter; for the Massachusetts legislature gave a new charter for a competing bridge virtually paralleling the first. The second bridge was so much more satisfactory to the users that it drained the first charter of all value. The first charter, or contract, was thus impaired not by repeal but by authorized competition. After years of deliberation the Court, through Chief Justice Taney, upheld the second charter.

Daniel Webster and his co-counsel presented the case for the first bridge with full recognition of its broad economic significance. They declared that they did not "seek to interrupt the progress of improvements," but they asked "a stay of revolution; a revolution against the foundations on which property rests." Webster's co-counsel said that if the second bridge were tolerated, "*what* and *where* is the security for other corporate property? More than four millions of dollars have been invested in three railroads, leading from Boston, under charters granted by the legislature. The title to these franchises is no other and no better, than that of the plaintiff. The same means may be employed to accomplish the same ends; and who can say that the same results will not follow?" Holding up the charter of the first bridge company, he described it as "once worth half a million dollars; and now not worth the parchment it is written upon."

Counsel for the second bridge declared that Webster would sacrifice the future for the past, and declared that all old public improvements are in necessary peril of suffering from new and better ones: "Railroads, perhaps, generally, supersede the highways near them, and render stages, wagons and other property to a great extent less valuable. They frustrate the views, and lessen the income of all who depend on the public travel for patronage and support."

Yet "the public convenience demands such improvements, and they are not to be obstructed from such causes."

The Court itself found that improved methods of transportation must succeed one upon the other: "Turnpike roads have been made in succession, on the same lines of travel; the later ones interfering materially with the profits of the first. These corporations have, in some instances, been utterly ruined by the introduction of newer and better modes of transportation, and travelling. In some cases, railroads have rendered the turnpike roads on the same line of travel so entirely useless, that the franchise of the turnpike corporation is not worth preserving. Yet in none of these cases have the corporations supposed that their privileges were invaded, or any contract violated on the part of the state." To let the first bridge complain of the competing second, said Chief Justice Taney, would jeopardize the millions of dollars which had been invested in railroads and canals: "We shall be thrown back to the improvements of the last century, and obliged to stand still, until the claims of the old turnpike corporations shall be satisfied; and they shall consent to permit these states to avail themselves of the lights of modern science, and to partake of the benefit of those improvements which are now adding to the wealth and prosperity, and the convenience and comfort, of every other part of the civilized world." [5]

And so the Court announced its limitation upon the obligations of the charters: what the charters gave to the corporations could not be taken away, but it must have been given clearly, directly, and precisely. The charter to the first bridge company did not bar later competitors, and therefore the Court would not read a restriction on competition into the first grant. Other cases also reserved to the

[5] *Charles River Bridge Co.* v. *Warren Bridge Co.*, 11 Pet. 420 (1837).

states the right to buy back from corporations at a fair price what the states might earlier have given,[6] and recognized the right of the states to reserve at the time of granting the original charter the power to make later changes.

In these cases the Court consciously dealt with fundamental economic problems and consciously made fundamental economic policy. It did the same thing with the commerce clause, developing a rule that, at least to some extent, the states could not regulate interstate business. This was almost pure judicial innovation; the Constitution declares that Congress shall have power to regulate commerce among the several states, but there is not a syllable in the document to suggest that the states may not do the same thing, at least until Congress exercises the power granted to it. Between 1824 and 1851 the Court partially restricted the state power to regulate commerce even where Congress had done nothing at all; and as Congress at this early period used its power only negligibly, this amounted to a general release of some business from any regulation.[7]

These state restrictions developed during the period of Jacksonian democracy, at a time when states were beginning to use their regulatory powers. The immunization of interstate business from state regulation required a very broad conception of the congressional commerce power. If the states were to be barred from an area, it might as well be a big area. John Marshall's conception of the federal commerce power was worded broadly enough to satisfy the judicial exponents of nationalism in the era of F.D.R., but with one practical difference: it never seriously occurred to Marshall that the federal commerce power which he was defining might actually be used.

[6] *West River Bridge Co.* v. *Dix,* 6 How. 507 (1948).
[7] For further discussion, see Chapters II and IX.

The great revolution came after 1886 when the Court invalidated certain state railroad regulations on the ground that only Congress might control this subject.[8] The regulatory vacuum thus created was too large to leave empty; by that comparatively recent date it was unthinkable that railroads and their rates should not be subject to any control. As a direct response to the Court's decision, Congress inaugurated the era of federal regulation of business with the adoption of the Interstate Commerce Act of 1887. Thereupon the Court, which had so broadly defined the federal commerce power when that power was *not* being used, proceeded almost at once to define that same power very narrowly once Congress began to exercise it. By 1895, after Congress had also adopted the Sherman Anti-Trust Act, the Court cut the federal commerce power down, finding this "essential to the preservation of the autonomy of the states," [9] an autonomy that had not worried the Court very severely a few years before.

These, then, were the two principal Court-made devices to protect business from legislative interference prior to the 1890's: the commerce clause, which also serves the large purpose of preventing "balkanization" of the country; and the contract clause, which prevents at least some interference with vested rights. Neither clause was good even from the standpoint of the business-protectionist. The contract clause was so extreme that it invited exceptions large enough to swallow it up. Unlike the contract clause, the commerce clause remains one of the most active portions of the Constitution to the present day, but it was nonetheless an unsatisfactory control, particularly when Congress began to use its own power.

8 *Wabash etc. R. Co.* v. *Illinois*, 118 U.S. 557 (1886).
9 *United States* v. *E. C. Knight Co.*, 156 U.S. 1 (1895).

The Court thus entered the era of mixed regulation and business sponsorship without an adequate arsenal of tools to control hostile economic legislation. What followed was from thirty to thirty-five years of judicial inventiveness, the most dynamic policy-making of any judicial body in history. In that time the Court went far indeed to insulate the multi-billion-dollar industry of the early twentieth century from popular control.

The principal architect of the new order was Stephen J. Field, a California Democrat who went to the Court by appointment of Abraham Lincoln and who served for thirty-five years. Field was crusty, ruthless, ill-tempered, arrogant —and immensely able. With the look of a Hebrew prophet and twice the sense of self-righteousness, he was a hard man. A messenger who once, for a joke, brought him a glass of water instead of a whisky punch when Field was working late one night was half paralyzed with fright at the tongue-lashing he received for his temerity,[1] and many an associate who gave less cause for offense found Field almost equally difficult.

The principal tool devised to control legislation was the conception of "due process of law." To quote a brilliant, concise comment on the history of due process, "It has come to be the symbol habitually invoked by private right, the barrier that guards the frontiers of business against the interference of the state, a sanction by which the judiciary reviews the work of the legislature. It has woven itself into the folkways of an industrial culture and called into being an august corpus of the law. Yet into an eminence that already showed signs of decay it has emerged out of an estate of little repute. The account of its coming up in the world is among the most

---

[1] Carl B. Swisher: *Stephen J. Field* (Washington, D.C.: The Brookings Institution; 1930), p. 439.

dramatic of stories. It bristles with color and conflict, with surprise and paradox. A novelist who made ideas his characters would not—for fear of provoking disbelief—have dared to allow his imagination to contrive such a series of events. . . . The brew of nullity, in the name of due process, was in the pot. Campbell was dead; Bradley stood fast; Miller came over; and Field, eternally right, marched with the marching doctrine." [2]

The story of the rise of due process is so intricate that here we can present only conclusions. The Fourteenth Amendment, with its provision that no person shall be deprived of life, liberty, or property without due process of law, was added to the Constitution in 1868 in the aftermath of the Civil War. Its obvious primary purpose was to protect ex-slaves. As Justice Miller once observed of all the Civil War amendments, "No one can fail to be impressed with the one pervading purpose found in them all, lying at the foundation of each, and without which none of them would have even been suggested; we mean the freedom of the slave race, the security and firm establishment of that freedom, and the protection of the newly made freeman and citizen from the oppressions of those who had formerly exercised unlimited dominion over him." [3]

The Court moved the amendment far from this simple purpose. By 1910 the due-process clause had been extended to cover corporations as well as living persons, and the Court had held that under it utility rates established by state regulatory agencies might be set aside if they were not high enough; that the states were severely restricted in their

---

2 Walton Hamilton: "The Path of Due Process of Law," in Conyers Reid, ed.: *The Constitution Reconsidered* (New York: Columbia University Press; 1938), p. 167. For the best account of Field, see Swisher: *Stephen J. Field.*

3 *Slaughter-house Cases,* 16 Wall. 36 (1873).

powers to put limits on hours of labor; and that Congress was powerless to forbid "yellow-dog contracts"—employment agreements whereby men were barred from joining labor unions. An almost endless number of state regulations of business were invalidated, and as recently as 1936 the clause was construed to forbid state minimum-wage regulation.

The late nineteenth and early twentieth centuries were the "let 'er rip" period of American economic history, the age of ultimate exploitation of natural resources and of human beings by the most powerful economic forces of the community. The Supreme Court proceeded to hammer out economic legal doctrine which would "let 'er rip," which proceeded to take every control off business and industry. In one year, 1895, the Court invalidated the income tax, put severe restrictions on labor unions, and substantially crippled the federal government's economic regulatory powers by confinement of the commerce power.[4] Not the extremest right-winger on the American scene would return to the constitutional doctrines of the turn of this century; the name of John Bricker, then Attorney General of Ohio, is on one of the briefs of the 1930's asking the Court to check these doctrines.[5] Today even the anti-tax faction wants merely to put a ceiling on the income tax and not to abolish it.

Because our own generation tends emotionally to enlist itself with Holmes, who began his dissents from the course of events just described near the beginning of this century, we sometimes fail to appreciate how remarkable the judicial craftsmanship of that period was. For sheer creativeness there has never been anything like it. The robber barons who

[4] Fred Rodell: *Nine Men* (New York: Random House; 1955) particularly develops the events of this dramatic year.
[5] *Nebbia v. New York*, 291 U.S. 502 (1934).

gave the permanent stamp to the era needed a body of law with which to fence their baronies, and the Supreme Court proceeded to give it to them. Whether for better or for worse is a matter of one's social point of view, but for the purpose of comprehending the function of the Court, we must recognize that when the era of serious regulation of business dawned in the 1870's there were at least some Justices to resist every step; and after 1890 they were dominant for more than forty years. It is true that these judicial victories left an appalling wake; the number of families of railroad workers who went uncompensated for the deaths of their wage-earners, the shortening of human life by excessive hours of labor, the loss in terms of malnutrition from striking down minimum-wage laws, and the excessive profits of utilities and particularly of railroads at the expense of farmers and shippers all represent conditions that few would desire deliberately to re-create.

Yet, can it be said that what the Court was then doing was less than what the country, or at least a large share of it, wanted? Was the Court doing any more than carrying out in the judicial department the policies of Hanna, and of Taft, and of Harding, and of Coolidge? As Carl Swisher has well said, Field "must be classified as one of the great men of the country—great as one of the master builders of the legal structure needed for the housing of a particular economic order through a dramatic era of our history." He helped make "a legal structure desired by and adapted to the needs of such men as Rockefeller in his kingdom of oil; Carnegie, Frick, and Morgan in the domain of steel; and Stanford, Huntington, Gould, Harriman and Hill in the realm of the railroad." [6]

The Court fell slowly into step with new times as the

6 Swisher: *Stephen J. Field,* pp. 431–3.

country passed from the era of mixed regulation and encouragement of business to the contemporary era of regulation. The New Deal had to win its second election in 1936 before the Court took its hand off the laws that had been passed after 1933, a simple recognition of the fact that a judiciary appointed for life neither is nor is supposed to be in immediate correspondence with the trend of its own times. The result was the Court-packing fight of 1937, a direct conflict over the function of the Court in respect to economic legislation of the federal government and of the states. Since approximately the spring of 1937, that function has been fundamentally and radically changed.

As new blood was infused, the Court totally reversed itself and began not to impede, but to promote regulation. From 1937 to the present time, the Constitution itself has virtually backed off the stage as a device to check business regulation. It remains virile principally in connection with the commerce clause, still used from time to time to strike down a state tax or other regulation, as, for example, the invalidation of an Arizona law concerning the length of trains. If any business-regulatory laws, either state or federal, have been invalidated since 1937 on due-process grounds in the same sense that the wage-and-hour laws had earlier been invalidated, I am unacquainted with them; and the contract clause has been quietly slumbering for some time. Not only have the constitutional roadblocks been stripped out of the way, but the Court has consistently interpreted the commerce power as concurrent with the economic needs of the nation. The purchase of a dozen sulpha tablets on doctor's orders from the corner drugstore is subject to federal regulation now, and so is the movement of wheat from the rear forty to the barn, there to be fed to the farmer's own stock. The Court toyed for a time with exempting picketing from regulation, but even that experiment in immunity has more recently been very largely given up.

If the era of regulation is unable to achieve the millennium that it sets for itself, it is *not* because the Court has placed the Constitution in its way. The elected representatives of the people have lost their whipping-boy; they must assume their own responsibilities. Yet the Court has not bowed itself off the economic scene; rather the focus of battle has shifted to a new point. Congress can regulate now, which means that it can pass statutes; but the room for interpretation of those statutes is so large that the judiciary continues to be very substantially felt.

Examples of the immense power and duty of the Court in the interpretation of statutes, including economic statutes, fill many volumes. Indeed, that is exactly what most of the volumes of the Supreme Court Reports now contain. Sometimes the problems arise in the context of co-operation with or discipline of a federal administrative agency. The general effectiveness of the early National Labor Relations Board was largely due to the week-in-week-out Court support of its orders. On the other hand, the hapless Interstate Commerce Commission, with its general policy of regulating transportation from the railroad point of view, has found itself almost constantly at odds with the Court, a circumstance that contributes to the inertia of economic regulation of ground and water transportation.

Two instances will illustrate the role of the Court both as a factor in the maintenance of the *status quo* and as a force for change. In *United States* v. *Columbia Steel Company* [7] the United States Supreme Court considered economic policy for the nation at least as much as did John Marshall when he passed upon the future of the Bank of the United

[7] 334 U.S. 495 (1948).

241

States. This was an anti-trust case in which the United States sought to block the United States Steel Corporation from purchasing the assets of an independent steel-fabricator on the West Coast. The government charged that U.S. Steel was already so big that the addition of this independent would lead to monopoly of the steel industry. The Court, five to four, decided in favor of U.S. Steel.

The particular expansion of U.S. Steel involved in this case was comparatively small. The company represents an investment of more than one and a half billion dollars, and it was purchasing a concern for a little more than eight million dollars. Justice Reed for the majority said: "It is not for courts to determine the course of the Nation's economic development. Economists may recommend, the legislative and executive branches may chart legal courses by which the competitive forces of business can seek to reduce costs and increase production so that a higher standard of living may be available to all. . . . No direction has appeared of a public policy that forbids, per se an expansion of facilities of an existing company to meet the needs of new markets of a community, whether that community is nation-wide or country-wide."

Basically, Justice Reed made clear, it was reasonable that Big Steel should expand to the west. "Size has significance also in an appraisal of alleged violations of the Sherman Act. But the steel industry is also of impressive size and the welcome westward expansion of that industry requires that the existing companies go into production there or abandon that market to other organizations."

Justice Douglas, dissenting for three other Justices, took a very different view of the economics of the matter. "This," he said, "is the most important anti-trust case which has been before the Court in years. . . . Here we have the pattern of the evolution of the great trusts. Little, independent units are gobbled up by bigger ones. At times the independent is driven to the wall and surrenders. At other times any number of 'sound business reasons' appear why the sale to or merger with the trust should be made." Douglas again told the story of *The Curse of Bigness,* the volume by Justice Brandeis directed against monopoly. Said the dissenters in a vigorous expression of economic policy: "Industrial power should be decentralized. It should be scattered into many hands so that fortunes of the people will not be dependent on the whim or caprice, the political prejudices, the emotional stability of a few self-appointed men. The fact that they are not vicious men but respectable and social-minded is irrelevant. That is the philosophy and the command of the Sherman Act. It is founded on a theory of hostility to the concentration in private hands of power so great that only a government of the people should have it." Reviewing the position of U.S. Steel in the economy, Douglas concluded: "The least I can say is that a company that has that tremendous leverage on our economy is big enough."

Sometimes in the field of restrictions on competition the die is cast the other way. In *Schwegmann Brothers* v. *Calvert Distillers Corp.,*[8] Justice Douglas expressed his philosophy of free enterprise in a majority opinion. The resultant decision at least for a time "rolled back" a greater volume of consumer-goods prices than the regulations of the World War II Office of Price Administration ever did. The issue was an interpretation of the Fair Trade laws exempting from the anti-trust laws contracts between manufacturers and retail outlets which prescribed minimum prices for retail sales. A pattern had grown up whereby a manufacturer could contract to fix prices with only one retailer in a state,

[8] 341 U.S. 384 (1951).

and thereafter all other retailers handling the same articles had to sell the goods at the same price; anyone who buys standard-brand items particularly in the drug and electrical fields has noticed how the system works. The opinion of Justice Douglas held that the price-fixing restrictions did *not* apply to stores that had not made an express agreement with the manufacturer. This case was decided on May 21, 1951. On May 28, Macy's, a New York department store, cut prices six per cent on 5,978 items. Gimbel's met the challenge, Klein's joined the fight, and there followed a price war that in several cities lasted until well into the summer of 1951. Thereafter Congress amended the law to put prices up again.

The details of the particular decisions may be put aside. Enough has been said to illustrate this point: from the earliest until the most recent day, the Supreme Court has been deciding cases that directly affect the pocketbook of the American public.

Chapter XIII

SPECIAL FUNCTIONS

OF THE COURT

4. INTERNATIONAL RELATIONS

On the 17th day of May 1784 the Chevalier de Longchamps got himself into trouble. On that day he went to call on the French Minister at his home in Philadelphia and there fell into a quarrel with him in which a servant overheard him say: *"Je vous deshonnerra Policon Coquin."*

On the 19th the affair passed from words to blows. Longchamps met the Minister near a coffeehouse on Market Street in Philadelphia, and this time Longchamps said to him: "You are a blackguard." Both men were carrying canes. Longchamps used his to hit the cane of the Minister, whereupon the Minister proved that he was able to give considerably better than he got, wielding his cane with such severity that Longchamps had to be rescued by passers-by. This incident occurred during the Confederation, before the adoption of the Constitution, and Longchamps came up for trial before a state court in Pennsylvania. On due consideration the Supreme Court of Pennsylvania gave Longchamps a sentence of two years and a fine of a hundred French crowns, noting that "The person of a public minister is sacred and inviolable. Whoever offers any violence to him, not only affronts the sovereign he represents, but also hurts the common safety and well-being of nations;—he is guilty of a crime against the whole world." [1]

The Longchamps case has significance in American history because it *might* have been decided the other way. The almost preposterously heavy sentence for this minor altercation was a sop to the French. If the court had happened to free Longchamps, however, the whole international position of the United States might have been jeopardized because of what might have been the whimsical consideration of one state court. The Longchamps incident, coming as it did only a few years before the Constitutional Convention, was much in the minds of the delegates; and it emphasized for them the necessity of having one national tribunal, rather than several local ones, to pass on those legal questions which inevitably arise and which can gravely affect foreign relations not merely of the state in which the incident occurs but of the country as a whole. In this case it was a matter of a French diplomat. It might have been (and frequently has been) a problem of foreign shipping or of some other foreign financial interest. Whatever it was, the founders of the republic wanted a national court to decide it.

The wisdom of this judgment has been fully demonstrated. In the general run of lawsuits there does from time to time turn up an incident with international complications. One of the very first cases before the Supreme Court was the matter of the French privateer *La Vengeance*.[2] A U.S. marshal had seized the vessel on the ground that it was being used to run cannon, muskets, and gunpowder in 1794 and 1795 from Sandy Hook, New Jersey, to the West Indies. A lower court found, and the Supreme Court affirmed, that the

---

[1] *Res Publica* v. *de Longchamps,* 1 Dall. 111 (1784).
[2] *United States* v. *La Vengeance,* 3 Dall. 297 (1796).

United States was wrong, and the vessel was released. It is immaterial for our purpose whether the Court was right or wrong (it found that the muskets were not being smuggled but were simply the private property of the passengers, an exceptionally well-armed lot). What matters is that decisions of this kind can have national consequences, and they deserve to be decided from a national standpoint.

The case of *La Vengeance* called for a routine application of principles of international law. In other cases the Court deals with treaties. The painful topic of payment of debts by Americans to their British creditors after the Revolution involved the treaty of peace with Great Britain. In a famous opinion concerning a migratory-bird treaty Justice Holmes used language so broad as to give Senator Bricker, many years later, the fear that the entire Constitution might be subverted by exercise of the treaty power.[3] The Senator offered a constitutional amendment of somewhat misty scope to correct the situation. In 1957 the Court explained that the treaty power is very definitely limited by other constitutional powers, so that perhaps the mind of the Senator is now at rest.[4] The opinion of Justice Black observes that "this Court has regularly and uniformly recognized the supremacy of the Constitution over a treaty" and makes most explicit that the treaty power does not permit "the United States to exercise power under an international agreement without observing Constitutional prohibitions." The opinion continues: "The prohibitions of the Constitution were designed to apply to all branches of the National Government and they cannot be nullified by the Executive or by the Executive and the Senate combined."

Other examples of the Court's international involvement

[3] *Missouri* v. *Holland*, 252 U.S. 416 (1920).
[4] *Reid* v. *Covert*, 354 U.S. 1 (1957).

are numerous. In the case of the American soldier Girard, charged with murdering a Japanese citizen, the Court was caught up in an intensely emotional area of international relations; so it was in the 1930's in passing on questions relating to the recognition of Russia.

The point remains, as developed in Chapter II, that the Court is on the periphery of international relations as compared with the other branches of government. The Secretary of State deals with more serious problems of international relations in a normal week than the Court does in twenty years. War or peace, to use the atomic bomb or not to use it, to annex conquered territory or let it go, to support the United Nations or to go it alone—these are not judicial problems.

For the most part, the Court's function in the international field is a *supporting* function; it is to make effective the policies of the other branches once they are established. Sometimes—rarely—this is on direct appeal from the State Department. The ejection of an African diplomat from an American restaurant does more harm to American relations than can be compensated for by a visit of the Vice-President to the diplomat's country; magnified by thousands of incidents, domestic American race relations are the greatest menace to America's international relations with the colored world, which is to say most of the world. Hence, in the school segregation cases the State Department made an express appeal for the result the Court reached.

But usually the connection is not quite so immediate. The principal support function of the Court is in mixed international-domestic matters, such as rigorous enforcement of inflation controls in wartime, and this the Court diligently provided in World War II. The harm that might be done a country at war by an uncooperative Court is enormous; if, in the *Prize Cases* in the Civil War, the Court had not, by a vote of five to four, upheld the system of Southern-port blockade by the American Navy, the result would have been either chaos or outright judicial-presidential conflict.[5] If Justice Burton's opinion for the Court had not upheld renegotiation, or the special system of control of profits on government contracts in World War II, the added cost of that war would have been enormous.[6]

Sometimes the support functions involve not economic but personal controls. The Justices, like the Presidents, the generals, and the leaders of Congress, are patriots, and sometimes, like the others, they allow their patriotism to run away with their common sense. In two unseemly instances of haste the Court has allowed itself to be stampeded. In the saboteur case of World War II the country became frenzied over eight Germans who landed on our shores from a submarine and were speedily caught by the F.B.I. To our allies, with their better-balanced sense of the realities of war, the sight of troops guarding the corridors of the Department of Justice while the Attorney General personally abandoned all other matters to try this passel of culprits before a group of major generals must have seemed odd. The Supreme Court itself then came into special and extraordinary session to pass on the cases, and sent the defendants to their deaths some months before Chief Justice Stone was able to get out an opinion telling why.[7] Again, in the *Rosenberg* espionage case, the Court, over several dissents, showed a positively indecent haste in having the defendants executed before it could possibly give serious consideration to their claims and

5 *The Prize Cases*, 2 Black 635 (1863).
6 *Lichter* v. *United States*, 334 U.S. 742 (1948).
7 *Ex parte Quirin*, 317 U.S. 1 (1942).

before an opinion could be prepared.[8] Even in a case of international implication, if the judges are to run a court of law and not a butcher shop, the reasons for killing a man should be expressed before he is dead; otherwise the proceedings are purely military and not for courts at all.

In each of these cases, my objection is not to the end results, which I think were right. But in neither case would the country have suffered if the course of law had been orderly as well as sound; and the cases illustrate that we are dealing with Justices who share the ardors and excitabilities of men who do not wear robes to do their work.

Wartime is likely to be a time of excesses, and it is noteworthy that the Court has a way of checking those excesses more *after* than *during* the event. Trials by military commissions were invalidated both for the Civil War and for World War II in Hawaii, but in each case the decision followed the war. Partly this is because litigation is slow business at best—by the time a case moves through the lower courts to its point of final disposition, years have usually passed. Yet partly this is because the Court does not always hasten the day. Justice Miller, long after the Civil War, reminisced about his efforts to delay decision in war-power cases in which he felt that "the most strenuous efforts were made to use the Court to embarrass the Government in its conduct of operations by endeavoring to get decisions upon such questions as the right of Mr. Seward to confine obnoxious persons in the forts. . . ."[9] In the First World War, Holmes and Brandeis themselves upheld convictions of war opponents which after the war they might well not have con-

[8] *Rosenberg* v. *United States,* 346 U.S. 273 (1953). For scholarly analysis supporting the conviction but not the sentence in this case see Howard Mann, Book Review, 67 *Yale Law Journal* 528 (1958).

[9] Charles Fairman: *Mr. Justice Miller* (Cambridge: Harvard University Press; 1939), p. 38.

doned. After several years of World War II had gone by, the Court flatly changed its treatment of conscientious objectors in a manner favorable to that group.[1] Justice Frankfurter in dissent in the second case pointedly observed "that it was during the crucial war years that the Act was thus interpreted and enforced . . . is of course no reason for misconstruing it now and relaxing the mode of administration which Congress deemed necessary for its effectiveness."

A tragic illustration of this very human tendency to "go along" with the military in the first flush of patriotism and to attempt later to salvage something from the wreckage is the treatment of Japanese Americans in World War II. The bombs at Pearl Harbor unleased a hysteria of fear and race hatred against both foreign- and American-born Japanese on our West Coast. Though more than seventy thousand American citizens were involved, as to whom there was not discovered then or later any substantial evidence of disloyalty, the government in an act of pure racism rounded up this horde of innocent people, took them from their homes and normal lives, and put them in concentration camps largely in interior America. There, in flagrant defiance of the American precept that guilt is personal, they were kept for years.

The matter first came before the Court in 1943. The case itself involved only the curfew for the West Coast Japanese Americans, but by the time of decision the movement to the camps was already on, and everyone realized that the issues were the same in the two situations. If, without any evidence of personal misdeed, the military could take American citizens selected solely on a racial basis off the streets by a certain time, it could probably also incarcerate them.

[1] Compare *Falbo* v. *United States,* 320 U.S. 549 (1944), with *Estep* v. *United States,* 327 U.S. 114 (1946).

All nine Justices upheld the result. Even Justice Murphy, though noting that the order "bears a melancholy resemblance to the treatment accorded to members of the Jewish race in Germany and in other parts of Europe," went along in an opinion stressing his reluctance to do so and the sharp limitations he meant to put upon the rule just adopted.[2] A year later the Court held that under the rule in the curfew decisions the Japanese Americans might, in the wartime emergency, be required to leave the West Coast. The Court's opinion in this later case said: "We cannot—by availing ourselves of the calm perspective of hindsight—now say that at the time these actions were justified." [3] On that same day the Court also held that loyal American citizens of Japanese descent could not be held in the camps, a result reached by closely construing the authority of the governmental agency involved; and the Court's opinion pointed to the splendid record of Japanese Americans in support of the war.[4] In other words, the 1944 decisions did cut off something of the effect of the 1943 determination, and the very hindsight that was denied contributed to the more sober perspective of the later date.

This same phenomenon of belated redemption is illustrated in the judicial reaction to the cold war.[5] As was developed in Chapter X, the McCarthy-McCarran era could scarcely roll the repression along fast enough to keep pace with the Vinson Court's approval of it; the Warren Court moves on a different tack. The Justices as human beings are affected by the excitement of their own days; as I once rather meanly observed on the relation of the Court to the

---

[2] *Hirabayashi* v. *United States,* 320 U.S. 81 (1943).
[3] *Korematsu* v. *United States,* 323 U.S. 214 (1944).
[4] *Ex parte Endo,* 323 U.S. 283 (1944).
[5] For an extended discussion of these cases, see Bernard Schwartz: *The Supreme Court* (New York: Ronald Press; 1957), Chapter IX.

history of civil rights, "The dominant lesson of our history on the relation of the judiciary to repressions is that courts love liberty most when it is under pressure least." [6]

This much stands clear: in the field of foreign relations the Court is an important auxiliary of policy, but not its maker. Its largest contributions have been support of international policy in moments of need, coupled with a tendency to attempt to right the boat after it has tipped in moments of excess. The Justices may not keep their heads when all about them are losing theirs, but they are very likely to be the first to recover balance.

[6] Edmond Cahn, ed.: *Supreme Court and Supreme Law* (Bloomington: Indiana University Press; 1954), p. 114.

Chapter XIV

THE JUSTICES AS MEN;

PERSONALITIES AND AMBITIONS

Justice Miller, that blunt old codger from the state of Iowa, was extremely candid about his colleagues. His Chief Justice, Waite, he thought "mediocre." "I can't make a great Chief Justice out of a small man," he told a friend, "I can't make Clifford and Swayne, who are too old, resign, or keep the Chief Justice from giving them cases to write opinions in which their garrulity is often mixed with mischief. I can't hinder Davis from governing every act of his life by his hope of the Presidency, though I admit him to be as honest a man as I ever knew." [1]

In other notes Miller observed: "It is vain to contend with judges who have been at the bar the advocates for forty years of railroad companies, and all the forms of associated capital, when they are called upon to decide cases where such interests are in contest." Justices Clifford and Swayne he particularly thought weak; "If I could content myself with such opinions as they write, and such investigation as they give to cases, and put no more solid mental product in them than they do, I could sit from one year to another without much source of fatigue, beyond the confinement to place and

[1] Charles Fairman: *Mr. Justice Miller* (Cambridge: Harvard University Press; 1939), pp. 349, 373, 374. The quotes from Justice Miller immediately following are also taken from this excellent work.

routine." Another member of this same court, Justice Hunt, Miller liked but thought "not a very strong man in intellect."

In short, at one point Miller thought his Chief poor, two of his colleagues weak, one affected in his judgment by his ambitions, and another not as bright as he might be. That was in the 1870's. In 1910, President Taft put down certain impressions that in part came to him from the Justices: "The condition of the Supreme Court is pitiable, and yet those old fools hold on with a tenacity that is most discouraging. Really the Chief Justice Fuller is almost senile; Harlan does no work; Brewer is so deaf that he cannot hear and has got beyond the point of the commonest accuracy in writing his opinions; Brewer and Harlan sleep almost through all the arguments. I don't know what can be done. It is most discouraging to the active men on the bench." [2] In the 1940's, Chief Justice Stone, like Miller a man given to very pronounced and highly critical views, thought poorly of almost every one of his colleagues. All of which is to say that at almost no time in the history of the Court has there been a riftless harmony and perfect respect among its members.

This is scarcely surprising. Nine men of different outlooks, backgrounds, and skills are put together in close quarters to do important work. The shortcomings of one necessarily create burdens for the others; to put it at its simplest, if some Justices are able to do less than their share, the other Justices must take up the slack. When this is complicated by factors of ego (and not all Justices are modest), of personality (some Justices are immensely colorful and have very strong personalities), and aggressiveness (some Justices have extremely positive points of view), it will surprise no

[2] Henry F. Pringle: *Life and Times of William Howard Taft* (New York: Farrar & Rinehart, Inc.; 1939), Vol. I, pp. 529, 530.

one that the Justices do not always give the same impression of lyric harmony as a boys' choir.

The community expects the Justices to do the impossible. Because they speak the voice of the law, which is assumed by the community to be fixed and immutable, something not made but discovered, the community expects the Court to speak with a personality-free voice. The Justices themselves are commonly aware of their duty to the institution in this respect, and seek to do their work impersonally and to hold as far from the public eye as possible their inevitable internal tensions.

The result is that out-and-out conflict among the Justices rarely spills over into the public gaze. Occasionally a dissent may be so biting that the country is aware of the wounds it has caused. When Justice Stone dissented from the invalidation of the Agricultural Adjustment Act, he said: "The only check upon our own exercise of power is our own sense of self-restraint." [3] A year later, when it became the turn of Justice Sutherland to dissent from an opinion in which Stone was in the majority, Sutherland said: "The suggestion that the only check upon the exercise of the judicial power, when properly invoked, to declare a constitutional right superior to an unconstitutional statute is the judge's own faculty of self-restraint, is both ill-considered and mischievous." [4] One may assume that Justice Sutherland spent the intervening year in a state of low boil over what he regarded as Stone's offense.

At the same time, decorum is preserved. To say that the other fellow's point of view is "ill-considered and mischievous" is not the most vigorous possible epithet. Normally the intra-Court reproaches are made with a gentle touch. A de-

[3] *United States* v. *Butler,* 297 U.S. 1 (1936).
[4] *West Coast Hotel Co.* v. *Parrish,* 300 U.S. 379 (1937).

vice occasionally used is to quote something one of the Justices has said in another place which appears to conflict with what he is saying in an opinion, as when Justice Jackson searched out observations that Justice Black as Senator Black had made on the floor of the Senate, or when Justice Black in dissenting from Justice Frankfurter quoted from a publication of onetime Professor Frankfurter. A devastating gentle cut was Justice Reed's opinion for the Court in the Texas white-primary case, holding that the Constitution barred exclusion of Negro voters from primaries.[5] Shortly before this case Justices Roberts and Frankfurter had vigorously sliced at the remainder of the Court for overruling an earlier decision. In the white-primary case Justice Roberts again dissented, incorporating what he had said on the matter of overruling shortly before, and adding the biting phrase that the majority decision in the primary case "tends to bring adjudication of this tribunal into the same class as a restricted railroad ticket, good for this day and train only."

The Roberts assault came with ill grace because Roberts, for all his splendid qualities as a lawyer and a jurist, is almost certainly the member of the judiciary who has the foremost reputation for inconsistency. It was, essentially, the switch of Roberts between 1936 and 1937 which killed Roosevelt's Court-packing plan by reinterpreting the Constitution to uphold the President's legislation. The phrase "a switch in time saves nine" referred to Justice Roberts.

Justice Reed, always a most gracious man, could not bring himself in his majority opinion to retort that Roberts was a poor pillar of consistency. Instead, Reed quietly observed that the practice of overruling decisions which were thought to be unsound, particularly on constitutional matters, "has long been accepted practice, and this practice has continued

[5] *Smith* v. *Allwright,* 321 U.S. 649 (1944).

to this day." Appended to the sentence was a footnote citing more than a dozen instances of overruling during the period of Roberts's own service, in most of which Roberts had concurred.

So refined are the techniques by which altercation among the Justices is commonly conducted that the general public may be wholly unaware that a war is on. The thrust and parry of battle is likely to consist of a barbed sentence met by a devastating citation. Instances of public dispute more severe than this are extremely rare. Two have been mentioned in this volume: the occasion in the 1840's when a newly formed Democratic majority in the Court discharged an old crony of Justice Story as court reporter, and the unseemly dispute between Chief Justice Taney and Justice Curtis over the *Dred Scott* decision in 1857.

Curtis's withdrawal from the Court led to the most marvelously acid communications in the Court's history. In his letter of resignation Curtis explained to President Buchanan that he was holding up his retirement till the end of the term to avoid inconvenience to litigants. Buchanan, who was on Taney's side of the controversy, replied: "The President gives you his thanks for postponing the time of your retirement to a period when no one will be inconvenienced by it." [6]

The most recent direct outbreak of one Justice against another was Jackson's attack on Black at the time of the appointment of Chief Justice Vinson in 1946. Jackson, who was abroad at Nuremberg trying German war criminals at the time and who had deeply desired the place for himself, apparently felt that Black was in some way responsible for the appointment of Vinson. He issued a vitriolic public state-

[6] Quoted in my "Appointment of Supreme Court Justices," 1941, *Wisconsin Law Review*, pp. 172, 176.

ment denouncing Black for having participated in a certain case in which Jackson felt that Black should have disqualified himself. This was certainly the first trans-Atlantic blast in Court history, and intimate friends of the brilliant but erratic Jackson have attributed the incident to the excessive nervous strain of his difficult work at Nuremberg. Black, who never under any circumstances discusses judicial matters off the bench, maintained a complete silence.

Far more striking than the Court's disputes over the years is the absence of personal friction among the judges, and the extent to which normal tendencies of irritability are controlled rather than exposed. When one considers how easily a bench of nine could march off in nine different directions, one's principal impression may well be not how often but how seldom this occurs. An instance of a McReynolds snarling in bare-toothed anti-Semitic hostility at his Jewish brothers of the Court is overbalanced by the real personal sympathy between a Marshall and a Story, a Taney and a Daniel, a Taft and a Sutherland. Moreover, this degree of respectful personal interrelation is by no means restricted to Justices who, like the pairs just mentioned, were essentially like-minded. Chief Justice Fuller and Justice Holmes stood on opposite sides of an enormous judicial chasm and yet were thoroughly respectful of each other in their personal relations. Brandeis was a man of great force and yet one who maintained impeccable relations with those about him; he sought to preserve the amenities even with McReynolds. Holmes's regular request for a story from Sutherland at the start of the conference was a matter of sheer good nature. The correspondence between Holmes and Hughes when Hughes became Chief Justice reflects a relationship of truly moving mutual respect.[7]

[7] This is one of the many delights in Merlo Pusey: *Charles Evans*

On the bench, as elsewhere, it takes two to quarrel, and there is usually one at least to try to avoid the conflict. By the time of his declining years in the 1870's, Justice Clifford was extremely querulous, and one of his complaints was turned away by Chief Justice Waite with a note beginning: "I trust you will believe me when I say that it caused me very great pain to learn from you this afternoon that my conduct toward you has been such as to give you offense. I can only say that it is the farthest from my heart that it should be so." Yet even the amiable Waite could be very firm, as when telling Field, who wanted to write a certain pro-railroad opinion, that Field's personal relations with the Central Pacific Railroad made this improper. Said Waite: "While I regret that you do not look at the matter as I do, I cannot but think that my judgment was for the best interests of us all." [8]

Partly this is because any good Justice maintains not merely an individual but also an institutional sense. Brandeis, who sharply disagreed with his colleagues on many serious matters, is an excellent case in point. He did his best to persuade the Justices in the conference room, and often even wrote long, formal opinions representing the utmost in careful labor, to be circulated only among them in the hope that one or another might be persuaded to his point of view. Sometimes he succeeded, moving the Court at least a little in his direction. Other times he failed entirely. Then, frequently he would go along with the majority he had failed to persuade, discarding enormous amounts of his own work

Hughes (New York: The Macmillan Company; 1951). Page 668 contains the exchange mentioned above, and is part of a substantial chapter on judicial interrelationships.

8 Quotes from Bruce R. Trimble: *Chief Justice Waite* (Princeton: Princeton University Press; 1938), pp. 259, 261.

to do so.[9] Chief Justice Taft, who as an ex-President had bitterly opposed the confirmation of Brandeis, later observed that Brandeis "thinks much of the Court and is anxious to have it consistent and strong, and he pulls his weight in the boat." Alpheus Mason, his biographer, tells us that Brandeis was so discreet that his clerks were left to deduce his views of his fellow Justices from a facial expression or a twinkle of the eye. Taking Brandeis as an example of the dedicated and vigorous judge, it is apparent that the forces which might have made him fly off in a direction of his own, a star in angry splendor, were more than balanced by factors of good breeding and good judgment which made him a good team man even when playing against a majority of his colleagues.

The tendency of Justices to group together in blocs, so that a given group of Justices are commonly found on the same side of a variety of seemingly unrelated questions is very nearly universal, and it is important in understanding the judicial function.

First as to the existence of the phenomenon. Take for example the pattern of dissenting opinions from 1837 to 1863.[1] There were 282 cases in which the Court was not unanimous out of 1,031 decided altogether in those years.

Various Justices served for different portions of this period, so very exact comparisons cannot be made. Nonetheless, some obvious combinations appear. For example, Chief Justice Taney served for almost all of that period with Associate Justice McLean. He agreed in dissent with McLean eight times. He served for about the same amount of time with

[9] Alexander Bickel: *The Unpublished Opinions of Justice Brandeis* (Cambridge: Belknap Press of Harvard University Press; 1957) is a revelation of the mountain of behind-the-scenes work which Brandeis threw aside as a contribution to Court solidarity.

[1] These figures are taken from unpublished work of Professor Charles Wright of the University of Texas.

Catron and Daniel, and he joined with those two Justices in dissent fifteen and twenty times respectively. He served for five years with Justice Curtis, and they never once agreed in dissent.

While Taney very rarely agreed with Justice Wayne, McLean almost always did. Catron and Daniel were almost always together, as were Catron and Grier for the portion of this period when Grier was on the Court. Daniel and Catron were very much in agreement with Campbell. McLean and Curtis were frequently together. Out of this jumble of names, it becomes apparent that for as long as they served together, Taney, Catron, Grier, and Daniel formed a bloc that tended to agree. Another bloc of McLean, Wayne, and, when he was there, Curtis reflected a separate alliance. None of these alignments was automatic, none was conclusive. Sometimes Daniel, as the most extreme agrarian on the bench, agreed with Curtis, the most extreme representative of the commercial interest. But most of the time the blocs were together.

This condition exists generally. In earlier years, Marshall and Story almost invariably agreed. After the Civil War, other blocs developed. In the 1920's, the extreme-conservative combination of Van Devanter, McReynolds, Sutherland, and Butler was known, unimaginatively, as the four horsemen, whose function it was to flatten out that dissenting trio Holmes, Brandeis, and Stone. From approximately 1940 to 1949, Black, Douglas, Murphy, and Rutledge (for slightly less than all of the period) were an established combination. In 1957, Chief Justice Warren and Justices Black, Douglas, and Brennan were very frequently in agreement.

A sample showing the tendency of particular colleagues to agree is shown in this analysis of a group of 1948–9 cases selected for their general importance:

AGREEMENTS AMONG JUSTICES IN MAJOR AND IMPORTANT CASES, 1948–9 [2]

	Vinson	Black	Reed	Frank-furter	Douglas	Murphy	Jack-son	Rut-ledge	Burton
Vinson	—	14	24	19	14	12	25	13	24
Black	14	—	17	12	25	20	10	20	13
Reed	24	17	—	18	15	15	20	16	21
Frankfurter	19	12	18	—	10	12	23	13	23
Douglas	14	25	15	10	—	0	12	18	13
Murphy	12	20	15	12	20	—	10	24	11
Jackson	25	10	20	23	12	10	—	9	24
Rutledge	13	20	16	13	18	24	9	—	12
Burton	24	13	21	23	13	11	24	12	—

[2] My "The United States Supreme Court," 17 *University of Chicago Law Review* 1, 45 (1949).

What makes these combinations, and how do they function? Obviously if judicial decisions were brought by the stork without the intervention of man, or if the task of deciding consisted of no more than consulting either the history books or the dictionary, these combinations could not exist. To follow the dictionary figure, it is simply inconceivable that, with all using the same dictionaries, one bloc of men would consistently get one set of meanings and the other a different set. Necessarily, attitude affects the business of judging. To use a single example, one set of judges may have a strong partiality for the jury system and another bloc a strong antipathy to it; in any case in which the issue is whether the jury was given a fair chance to decide the case, the pro-jury judges are going to be more mindful of the powers of the jury than are the judges who are either indifferent or hostile.

Hence, blocs come into being fundamentally from like-mindedness. It should not be confused with blocs in legislative bodies, where a party discipline is imposed, and where the members of a given faction are expected to "go along" with the leader. Such devices as party structure, whips, policy committees, leadership are factors of size and are unrelated to the co-ordinated operations of two or three or four men whose offices are within a few feet of one another and who can perfectly well talk things over either in private or in the general conference of the Court.

Blocs heighten the probability that things will be talked over, and like-minded men are more apt to reach agreement when they talk things over than when they leave the subject alone. Professor Mason's biography of Stone describes the manner in which, when Stone was first appointed, he was welcomed into the little extra-Court meetings of the Taft bloc of conservative Justices, and then, after a time, was dropped from those conversations when it appeared that he might be dangerously "progressive."

Although there is no system of bloc caucuses, after the legislative fashion in which the members may agree in advance to be bound by the conclusion of the majority, there is a certain amount of almost unconscious yielding of one to another on lesser matters. Each Justice has points about which he feels particularly strongly, as well as those on which he tends to be neutral or not much concerned; in those circumstances, any group of good friends will on occasion yield, one to another, in a spirit of general harmony. However, there is no evidence that at any point in the Supreme Court's history this normal tendency has spilled over into real sacrifice of principle. Chief Justice Taft did claim that Brandeis dominated Holmes in the latter's last years. In the Holmes-Laski correspondence, these scattered phrases by Holmes appear: "unless I let Brandeis egg me on to write a dissent in advance": "on that day came down an opinion that stirred the innards of Brandeis and me and he spurred me to write a dissent"; "when I can get calm I am catspawed by Brandeis to do another dissent on burning themes"; "Brandeis . . . reminded me of a case argued last term in which he said I should have to write a dissent"; "but meantime a dissent that the ever active Brandeis put upon my conscience waits untouched." [3] They indicate a good-humored acknowledgment of the restless energy of Brandeis rather than any dominance, but they also suggest that a harmonious personal relationship does make for collaboration.

Because the public and the commentators tend to transfer to the Court their conceptions of legislative institutions,

[3] These phrases are collected in an instructive essay by Samuel J. Konefsky: "Holmes and Brandeis, Companions in Dissent," 10 *Vanderbilt Law Review*, 269, 270 (1957).

they assume that there is a leadership within the Court. The facts do not confirm this. The senior Justice of a bloc undoubtedly has some advantage; in the days of the Black-Douglas-Murphy-Rutledge regime, for example, Black as the senior might assign opinions to members of his own group. At the same time, the blocs are normally made up of strong and independent men who are not the pawns of anyone.

This is evidenced by the large number of disagreements occurring within the blocs and by the absence of anything like total uniformity in views among their members. On the contemporary Court, for example, Chief Justice Warren and Justices Black, Douglas, and Brennan may be tending to form a bloc, but in the obscenity cases of 1957 they marched in very different directions. In the vital 1958 denaturalization cases, Justice Whittaker left his usual ally, Justice Harlan, to stand much closer to Warren, Black, and Douglas; and yet the power to denaturalize a citizen for voting in a foreign election was upheld, five to four, because Justice Brennan joined in the majority opinion of Justice Frankfurter.[4] In both the John L. Lewis contempt case and the case of the conviction of the Japanese General Yamashita, Justices Murphy and Rutledge were opposed to Justices Black and Douglas. In Justice Rutledge's last year on the bench, he agreed with Justices Black and Douglas in only about half of the divided cases. In the greatest free-speech opinion that he ever wrote, the matter of Miss Whitney, Justice Brandeis was with Justice Holmes, but not with Justice Stone. On the pre-Civil War Court, Taney and Daniel, basically like-minded and thoroughly harmonious men, disagreed

[4] *Perez* v. *Brownell,* 78 S. Ct. 568 (1958). That the difference between Brennan and the others was narrow is illustrated by the fact that in two other denaturalization cases decided on the same day, he was back with his usual cohorts. *Trop* v. *Dulles,* id., 590; *Nishikawa* v. *Dulles,* id. 612.

consistently on important matters of corporate policy. The table for the 1948 term shows that Chief Justice Vinson and Justice Reed were together in twenty-four cases; but they were also *not* together in a few. Justice Frankfurter was with Justice Jackson in twenty-three cases, but not in all of the cases. In other words, the blocs are fluid, not rigid; and at all times counsel must remember that they are dealing with nine Justices and not two or three.

Of all the corruptions that can tempt a Justice, the most practically dangerous is ambition. It is when a brother is chasing some other star than the law that respect for him diminishes. An example is the slap, quoted at the beginning of this chapter, in which Justice Miller charged his colleague Davis with aspiring to the Presidency.

This raises the whole problem of the extra-judicial duties or aspirations of the judges. First as to those duties which a Justice may perform without leaving the bench. The Constitution provides that the Justices shall be Justices, and, with the exception of the provision that the Chief Justice shall preside over proceedings in the Senate for impeachment of the President, it sets up no other duties. As one of its first acts, the Court held that the Justices could not be compelled to undertake any side assignments. But while such side duties cannot be made compulsory, a Justice may undertake them as a matter of choice, and here there is full range for individual judgment. Cardozo, while still on the high court of the State of New York, declined to serve as a member of the Permanent Court of Arbitration at The Hague. On the other hand, Justice Joseph Lamar did choose to hear an international arbitration. Justice Jackson left his judicial duties for a year to prosecute the war criminals at Nuremberg, and Justice Roberts undertook to investigate the causes of the disaster at Pearl Harbor.

The last two instances both involved judgments that an emergency warranted deviation from normal practice. In the Pearl Harbor instance, national confidence was jeopardized, and any investigation by a Democrat would have been regarded as a whitewash. The high character of Justice Roberts guaranteed a maximum respect for his conclusions. The war trials doubtless seemed of equal importance to Justice Jackson.

Yet Justice Roberts later candidly declared that his action had been a mistake. Chief Justice Stone was also offered extra-judicial duties during the war and, after giving the matter the deepest thought, refused. He was willing to undertake duties of some substance—as, for example, his work with the Mellon Art Gallery—but not even his devoted patriotism would take him into the war program and away from the bench. In his letter declining President Roosevelt's request that he review the rubber program, Stone recalled the errors of the past when Justices had accepted outside duties, and concluded:

> I hope, Mr. President, that you will fully understand how deeply I regret my inability to render this service for you, and that it is only a sense of public obligation transcending all personal considerations which prevents. I console myself by the assurance that there are others, not judges, more capable than I, of doing this particular task. . . .[5]

I believe that Roberts's second guess was right, and that Stone was correct in keeping to his judicial labors. Surely

[5] Quoted in Alpheus Mason: *Harlan Fiske Stone* (New York: The Viking Press; 1957), pp. 710, 711. A variation of Stone's problem confronted Justice Reed, who after his retirement from the Court but while still subject to service as a judge was appointed to head the federal Civil Rights Commission. Reed at first accepted, but soon withdrew because of doubts as to whether it was proper for even a retired Justice to undertake a non-judicial task.

in a country as large as this one, the business of judging is sufficiently important that we can devote the full time of nine men to it. Taking a Justice away from his primary duty can be done only at the expense of that duty. Stone's acute bitterness over the burdens placed upon the Court by the absence of Jackson (who, Stone sputtered, was off running a lynching bee at Nuremberg) is understandable. Such extra-judicial work may also involve Justices in controversies that lower the prestige so valuable to the Court. The experience of Roberts when he was required to account to congressional committees concerning his Pearl Harbor investigation is an example of these vexations. Finally, such participation can disqualify a Justice from deciding cases when some aspect of that very matter comes before his Court.

But suppose that a Justice, instead of taking a vacation from his judicial work and then coming back to it, aspires to an assignment that would take him off the bench entirely. In the beginning, a comparatively minor lure was sufficient to pull a man away. The first Chief Justice, John Jay, resigned to become Governor of New York. After the Court had gained in prestige, and particularly after the onerous circuit-riding duty had been eliminated, the attraction of lesser posts disappeared, although in recent times there was some talk, at least, of the possibility that Justice Douglas might become Secretary of the Interior. Normally, if a Justice aspires to another post, it is to the Chief Justiceship or the Presidency.

The ambition for promotion to the Chief Justiceship has been a problem since the 1870's. Prior to that time the circumstances of the particular appointments left no real room for rivalry on the bench. Chief Justice Chase died in 1873 after an illness that made his replacement a topic of gossip as long as three years before his death. John M. Harlan, later a Justice himself, wrote President Grant that some one of the Associates should be made Chief. He thought it a bad thing to say that an Associate, "however faithful he may have been in the discharge of his duties and however eminent his ability—could never proceed to the office of Chief Justice." [6]

Hungry to succeed Chase was Justice Miller, who watched with gratification the demand for his promotion in both legal and general newspapers. When President Grant instead chose Attorney General Williams, Miller's disappointment was acute; and when opposition caused that nomination to be withdrawn, he was far from distressed. Grant's next choice was Caleb Cushing of Massachusetts, and although Miller had not used his own political influence to obstruct the Williams appointment, he threw himself all out against Cushing. This nomination also was withdrawn under pressure, and Grant then chose Waite, who was confirmed.

That Miller wanted the position, and that his wanting it made trouble, is clear from his own statements. Miller's son-in-law ran a Washington newspaper which violently attacked Cushing—evidence to other papers that Miller was in the anti-administration camp. Miller himself thought his failure to be appointed was due to the efforts of two colleagues. Of one of them, Justice Swayne, Miller said that he "has artfully beslobbered the President since Chase was stricken with paralysis in a way that no one was aware until now." His colleague Bradley he thought to be in alliance with Swayne because, said Miller, Bradley "from the hour he entered the Court entertained the hope that he might succeed Chase as Chief Justice." [7] To this ambition Miller at-

[6] Harlan to Grant, August 28, 1873, unpublished MS., National Archives.

[7] The two Miller quotations are taken from Fairman: *Mr. Justice Miller,* pp. 265, 276.

tributed the circumstance that he was unable to achieve any close relations with Bradley until after the appointment had gone to a third person. Thereafter he found that what he regarded as Bradley's antagonism to him had ceased.

Waite's term ended during a Democratic Presidency, and the ranking Democrat on the Court, Stephen J. Field, aspired to succeed him. Field's biographer tells us that when Cleveland went outside the Court to choose a successor, Field never forgave him for it and charged, probably accurately, that Cleveland made his choice to pick up political support for himself.[8]

Until 1910 the Chief Justice was invariably chosen from outside the Court. Cleveland had at least paid lip service to the proposition that the appointment, as a matter of policy, should not come from within. But any tradition that the Chief Justice should always come from outside was irretrievably blasted when President Taft appointed Associate Justice White to the Chief Justiceship in 1910. Taft, an experienced judge himself before he became President, apparently did not even consider whether an appointment from the bench might harm the whole Court. Some months before Fuller left the bench, Taft had appointed Charles Evans Hughes, then Governor of New York, as an Associate Justice and had come close to promising Hughes that he would raise him to the Chief Justiceship as soon as Fuller left. When the time came, former President Theodore Roosevelt opposed Hughes, and Taft turned to other possibilities. Some suggestion was made that he ought to appoint Associate Justice Harlan, who had been on the bench for more than thirty years. Taft's biographer quotes him as saying: "I'll do no such damned thing. I won't make the position of

[8] Carl B. Swisher: *Stephen J. Field* (Washington: The Brookings Institution; 1930), p. 319.

Chief Justice a blue ribbon for the final years of any member of the Court. I want someone who will coordinate the activities of the Court and who has a reasonable expectation of serving ten or twenty years on the bench." [9] Taft's Attorney General then consulted members of the Court, who preferred White, and White was appointed.

Taft himself, by then an ex-President, succeeded White in 1921, and by the end of his own term he was greatly alarmed that President Hoover might appoint Associate Justice Stone to take his place. Hoover did not, choosing Charles Evans Hughes instead, so that the honor of making the Stone advancement fell to President Roosevelt ten years later. In making that appointment, F.D.R. passed over Associate Justice Jackson, who also had hopes of the preferment. It was these ambitions of Jackson which erupted into the explosion of 1946 when Jackson was *not* chosen by President Truman. Had any Justice been chosen at that time, several members of the Court would have preferred Stanley Reed.

In the light of this experience, it is always possible that an Associate will be made Chief Justice, and there is no possibility now of creating a tradition to the contrary. Even if two or three Presidents should deliberately refuse to appoint an Associate on the very ground that he was an Associate, there would always be the possibility that a fourth President might revert to the earlier practice. It also is painfully clear that the Court would have profited if such an appointment had been barred from the beginning. The two Associates who were advanced to the center position do not rank among the more distinguished holders of that office, and the hard feelings caused by the very existence of the possibility have been out of all proportion to the good done the country by

[9] Pringle: *Life and Times of William Howard Taft*, Vol. I, 534.

its existence. Overwhelming experience has demonstrated that an incoming Chief Justice does not need previous experience on the bench to be able rapidly to pick up the reins of office.

Most glittering of all the baubles for a roving judicial eye has been the greatest honor of all, the Presidency.

McLean, whose biographer has discerningly subtitled the book about him *A Politician on the United States Supreme Court*, went to the bench in 1829 and died there in 1861, having aspired to the Presidency at every four-year interval in the meantime.[1] I have personally gone through the many boxes of McLean papers in the Library of Congress, and have found there substantially nothing on the business of being a judge, and an endless stream of observations on his candidacy. Appointed by President Jackson in 1829, he was one of the persons whom Lincoln had to shoulder aside for the Republican nomination in 1860. In the intervening years he attempted to win office with the supporters of John C. Calhoun, toyed with the possibility of joining the Antimasonic Party, and built himself up as a Whig. McLean's activities were so indiscreet that in 1849 there was a Congressional debate over whether the Supreme Court Justices should be allowed to send letters without postage, because McLean allegedly engaged in so much political correspondence. This perpetual candidate frequently discussed legal matters in public letters despite the fact that he might have to pass on the same questions from the bench.

Shortly after McLean went off the Court, Chief Justice Chase came on. Chase as an Ohio Senator had fought hard for the presidential nomination that went to Lincoln in 1860, and as a member of Lincoln's cabinet he had taken every

---

[1] Francis P. Weisenburger: *The Life of John McLean* (Columbus: Ohio State University Press; 1937).

possible advantage of his seat to build up support for himself for the nomination in 1864. His ambitions were not stilled by his ascension to the bench, leading to the savage and probably accurate comment of Justice Miller: "I doubt if for years before his death, his first thought in meeting any man of force, was, not invariably, how can I utilize him for my Presidential aspirations." [2]

Another presidential hopeful was Stephen J. Field, who served with Chase and for many years thereafter. In 1877 Field turned out his *Personal Reminiscences of Early Days in California*, published as a campaign pamphlet in 1880. In that year his powerful family pushed him hard for the nomination, and he personally entertained his own delegation from California to lure it into his fold. After a vigorous preconvention build-up, including an enormous expenditure of money by the standards of that day, he made a fair showing at the convention. Thereafter from time to time he was spoken of again, but never so strongly. His great difficulty was his inability to muster a united delegation from his own state—a result, he thought, of dissatisfaction of some interests in California with his judicial opinions on several subjects. He contented himself with the belief that "one of these days our good people will see their error, and then they will do me full justice." [3]

Poor Field hoped in vain. He discovered in 1884 that it was to be a considerable time before he would receive that "ultimate judgment of approval" from the home folks. His state convention adopted a resolution "that the democracy of California unanimously repudiates the Presidential aspirations of Stephen J. Field, and that we hereby pledge ourselves to vote for no man as a delegate to the National Con-

[2] Fairman: *Mr. Justice Miller,* pp. 251, 252.
[3] Swisher: *Stephen J. Field,* p. 302, from which the next quotation is also taken.

vention of July 8, 1884, who will not before this convention pledge himself to use his earnest endeavors to defeat these aspirations." The resolution carried by a vote of 453 to 19 after a lengthy discussion of the judicial opinions of the Justice.

In 1916 a Justice very nearly made it. In that year Charles Evans Hughes received the Republican nomination for the Presidency. It was a hard year for his party, which had split in 1912 with Theodore Roosevelt leading one wing and William Howard Taft the other. In the resultant melee, Woodrow Wilson had slipped into office as a minority candidate. The Republicans in 1916 desperately needed a candidate not associated with the two factions of 1912, and Hughes was ideal because he had been on the Court at the time and out of the campaign. Hughes retired from the Court on acceptance of the nomination, and was defeated. He returned to the Court as its Chief Justice in 1931.

Taft, Chief Justice in the 1920's, had already been President and had had quite enough of it. From 1932 to 1944 the Democrats thought only of F.D.R., but the Republicans very frequently spoke of the possibility of a campaign by Justice Owen J. Roberts, particularly in 1936. In 1944 Justice Douglas was named by President Roosevelt as acceptable, along with Harry Truman, for the Vice-Presidency, and President Truman himself offered the Vice-Presidency to Douglas in 1948.

This little chronology adds up to one proposition: for at least one hundred and twenty-five years, there has been no ten-year period in which a Supreme Court Justice has not been seriously and soberly considered for the presidential office.

While some Justices have flirted with the position, others have taken a very different view of the matter. In 1876 Chief

Justice Waite might well have had the nomination which went to Hayes. Declining to be considered, Waite issued this statement:

> The office came down to me covered with honor, and when I accepted it, my duty was not to make it a stepping-stone to something else, but to preserve its purity, and make my own name as honorable, if possible, as that of my predecessors. . . . No man ought to accept this place unless he shall take a vow to leave it as honorable as he found it. There ought never to be any necessity for re-building from below. All additions should be above.

And when his first rejection did not seem to hold the matter down, Waite told an organized Waite for President Club: "I am one of those who *know* that a Chief Justice cannot be a candidate for the Presidency without damaging the office he holds and himself too. . . . There ought to have been a constitutional prohibition against the political advancement of judges. I am as ambitious as anyone can be. But it is to make my name honorable in the task of those who have and who are to receive my present place. When I accepted this office it was with the understanding that I was not to look for fame except in the line of its duties. The Chief Justiceship is damaged if it is permitted to enter the political whirlpool." [4]

When it appeared that President Eisenhower might be unable because of ill-health to undertake a second term, many Republicans turned to Chief Justice Warren as the next-strongest man in their party. Warren made clear that he regarded it as undesirable for a Chief Justice to take any other post, a view with which President Eisenhower expressed some agreement.

Only some positive rule of law, probably a constitutional

---

4 The quotations are from Trimble: *Chief Justice Waite,* pp. 142, 144.

amendment, could completely bar Supreme Court Justices from accepting any other position. Should there be such a law? The hardest case for those who think so is that of Justice Byrnes, who was appointed to the Court in 1941, not long before the United States became directly involved in World War II. Byrnes had been a most influential Senator. In his autobiography he wryly observed that as a Supreme Court Justice he was considering a belated problem of profit control arising from World War I at the very moment when the Japanese bombed Pearl Harbor. Byrnes desired to be in the present and not in the past war, and because of his extraordinary personal influence his office in the Supreme Court during early 1942 became a clearinghouse for much of the wartime program. Finally in the fall of 1942 Byrnes resigned from the bench to become "Assistant President," a position in which, as the person principally in charge of the domestic side of the war effort, he made an enormous contribution. It is possible that Byrnes as an Assistant President did a better job for the country in its worst hours than any other person could have done.

And yet these are questions which must be decided on balance, and on balance the possibility that a Justice might accept another office has done far more harm than good. The men who wrote the Constitution did everything within their power to make the Justices absolutely independent of the temptations of life. They did this because they believed that independence was of high value. Therefore they provided that "the judges, both of the Supreme and inferior courts, shall hold their offices during good behavior, and shall, at stated times, receive for their services, a compensation, which shall not be diminished during their continuance in office." In other words, the Justices hold office for life and their pay cannot be cut.

I suspect that if it had occurred to the founding fathers that Justices might seek any other office, they would have prohibited that as well. We cannot be sure, however; early Justices engaged actively in politics to an extent that would be shocking today. Marshall regularly participated in party conventions; Daniel as district judge was a partisan pamphleteer and leader of the most extreme sort; Wayne remained active in Georgia politics. As Hughes has accurately said, "What we have come to recognize as the appropriate judicial demeanor was not an early tradition, and is due more to the response which became necessary to the public demand for complete impartiality in judges, and for their aloofness from politics, than to any magic effect of the wearing of the judicial role." [5]

This is a matter which is beyond the power of any individual Justice to control. For a given Justice to say that he will not accept any other office might only result in costing the country the services of the most worthy while putting no check upon the perpetual candidates like McLean. It is too late for the matter to be solved by the creation of a tradition or by good example. On the Court of the 1870's and 1880's, Chief Justice Waite took the view that it was wrong for a Justice to seek the Presidency, but Justice Davis of that very same Court ran for the Presidency on a minor-party ticket, and Justice Field was stopped only by the voters and not by his own sense of discretion. Hughes *did* run; thereafter certainly anyone else may.

Justice Roberts, after he left the Court, addressed himself to this problem. He had accepted two extra-judicial positions, serving on a claims commission as well as in the Pearl Harbor investigation. In 1949 he said: "I had every reason

[5] Charles Evans Hughes: *The Supreme Court of the United States* (New York: Columbia University Press; 1928), p. 173.

to regret that I ever did so. I do not think it was good for my position as Justice nor do I think it was a good thing for the Court." [6] Roberts advocated a constitutional amendment that would bar a Justice from being eligible for the Presidency, Vice-Presidency, or any other government office or position. Senator Butler of Maryland had pressed a constitutional amendment that, among other things, would prohibit a Justice from becoming President or Vice-President within five years of leaving the Court, and this proposal passed the Senate overwhelmingly in 1954.

I do not think that political aspirations of the Justices, either for the Presidency or the Chief Justiceship, have in fact been a corrupting influence to any great extent. The McLeans are rare. But the appearance of such corruption has done a disservice to the Court, and who can be sure how great the damage? Once a Field got the Presidential bug, and once he learned that the course of his decisions was adversely affecting his prospects and that what he said on the bench would be the subject of debate on the hustings, could even so tough a figure as Field ever be absolutely sure that he never wavered in any degree because of hope of preferment?

The Constitution was intended to free the Justices to satisfy just one ambition, the ambition to do a good judicial job. As Chief Justice Waite said in 1876, "Certainly no man should have the place who is willing to exchange it for another." [7]

---

[6] Owen J. Roberts: "Fortifying the Supreme Court's Independence," 35 *American Bar Association Journal* 2 (1949).

[7] Trimble: *Chief Justice Waite*, p. 145 n.

Chapter XV

THE FUTURE OF THE COURT

In 1943 a soldier named Peak disappeared from his Army unit and was never seen again. In 1954 his mother sued the United States to recover on the boy's National Service Life Insurance policy. Her evidence that the boy was dead was his absence for seven years, so that he could be presumed to be dead in 1950.

Mrs. Peak was in a dilemma. A National Service Life policy can lapse for non-payment of premiums. Any claims on the policy must be made within six years of death. If the boy was considered dead as of 1950, then she could not recover because there had been no premiums paid between 1943 and 1950. On the other hand, if she were to contend that he died in 1943, she would lose because the suit was brought more than six years after 1943. Moreover, she would have no practical way of proving that the boy did die in 1943 because he was a missing person, and the only way she could prove death was by relying on the presumption of seven years of absence. Mrs. Peak was thus caught in a circle in which every exit appeared barred.

The Court divided, five to three (Justice Whittaker not participating), in favor of the mother. Justice Douglas, for the majority, observed that this "seems to us to be the common sense of the matter; and common sense often makes good law"; and he held in effect that the death would be

280

dated at two different times for two different purposes. For purposes of measuring the time within which to bring the claim, death would be measured from the end of the seven years, since the mother could not bring the suit in a case of a disappearance without the aid of the presumption of death. On the other hand, to avoid the lapsing of the policy for non-payment of premiums, a jury might conclude that the soldier died much earlier, before lapse of the policy for failure to make the payments. Justice Harlan, in dissent, took the opposite point of view.

As it happens, the majority is almost certainly right, but for the wrong reasons. The ruling no longer needs to depend on "common sense," though it is always a comfort to find common sense on the side of the law. This problem has been considered by courts for as long as there have been both insurance companies and a presumption of death from seven years' absence. The problem repeatedly arises in cases where there is no practical way of proving death until the end of the seven years and where premiums have not been paid in the meantime. A mountain of decided case law supports the position the majority took. Whether either the majority or the dissent was aware of all of the law on the side of the majority, and simply chose not to talk about it, is not clear; but it is difficult to suppose that as good a technical lawyer as Justice Harlan would have dissented if he had realized how frequently the questions he raised had been decided against the position he held.[1]

On the other hand, consider the case of a man named Smith, a shareholder in Warner Brothers Pictures, Inc., who brought a suit against Warner Brothers and a second film

---

[1] *Peak* v. *United States*, 353 U.S. 43 (1957). The leading article cites some two dozen cases to the same general effect as the court majority, and none the other way. Paul M. Roca, 23 *George Washington Law Review* 172, 190, n. 26 (1954).

company. He alleged that Warner Brothers was making a special deal on behalf of a relative of one of its directors which was harmful to the best interests of the company and, consequently, harmful to his interests as a shareholder. The issue in the case as it came to the Supreme Court was whether such a suit could be brought in a federal court at all. The majority, in an opinion by Justice Douglas, held that this was a proper place for the suit. Justice Frankfurter, dissenting for three other Justices, argued to the contrary. On both sides of this difficult question, the argument is closely reasoned and well supported; one puts the case down with the sense that a hard problem has had the best and most careful handling that could be desired for it.[2]

The two cases illustrate the modern skills of the Supreme Court. The insurance question is the kind of question which state supreme courts must decide regularly, but which comes to the United States Supreme Court only by the accident that one of the endless activities of the federal government involves it in the insurance business. A hundred years ago this kind of question might have come before the Supreme Court with some frequency, and that Court might then have exhausted the subject; but not now. On the other hand, in the Warner Brothers case of federal jurisdiction, the Court was completely at home, and no other tribunal in the country would have come close to giving as good a treatment to the subject. Only occasionally now—perhaps once every few years—does the Court shine in treating the state-court kind of question. An opinion a few years ago on a matter of criminal intent, an occasional very thoughtful and analytical opinion on some phase of the law of accidents—these are the rare exceptions. The wave of the future is a continuation of the Court's preoccupation, particularly in the last twenty

[2] *Smith* v. *Sperling,* 354 U.S. 91 (1957).

years, with questions of pure federal law, the interpretation of the Constitution and the acts of Congress.

What the Court will do with these federal questions in the next few years is anyone's guess. Shifting personnel obviously make a difference. The 1960 election can be of great importance to the Court; several vacancies may well occur between 1961 and 1965.

By way of short-term forecast on three matters of general policy or attitude, I would predict:

1. The Court will continue the path of moderation in the interpretation of economic regulatory statutes. We have at the moment a middle-of-the-road Court in a middle-of-the-road country with little crusading zeal for drastic social reform anywhere. The anti-trust laws, the securities laws, the labor laws, and the laws regulating trade practices are unlikely to receive any radical new interpretations, and the Constitution will not be interpreted to strike down state labor restrictions. On the other hand, the states will continue to be required to stay out of the field of labor relations covered by the National Labor Relations Act.

One of the largest state problems is the snowballing tendency to license all domestic industries, from the traditional professions of law and medicine to the newer trades of beautician and plumber. These licensed industries are commonly turned over to their own members for regulation. No constitutional check of this state creation of a guild system of trade appears in the offing, though the Court may very rarely review licensing procedures.

2. In the field of race relations, the Court may be expected to hew to the now established line. The Court's policy of eliminating second-class citizenship for Negroes has been so firm and so steady for so many years, through several administrations and through drastic changes of Court person-

nel, that no shift is even remotely likely to occur. Those persons, if such there be, who hope that this problem may be solved by the simple expedient of persuading the Constitution either to lie down or to go away are doomed to disappointment.

3. Most difficult to predict is whether the Court will continue to ameliorate the effects of the recent repression. As the nation fights its way out of the gigantic hangover left from the days of the McCarthy-McCarran binge, the Court may be expected to provide moderate leadership back toward emotional stability. As one of the Court's closest journalistic observers puts it, "More than any single force, the Court has helped to abate the extremes of McCarthyism." [3] The path of restoration is inevitably moderate; the country may never restore to their original shape a Constitution and a Bill of Rights as bruised and battered as ours have been in recent years. There is no reasonable prospect that the constitutional views of Justices Black and Douglas will prevail and that the entire national program of speech and thought restriction will be torn out by its roots. There is, however, a great likelihood that a voice of general moderation will prevail; it is significant, as was observed in Chapter VIII, that the role of the Warren Court in this regard is usually supported by such voices as *The New York Times*, the *Washington Post* and *Times-Herald*, the *Milwaukee Journal*, the *St. Louis Post-Dispatch*, the *Louisville Courier-Journal*, the *Arizona Daily Star*, and the *Atlanta Constitution*. All of these are voices of moderation, voices sometimes Republican and sometimes Democratic, but never radical. The weight of the Court may

[3] Marquis Childs, St. Louis *Post-Dispatch*, May 2, 1958, Part III, p. 1. As Professor Edmond Cahn puts it, "Though the courts, as guardians of the [First] Amendment have occasionally yielded or retreated, it is clear that without their intervention, fundamental liberties would have been stripped bare." (*The New York Times Book Review*, January 19, 1958, p. 24.)

be expected to stay generally in line with the spirit of these and similar voices.

In this respect, as was more fully developed in Chapter X, the incident of the *Jencks* case on the examination of reports of government witnesses in criminal cases may well prove to be a turning-point. The significant feature of the bitter outpouring against the decision from the Fulton Lewises and the Lawrences is that it did *not* prevail and that the resultant legislation confirms rather than detracts from the Court's decision. In this and other cases of criticism of the Court, there is a contemporary marriage of those outspokenly opposed to the segregation decision and those who are the Mc-Carthyite residue. While the Court's position on segregation may be unshakable, it is possible that this combine may so change the laws as to upset the line of recovery in respect to other civil rights. However, in the early summer of 1958, at least, it appears that these forces will be unable substantially to alter the developing course.

These are short-term predictions so heavily dependent on personnel as to be of little value. What of the long haul? What is the likely role of the Supreme Court in American life over the many years ahead?

Here the great question is the one repeatedly adverted to in this volume: can the Court keep pace with the sheer physical growth of America? Our basic institutions were established for a nation of 3,000,000 people along the Atlantic Seaboard. We are now a nation of 173,000,000 people covering a large part of one continent, reaching into several more, and perhaps even taking on the universe. Each institution of government must make adjustments to changing size. The office of the President grows with the expanding country by the creation of a stupendous executive establishment; that mysterious something, the "White House," is ever larger both in terms of physical size and in terms of the number of persons who serve the President within it. Congress attempts to keep pace with the expanding country by reorganization of its functions and methods, and by the work of an ever increasing staff of individual and committee assistants. One congressional investigating committee may have more civilian personnel than the whole executive department in Washington's day.

Over a hundred years ago there were nine Justices, and there are still nine Justices. The only important personnel difference over the years is the addition of a few law clerks. As we saw in the beginning, this is an institution which some seventy-five years ago found two hundred to be the maximum number of cases which it could decide and write on each year, and meanwhile the number of disputes to be decided within the country has risen astronomically. Moreover, the country is just beginning to grow; its population will be the Lord knows what by the end of the century. In the circumstances, is the Court to occupy a dwindling proportional place in American life? If not, what steps are to be taken to avoid this?

There is no complete solution. To hark back to the discussion of the patent system in Chapter II, for example, the Court is so utterly overwhelmed by the volume of cases that nothing is likely to help. Nonetheless, there are at least five devices that the Court can use to try to cope with volume. Some of them must be used if the Court is not in the course of time to become a flea on the back of an elephant so large that the elephant scarcely knows the flea is there, or, to use a less offensive symbol, if it is not to become simply a place of ceremony.

1. The Court can increase its output by increased delegation to staff within itself. Basically, this is the way the ad-

ministrative agencies handle the volume problem. Each Justice can be given, instead of a law clerk or two, a whole corps, like a member of the National Labor Relations Board who has a coterie so large he can barely remember their names. There can then emerge from the Court opinions which are in form those of the Justice but which in fact are not.

Any such solution is so wholly contrary to the tradition of the Court and seems so completely undesirable that no more should be said about it. Nonetheless, it is a painfully obvious solution, and unless others are found, this may well be the pattern of development. It is, after all, the solution that has been adopted by Congress and the executive; and in the last twenty years the Court itself has shown a faint tendency in that direction by doubling the number of its clerks. It is a possible solution, but one would be hard put to think of a worse one.

2. Another device is the more widespread use of orders without opinions. The gods on Olympus tended to be talkative, and, if Homer is to be believed, there was a strong tendency to lengthy conference before opinions were announced. Nonetheless, every now and again Zeus simply banished opposition with a thunderbolt. The Court's reversals without opinion are its thunderbolts; a case comes up from a lower court in which that court is quite clearly wrong, and without any oral argument or extensive briefing the Supreme Court simply reverses the opinion below, perhaps citing one or two precedents so that the lower court will recognize its error. In 1957, for example, this device was very well used in guiding state supreme courts to find the border where state labor law ends and the power of the National Labor Relations Board begins. In two instances the Supreme Court of Idaho was reversed out of hand.

The summary reversal is an excellent method for policing

the law in the big-quantity areas. It is used in the appellate system of New York State with great frequency. It could easily be abused, because the device of simply saying "No" without having to give reasons is an invitation to arbitrariness and renders it almost certain that the Court will from time to time fail to note important distinctions and will thus perplex the bar and the lower courts. Nonetheless, harking back to the instances discussed earlier, the fields of patents and of jury trials, in which the sheer flood of business so overpowers the Court that it is unable effectively to carry out its policies, the Court's practical choices are either to give up the battle and accept defeat or to say "No, no, no."

3. Both methods just suggested have, among their other limitations, the further vice that they conflict with the traditions of the Court. A third method, happily free of that vice, is that the Court might return to its best tradition by eliminating time-consuming diversions which have cut into its productivity in the past fifteen years.

The Court is responding to the quantity problem by deciding not more cases, but fewer. The production curve described in Chapter I shows that the Court had almost nothing to do in its first few years; that it began to encounter a real demand on its time about 1850; and that it reached a point of full production and was becoming swamped about 1875. At that time the Court was turning out something like two hundred opinions a year and could not keep up with the flood of new work. But today, in a country with more than twice the population of that of 1875, the Court's opinion output is below one hundred a year. In 1950 the Court produced fewer opinions than in any year since 1850.

The Court of the 1930's turned out twice as many opinions as the Court of the 1950's. This quantity decline is extremely recent; it is approximately accurate to say that

Chief Justice Stone and Justices Black, Douglas, and Roberts among them turned out as many opinions in 1940 or 1941 as does the entire Court now. Moreover, there has been no increase in the quality of opinions to account for the difference.

There are at least three mechanical factors to which this decrease is attributable, and as to each there is room for doubt as to whether it is worth the cost. First, many opinions are much more extensive than they need to be. This is not a matter only of length, for it commonly takes more time to be concise than to be verbose. It is a matter of learned discussion that could perhaps be omitted entirely, and some responsibility is attributable to the use of the footnote. As is noted in Chapter VII, this is a recent device in Supreme Court opinions; it was not unknown before 1940, but it was by no means as nearly universal as it is today. It is a device for adding supplementary knowledge which, because of its very neatness perched at the bottom of the page, invites excursions and the dissipation of time. Much that is contained in the notes would never stand the test of survival if it had to be worked into the text. Most of the time spent in creating these monuments of knowledge is that of the law clerks, but some, at least, is that of the Justices. There will always be some cases which deserve the full treatment, but by no means all of them do. Justice Brandeis was the great progenitor of the footnote, and in his hands it was most useful and not an impediment, but a President does not often pick a Brandeis.

The other two factors depressing production are the dissents and concurrences. Promiscuous dissent and promiscuous concurrence involve evils wholly apart from the amount of time consumed by them. For purposes of immediate discussion, however, the time element is enough to call them into question. The general principle that he who minds the other fellow's business will have great trouble minding his own is true even of august personages. The limits of human energy being what they are, if a Justice writes thirty or forty opinions of his own in cases that the Chief Justice has assigned to someone else, then necessarily he will do far fewer opinions for the Court than he otherwise could.

4. The Court can meet the problem by hitting hard when it does hit. Every blow must count. A law that is a tissue of delicate distinctions may be a lovely sight to the initiate, but it is a vain thing. The nature of the problem of quantity requires that the Court be more significant for what it leads others to decide than for what it decides itself; properly understood, the Court is not so much the great arbiter as the great educator on the American scene. For example, in the grade-school segregation cases the Court decided only a handful of cases about a few children, none of them from Arkansas. What the Court did was significant in Arkansas because by its decision the Court educated a federal district judge, who proceeded to apply in Arkansas the lesson he had learned.

The Court teaches a large class, whose members come to its lessons only piecemeal and sporadically, as particular problems arise. Such education, to be effective, must be broad. The merely erudite or precious will not do the job. This does not mean that the Court must take the ax to all of its problems and never use the scalpel. It means merely that the big problems must be solved in a big way if they are to be solved at all.

5. The Court can use its discretionary power by choosing to hear more cases. It is an important part of the Court's symbolism, of its role in the community concept, that, in addition to being a court which makes great policies, it is also a court of law. Hence, its great decisions must be in a

matrix or context of more nearly conventional matters. A Congress is able to pass declarations of war or atomic-energy acts, but it is also still able to pass a bill for the relief of Minnie Smith, and the same President who makes policy over space satellites can give a moment's thought to the welfare of the most minor Indian reservation. Each year, between fifty and a hundred cases knock for admission to the Court which are, by the older standards at least, Court-worthy and which, on the demonstrated record of the past, could be handled by the Court. The big matters that need the big treatment might well have more favorable public response if the same Court at the same time were giving a lesser treatment to more matters of the second rank.

This is, let it be hoped, not wanton criticism. That the Court receives too often, and can never deserve. The Supreme Court is a uniquely American institution; when it exists elsewhere, as in Australia, it exists as a copy of our own. The Court's everlasting value and its guarantee of perpetuity lie in the circumstance that it has always been a seat for men of courage and ability, each devoted in his own way to the American tradition as he understands it, each giving of his best thought and effort. It would be sanctimony, and falsehood as well, to say that *all* of its members have had either courage or ability, though it would be less than just not to acknowledge that very nearly all have had dedication; but the Court has always had men of courage and ability on it, and always men of independence. As Charles Evans Hughes said of the Justices, "One cannot study their lives and decisions without confidence in their sincerity and independence. The Supreme Court has the inevitable failings of any human institution, but it has vindicated the confidence, which underlies the success of democratic effort, that you can find in imperfect human beings, for the essential administration of justice, a rectitude of purpose, a clarity of vision and a capacity for independence which will render impotent the solicitation of friends, the appeals of erstwhile political associates, and the threats of enemies." [4]

It is inconceivable that any institution with so many glorious days in its past should not have many good days left. There have always been on this bench men prepared to face the tides of their own day, men to remind Americans of their basic values and damn the passions of the moment. William Johnson, facing the nullificationists in his home state of South Carolina in the 1830's; Roger Taney, standing even against Abraham Lincoln over the rights of a man named Merryman in Baltimore in 1861; David Davis, invalidating military trials in the case of Milligan in 1866 and thereby bringing down upon his shoulders the outraged wrath of his own party, for the moment lost to reason; Stephen J. Field, upholding the rights of Chinese in California and thereby junking his own chances for the Presidency because of the prejudices of the white population of that state; Holmes, Brandeis, Hughes, and Sutherland opposing Hughes, for that matter—from the day when John Marshall took on Thomas Jefferson in the case of Aaron Burr to the opinion of Hugo Black striking down the steel seizure by President Truman or the opinions invalidating segregation in higher education by Fred Vinson and in the grade schools by Earl Warren, the record is one of crises surmounted and traditions maintained. Felix Frankfurter rebuking the neo-folk idol Judge Medina for trial abuses; William O. Douglas dissenting in the principal Communist case; Harold Burton going against his impulses and rejecting the so-called Attorney General's list; Tom Clark finding in Oklahoma a loyalty

[4] Charles Evans Hughes: *The Supreme Court of the United States* (New York: Columbia University Press; 1928), pp. 45–6.

program he could not stomach; John Harlan setting aside Communist convictions; William Brennan and his decision on the F.B.I. files—every sitting Justice has on occasion done the hard thing in order to do what seemed to him the right thing, and Charles Whittaker, as his 1958 denaturalization opinions suggest, will reveal that same stern quality of independence when he has the chance. Indeed, the Court as a whole showed its customary fortitude when in May of 1958, shortly after a Senate committee had recommended alteration of the Court's rule on contempt of Congressional committees, the Court gave a renewed application of the rule in a difficult case. There was no impulse to turn tail here.

This is the fundamental utility of the Supreme Court in the American past. In the American future what we may expect of it—at least what we may ask of it—is the courage, the ability, and the will not to maintain but to help maintain the American tradition of liberty. No five or nine men could stop any country bent on rushing to its own destruction; the power is simply not there. But leadership and guidance may be there. That guidance may be a summons to fundamentals especially in the immediate future when the country has something of the will to stagger out of the season of illiberality which has so recently gripped it.

As Jefferson said in a passage quoted earlier, it is the function of a written constitution to provide a point of rally after moments of passion or delusion. In 1866, Jeremiah Sullivan Black, in what some have thought was the greatest argument ever made in the Supreme Court, argued to the Court the invalidity of military trials. Black was the most famous lawyer of his day, and the story is that a spectator listening to this argument rushed out to the House of Representatives where a good friend was addressing that body and whispered to his friend: "Wind her up, Bill! Wind her up, and come over and listen to old Jerry Black giving 'em hell."

What Black was saying to the Court as he spoke for Milligan was: "I shall necessarily refer to the mere rudiments of constitutional law, common topics of history, plain rules of justice. I beg your Honors to believe that this is not done because I think that the Court is less familiar with these things than I am but simply and only because there is absolutely no other way of dealing with it. If the fundamental principles of American liberty are attacked, and we are driven behind the inner walls of the Constitution to defend them, we can repel the assault only with those same old weapons which our ancestors used one hundred years ago. You must not think the worse of our armor because it happens to be old-fashioned and looks a little rusty from long disuse."

Appendix

SAMPLES OF JUDICIAL PROSE

I. *Legal Lumpy*

Instances from Justice Shiras mentioned in the text:

It is argued that, even if this Court will not take notice of the contents of the petition for a rehearing, in which the protection of the Constitution of the United States was in terms invoked, yet that, as well by the recitals in the opinion as by the said averments in the answers of the railway company and of Houck, it affirmatively appears that the Federal questions were raised, and that no formal objection or exception to the action of the Court in striking out those averments was necessary. We do not think it necessary to narrowly inquire whether the record formally discloses that the respondents relied upon and pleaded rights under the Constitution of the United States, because we are of opinion that, even if it be conceded that the respondents did, in form, invoke the provisions of the Federal Constitution, yet no Federal question was really raised.[1]

Or take a paragraph from another case:

The case is thus brought within the rule, which this Court has so often had occasion to lay down, that the remedies in the courts of the United States are, at common law or in equity, not according to the practice of state courts,

[1] *St. Louis C. G. & Ft. S. Ry. Co. v. Missouri,* 156 U.S. 478 (1895).

but according to the principles of common law and equity, as distinguished and defined in that country from which we derive our knowledge of these principles, and that, although the forms of proceedings and practice in the state courts shall have been adopted in the circuit courts of the United States, yet the adoption of the state practice must not be understood as confounding the principles of law and equity, nor as authorizing legal and equitable claims to be blended together in one suit.[2]

That is quite a load for one sentence to carry.

Justice Shiras was also an exponent of that ultimate clumsyism, the multiple negative:

Whether, if the power of the state to fix and regulate the passenger and freight charges of railroad corporations has not been restricted by contract, there can be found by judicial inquiry, a limit to such power in the practical effect its exercise may have on the earnings of the corporations, presents a question not free from difficulty.[3]

Another inclined to mushy mouthfuls was Justice Woodbury, whose most famous opinion is *Planters Bank* v. *Sharp.*[4] This case invalidated a Mississippi law that prohibited banks from transferring to others bills and notes which they had received. Here are samples:

Doing business with these powers, amounting, as it has been repeatedly settled, to a contract in the charter for

[2] *Lindsay* v. *First National Bank,* 156 U.S. 485 (1895).
[3] *St. Louis & S. F. Ry. Co.* v. *Gill,* 156 U.S. 649 (1895). Shiras was a useful member of the Court. His biographer points out the difference between the lively personal Shiras and the tedious judge: "While Shiras's experience had equipped him to deal with the legal substance of the cases that came before him, it gave him no advantage as a stylist. His way of presenting his view was more competent than charming, and not even a lawyer will be likely to read his opinions for the fun of it. The wry humor and pungent expression which often characterized his letters and speech are totally lacking in the opinions." Winfield Shiras: *Justice George Shiras, Jr., of Pittsburgh* (Pittsburgh: University of Pittsburgh Press; 1953), pp. 184, 185.
[4] 6 How. 301 (1848).

the use of them (see cases in The West River Bridge, at this term), the bank, on the 24th of May, 1839, took the promissory note on which the present suit was instituted, and, on the 10th day of June, 1842, transferred it to the United States Bank, having first commenced this action on it, the 11th of October, 1841. . . .

These two acts, though undoubtedly well meant, and designed to give an honest preference to billholders (see Sharkey's dissenting opinion) as to a paper currency which ought always to be kept on a par with specie, were unfortunately, in the laudable zeal to avert a great apprehended evil, passed, without sufficient consideration of the limitations of the powers imposed by the Constitution of the Union on the state legislatures, not to impair the obligation of existing contracts.

II. *Legal Massive*

An excellent massivist was Justice Stone, whose dissent to the effect that states have power to regulate the rates of employment agencies has since become the accepted law: [5]

Apart from the cases involving the historic public callings, immemorially subject to the closest regulation, this court has sustained regulations of the price in cases where the legislature fixed the charges which grain elevators, *Brass v. North Dakota*, 153 U.S. 391; *Budd v. New York*, 143 U.S. 517, and insurance companies might take, *German Alliance Ins. Co. v. Lewis*, supra; or required miners to be paid per ton of coal unscreened instead of screened, *McLean v. Arkansas*, supra; *Rail & River Coal Co. v. Yaple*, 236 U.S. 338; or required employers who paid their men in store orders to redeem them in cash, *Knoxville Iron Co. v. Harbison*, 183 U.S. 13; *Dayton Coal & I. Co. v. Barton*, 183 U.S. 23; *Keokee Consol. Coke Co. v.*

[5] *Ribnik* v. *McBride,* 277 U.S. 350 (1928).

Taylor, 234 U.S. 224; or fixed the fees chargeable by attorneys appearing for injured employees before workmen's compensation commissions, *Yeiser v. Dysart*, 267 U.S. 540; or fixed the rate of pay for overtime work, *Bunting v. Oregon*, 243 U.S. 426; or fixed the time within which the services of employees must be paid for, *Erie R. Co. v. Williams*, 233 U.S. 685; or established maximum rents, *Block v. Hirsh*, 256 U.S. 135; *Marcus Brown Holding Co. v. Feldman*, 256 U.S. 170; or fixed the maximum rate of interest chargeable on loans, *Griffith v. Connecticut*, 218 U.S. 563. It has sustained restrictions on the other element in the bargain where legislatures have established maximum hours of labor for men, *Holden v. Hardy*, 169 U.S. 366; or for women, *Muller v. Oregon*, 208 U.S. 412; *Hawley v. Walker*, 232 U.S. 718; *Riley v. Massachusetts*, 232 U.S. 671; *Miller v. Wilson*, 236 U.S. 373; or prohibited the payment of wages in advance, *Patterson v. The Eudora*, 190 U.S. 169; *Strathearn S. S. Co. v. Dillon*, 252 U.S. 348; or required loaves of bread to be a certain size, *Schmidinger v. Chicago*, 226 U.S. 578. In each of these cases the police power of the state was held broad enough to warrant an interference with free bargaining in cases where, despite the competition that ordinarily attends that freedom, serious evils persisted.

III. *Rock-Bottom Contemporary*

A sample of what might be described as rock-bottom contemporary is this group of excerpts from the opinion of Chief Justice Vinson in a case in which the issue was whether an alien twice convicted of liquor-tax avoidance had been guilty of "moral turpitude." If so, he might be deported, as aliens who commit offenses of "moral turpitude" are deportable. These quotations are strung together from a short opinion:

Our inquiry in this case is narrowed to determining whether this particular offense involves moral turpitude. . . . Without exception, federal and state courts have held that a crime in which fraud is an ingredient involves moral turpitude. In the construction of the specific section of the Statute before us, a court of appeals has stated that fraud has ordinarily been the test to determine whether crimes not of the gravest character involve moral turpitude. In every deportation case where fraud has been proved, federal courts have held that the crime in issue involved moral turpitude. . . . In the state courts, crimes involving fraud have universally been held to involve moral turpitude. . . . In view of these decisions, it can be concluded that fraud has consistently been regarded as such a contaminating component in any crime that American courts have, without exception, included such crimes within the scope of moral turpitude. It is therefore clear, under an unbroken course of judicial decisions, that the crime of conspiring to defraud the United States is a "crime involving moral turpitude." . . . Whatever else the phrase "crime involving moral turpitude" may mean in peripheral cases, the decided cases make it plain the crimes in which fraud was an ingredient have always been regarded as involving moral turpitude. . . . Fraud is the touchstone by which this case should be judged. The phrase "crime involving moral turpitude" has without exception been construed to embrace fraudulent conduct.[6]

One gets the impression that there is some connection between fraud and moral turpitude.

IV. *Legal Lucid*

In *Abrams* v. *United States* the Court upheld the conviction of five persons who distributed some five thousand copies

[6] *Jordan* v. *De George,* 341 U.S. 223 (1951).

of a leaflet opposing American intervention in Soviet Russia
after World War I. Justice Holmes, in dissent, said in part:

> In this case sentences of twenty years' imprisonment have
> been imposed for the publishing of two leaflets that I be-
> lieve the defendants had as much right to publish as the
> Government has to publish the Constitution of the United
> States now vainly invoked by them. Even if I am techni-
> cally wrong, and enough can be squeezed from these poor
> and puny anonymities to turn the color of legal litmus
> paper; I will add, even if what I think the necessary in-
> tent were shown; the most nominal punishment seems to
> me all that could possibly be inflicted, unless the defend-
> ants are to be made to suffer not for what the indictment
> alleges but for the creed that they avow—a creed that I
> believe to be the creed of ignorance and immaturity when
> honestly held, as I see no reason to doubt that it was held
> here, but which, although made the subject of examination
> at the trial, no one has a right to even consider in dealing
> with the charges before the Court.
> Persecution for the expression of opinions seems to me
> perfectly logical. If you have no doubt of your premises
> or your power and want a certain result with all your
> heart you naturally express your wishes in law and sweep
> away all opposition. To allow opposition by speech
> seems to indicate that you think the speech impotent, as
> when a man says that he has squared the circle, or that
> you do not care whole-heartedly for the result, or that you
> doubt either your power or your premises. But when men
> have realized that time has upset many fighting faiths,
> they may come to believe even more than they believe the
> very foundations of their own conduct that the ultimate
> good desired is better reached by free trade in ideas—
> that the best test of truth is the power of the thought to
> get itself accepted in the competition of the market; and
> the truth is the only ground upon which their wishes safely
> can be carried out. That, at any rate, is the theory of our
> Constitution. It is an experiment as all life is an experi-

ment. Every year, if not every day, we have to wager our salvation upon some prophecy based upon imperfect knowledge. While that experiment is part of our system I think that we should be eternally vigilant against attempts to check the expression of opinions that we loathe and believe to be fraught with death, unless they so immensely threaten immediate interference with the lawful and pressing purposes of the law that an immediate check is required to save the country.[7]

A more recent instance of eloquence on the same topic is the dissent of Justice Douglas in one of the principal Communist trials of recent years. Justice Douglas, dissenting, advanced the opinion that, while world Communism presented a great threat to the United States, domestic Communism did not. In part he said:

Communism in the world scene is no bogey-man; but Communism as a political faction or party in this country plainly is. Communism has been so thoroughly exposed in this country that it has been crippled as a political force. Free speech has destroyed it as an effective political party. It is inconceivable that those who went up and down this country preaching the doctrine of revolution which petitioners espouse would have any success. . . . Some nations less resilient than the United States, where illiteracy is high and where democratic traditions are only budding, may have to take drastic steps and jail these men for merely speaking their creed, but in America they are miserable merchants of unwanted ideas; their wares remain unsold. The fact that their ideas are abhorrent does not make them powerful.

The political impotence of the Communists in this country does not, of course, dispose of the problem. . . . If we are to proceed on the basis of judicial notice, it is impossible for me to say that the Communists in this country are so potent or so strategically deployed that they must

[7] *Abrams* v. *United States,* 250 U.S. 616 (1919).

be suppressed for their speech. I could not so hold unless I were willing to conclude that the activities of recent years of committees of Congress, of the Attorney General, of labor unions, of state legislatures, and of loyalty boards were so futile as to leave the country on the edge of grave peril. To believe that petitioners and their following are placed in such critical positions as to endanger the Nation is to believe the incredible. It is safe to say that the followers of the creed of Soviet Communism are known to the F.B.I.; that in case of war with Russia they will be picked up overnight as were all prospective sabateurs at the commencement of World War II; that the invisible army of petitioners is the best known, the most beset, and the least thriving of any Fifth column in history. Only those held by fear and panic could think otherwise.[8]

---

[8] *Dennis* v. *United States,* 341 U.S. 494 (1951).

INDEX

Abolition, 172
Abrams v. *United States*, 299–301
Adams, John, 45, 56, 180, 184
Adams, John Quincy, 183, 203
Administrative office, 18
Administrative problems, 71, 74
Admiralty, 11
Africa, 248
Alabama, 215
Alien and Sedition Acts, 181, 197
Aliens, 180, 189, 198–9
Allison, William, 56
Altgeld, John Peter, 183
American Bar Association, 53, 152, 195
American Civil Liberties Union, 51
American Communications Association v. *Doud*, 142
American Legion, 51
Anderson, Marian, 213
Anti-Masonry, 182, 273
Anti-Semitism, 48
Appeals, 15
Argument of cases, Chapter V, *passim*
Arizona, 29
Arizona Daily Star, 159, *quoted* 163, 284
Arizona v. *California*, 162–3
Arkansas, 54, 151, 177, 214, 290
Arkansas, University of, 214
Atlanta Constitution, 284
Atomic energy, 3, 4, 9, 248, 291
Attachés of Court, 109
Australia, 291
Auto Light, 103

Baltimore, George Calvert, Lord, 161
Baltimore & Ohio Railway Co. v. *Jackson*, 156
Bank of Augusta v. *Earle*, 228–9
Bank of United States v. *Deveaux*, 227
Bank of United States v. *United States*, 83
Bankruptcy, 229
Barbour, Philip P., 53, 107, 112
Baseball, 6
Basler, Roy, 35n
Beal v. *Missouri*, 170

Benny, Jack, 103
Bergman, Ingrid, 103
Betts v. *Brady*, 221n
Beveridge, Albert J., *quoted* 87–8
Bickel, Alexander, 111, 261
Biddle, Francis, 59, *quoted* 141; and free speech, 187, 217
Bill of Rights: currency of, 197–9; future of, 248; *see also* particular subdivisions, as Freedom of Speech and Press
Black, Hugo L.: and civil juries, 31–2; length of service, 42; 45, 54, 56, 59; creativeness, 63; 64, 66, 77; questions by, 104; 113, 114; clerks, 116–17; 122, 124, 125, 128; style, 132–3; 143, 152, 189, 191, *quoted* 196–7; 199; military trials, 218–19; 221; *quoted* on treaties, 247; 257, 258–9, 262, 263, 266, 284, 289, 292
Black, Jeremiah S., 94, 96–7, 293–4
Blatchford, Samuel, 69
Boyer, Charles, 103
Braden, George, *quoted* 29–30
Bradley, Joseph, 43, 61, 69, 73, 102, *quoted* 119, 237; and Miller, 270–1
Brandeis, Louis D.: *quoted* 23; 43, 48, 49; creativeness, 63; 64, 65, 68; and Taft, 84; 114; Brandeis Brief, 115; 116, 125, 126, 152; and free speech, 186; 190, 196, 243, 250, 262; and Holmes, 265–6; footnotes, 289; 292
Brennan, William, 32, 43, 48, 53, 54, 55; brevity, 133; 191; and *Jencks* case, 193–5; 262, 266, 293
Brewer, David J., 66; Taft on, 255
Bricker, John, 238, 247
Briefing of cases, Chapter V, *passim*
Brigance, William N., 97n
Broun, Heywood, 132
Brown, Catherine, 205, 208
Brown, Henry B., 125, 202n
Brown, Ralph S., *quoted* 190–1
Brown v. *Board of Education*, 212
Buchanan, James, 46, 203, *quoted* 258
Buchanan v. *Worley*, 207
Budget, 3, 5
Bulganin, 3
Burr, Aaron, 292

i

Index

Index

Index

Index

Index

Index

Warren, Earl (*continued*)
  style, 134; 152, 158; effect of appointment, 191; 196, 198; segregation cases, 212; 252, 262, 266, 276, 284, 292
Washington, Bushrod, 79
Washington, George, 9, 55, 68
Washington Post and Times-Herald, 159, 284
Watkins v. *United States*, 134, 191
Wayne, James M., 53, 109, 133, 203, 204, 262, 278
Webster, Daniel, 68; argument in *Dartmouth College* case, 87–8; 92, 99–100, 109, 173, 228; on contract clause, 232–3
Weed, Thurlow, 182
Weisenburger, Francis P., 273
West Coast Hotel Co. v. *Parrish*, 256
West River Bridge Co. v. *Dix*, 234
West Virginia, 214
West Virginia State Board v. *Barnette*, 143
Westmoreland County, 160
Wheeler, Burton K., 50

Whig Party, 53–4, 99–100, 273
White, Edward D., 57, 72, 76, 79, 202n; appointment as Chief Justice, 271–2
White, William Allen, 66
White primaries, 209, 257
Whitney v. *California*, 266
Whittaker, Charles, 43, 54, 266, 280, 293
Wickard v. *Filburn*, 176
Wickersham, George, 72
Williams, George H., 52, 270
Willkie, Wendell, 89–91, 104
Wilson, James, 47, 66
Wilson, Woodrow, 45, 46, 57, 71, 225, 275
Wisconsin, 56
Wolf v. *Colorado*, 222
Woodbury, Levi, 99, 296
Woods, William, 69, 92
Wright, Charles A., 261n
Wyoming v. *Colorado*, 120–1
Wyoming Valley, 160

Yamashita, In re, 135–7, 266
Yates v. *United States*, 133, 191

A NOTE ABOUT THE AUTHOR

John P. Frank has in rare degree combined theoretical and practical knowledge of the United States Supreme Court. For eight years he taught constitutional law and Supreme Court studies at Indiana University and at the Yale Law School. He is now practicing law in Phoenix, Arizona, and has briefed or argued numerous cases in the Supreme Court. His technical books in constitutional law are used in colleges and law schools. His first book, *Mr. Justice Black: The Man and His Opinions*, published in 1949, describes the Justice whom he served as law clerk in 1942. He has written widely in periodicals on Supreme Court subjects.

He was born in Appleton, Wisconsin, in 1917, and received B.A., M.A., and LL.B. degrees from the University of Wisconsin and a J.S.D. from Yale. When asked about his extracurricular interests, he said that outside of his wife, children, and good restaurants, his almost exclusive interest is the law, with a special concentration on the history of the Supreme Court. As what is sometimes called a "lawyer's lawyer," he devotes much of his time to handling appeals for his partners and for other attorneys.

A NOTE ON THE TYPE

This book was set on the Linotype in *Scotch,* a type-face that has been in continuous service for more than one hundred years. It is usually considered that the style followed in our present-day cuttings of Scotch was developed in the foundry of Alexander Wilson and Sons of Glasgow early in the nineteenth century. The new Wilson patterns were made to meet the requirements of the new fashion in printing that had been set going at the beginning of the century by the "modern" types of Didot in France, of Bodoni in Italy, and of Baskerville in England. It is to be observed that the *modern* in these matters is a modernity of A.D. 1800, not of today.

The book was composed, printed, and bound by The Plimpton Press, Norwood, Massachusetts. Paper manufactured by S. D. Warren Company, Boston. Typography and binding based on original designs by W. A. Dwiggins.

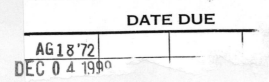